INSIDE THE HARE KRISHNA MOVEMENT

INSIDE THE HARE KRISHNA MOVEMENT

an ancient eastern religious tradition comes of age in the western world

mukunda goswami

TORCHLIGHT PUBLISHING

Cover and interior design by Yamaraja Dasa

Printed in India

Published simultaneously in the United States of America and Canada by Torchlight Publishing, Inc.

Photo credits:
Chapter 27—London's *Daily Telegraph;*
Chapter 31—Radha Krishna Dasa

Library of Congress Cataloging-in-Publication Data

Goswami, Mukunda, 1942-
Inside the Hare Krishna movement / an ancient eastern religious tradition comes of age in the western world / Mukunda Goswami.
p. cm.
Includes index.
ISBN 1-887089-28-4
1 International Society for Krishna Consciousness—History. I. Title.

BL1285.83 .G67 2000
294.5'512—dc21
00-037732

Attention Colleges, Universities, Corporations, Associations, and Professional Organizations: *Inside the Hare Krishna Movement* is available at special discounts for bulk purchases for fund-raising or educational use. Special books, booklets, or excerpts can be created to suit your specific needs.

For more information, contact the Publisher:

Torchlight Publishing
PO Box 52
Badger, CA 93603
Telephone: (559) 337-2200
Fax: (559) 337-2354
Email: Torchlight@spiralcomm.net
Web: www.Torchlight.com

To my spiritual master

HIS DIVINE GRACE
A. C. BHAKTIVEDANTA SWAMI

Contents

CHAPTER 4—1992

A Post-Secular World?

CHAPTER 5—1993

Walking Our Talk

CHAPTER 6—1994

PR Versus Reputation

CHAPTER 7—1995

Relevance

CHAPTER 8—1996

Creating an Infrastructure

CHAPTER 9—1997

Players on the Field

CHAPTER 10—1998

A Global Perspective

Preface

I first saw Hare Krishna devotees chanting and dancing along Oxford Street in the '60s. Mukunda dasa Adhikari was probably there. I was training to be a clinical psychologist but going through a very God-conscious period of my life, wanting to be a missionary, yet not sure about just preaching Christianity. Most weekends I would stand and watch the devotees before I frequented one of London's new vegetarian restaurants. Someone told me the Hare Krishnas provided delicious, vegetarian food but then added, "The food is incredible, but be careful; people go for the meal and never return." For some reason I heeded this warning and did not seek out the devotees nor meet Srila Prabhupada (the founder-*acharya,* or founding spiritual master, of the International Society for Krishna Consciousness, or ISKCON).

It was many years later that my daughter introduced me to Krishna consciousness, and I came to the United States to work for ISKCON Communications Global (ICG). I am excited that ISKCON's communications ministry is not merely a transatlantic alliance but a true global team. As a full-time worker at the ICG center, I want to emphasize the profound relevance of the cutting-edge communications principles described in this book.

On April 5, 1998, ISKCON's Glory of India project opened in Delhi in the presence of the prime minister and other leading dignitaries. It received world media coverage. The foundations of this temple had to be installed on rock as hard as granite. Contractors were forced to use explosives to blast parts of it, while hundreds of workers had to chip and chisel away by hand. The temple, sculptured on the skyline, now reminds those who visit that India's spiritual heritage is alive and well in the hands of the Hare Krishnas—a remarkable fact when you consider that members of India's parliament were convinced that the first Americans who came to India with Srila Prabhupada in 1971 were CIA agents.

Mukunda Goswami's initiation into the ISKCON communications field began with organizing the media coverage for the Mumbai temple grand opening in January, 1978. Barely a month after Srila Prabhupada's departure from our mortal view, Mukunda was summoned to India to publicize the Mumbai opening. He was determined to fulfill the founder-*acharya*'s desire to make the temple opening a glorious, global event. He spent most of his time in the capital city of New Delhi, negotiating his way through media offices scattered throughout the urban sprawl. Separated from even the minimal comforts ISKCON afforded in those days, he rose early and returned late at night, often snatching only a few hours of sleep before the daily 4:30 AM *mangala arotika* ceremony in a cold Delhi temple. After a breakfast of steamy, spicy *sambhar*, he set out alone, hailing three-wheeled scooter-taxis everywhere he went, finding out where to go and what to look for as the day unfolded.

In ISKCON there is a military-style component in our communications work: a need for leadership and loyal allies, grand strategies, regulation, discipline, and confrontation. There is the need to protect from attack. Fighting for spiritual justice, however, brings major rewards in reputation management. Such was the case with the Bhaktivedanta Manor campaign in England. Far more people in the UK are aware of the Hare Krishnas than would have been without the battle.

Of course, Srila Prabhupada reminds us that the greater enemy is within: our eternally conditioned desire to play and to be a "plaything in the hands of *maya*" (Cc. Adi 5.232 purport). I think he would have endorsed the inimitable words of Pogo Possum, "We have met the enemy, and he is us."

Within and without, ICG has been making links that secure our principles and refine our purpose. The links strengthen our Society and create environments favorable for advancing the goals of the Krishna consciousness movement. ISKCON is busy building a comprehensive infrastructure for the next century.

This book explains how ISKCON quietly developed its "corporate" identity. ICG floated the idea of a global logo first in 1992. In 1998, ISKCON's Governing Body Commission approved Mukunda Goswami's presentation, one that became the "official" ISKCON logo. In business culture, the logo, along with the name of the company and the mission statement, is a top priority. From 1992–98, ICG patiently and steadily worked its way toward a global logo, steering the concept and design through the appropriate channels.

Communications helps us remember that we must unceasingly strive for unity. ICG's most important audience is probably the devotees themselves. It is essential to realize that loyalty to Srila Prabhupada does mean loyalty to ISKCON. A major part of ICG's activity is to make sure that devotees can connect, share information, debate issues, and generally know what is happening in all parts of the ISKCON world and feel a part of what is our living inheritance, Srila Prabhupada's own organization.

Helping devotees participate in the world, after initially adopting a somewhat phobic and fearful attitude toward "outsiders," is essential. It is spiritual stagnation not to engage with the world we live in.

Inside's author often stresses the importance of learning from anyone and everyone, if it will help create a God-conscious world. This reminds us of the *avadhuta brahmana* telling Maharaja Yadu of his "twenty-four gurus," including the earth, pigeon, python, prostitute, and the arrow-maker (*Srimad-Bhagavatam* 11.7.33–35). The author has introduced methods of communications, management, and learning that will improve ISKCON. I believe this work will serve to establish a more effective and healthier organization.

Many devotees around the world have contributed to Mukunda

Goswami's work, shaped and sharpened his thoughts and words, inspired and engaged him. Thus, ICG embodies the art and technology of communicating. It's about transmitting information, but it is also about relationships.

Many of ISKCON's "second-generation" devotees' biological children manifest a resurgence of the sheer enjoyment of Krishna consciousness. These and other young people will take over from us. Mukunda Goswami sees it as his duty to responsibly impart what he knows to them in a way that will make sense. He is particularly encouraged by their capacity to relate in a personal way to each other, to debate and question issues that require attention, and to have high expectations of Srila Prabhupada's movement. He respects their doubts and knows some of them will prove to be our enlightened and intelligent leaders in the future. Once I watched him tutor some under-twelves during a *Srimad-Bhagavatam* class. It was another demonstration of his "professorial role." He coaxed from his apparently distracted and fidgety audience questions and answers that stimulated everyone's interest in the philosophy. He recognizes that education, in every sense, holds the key to the future of the movement.

As we approach the twenty-first century, it has become apparent that ISKCON's reputation increasingly depends on our ability to relate to ourselves, other devotees, and the world in general in an honest and compassionate way. In many ways, this book foreshadows events that are now happening and processes that will become part of the movement's modus operandi.

The millennium will see the Mayapura temple as a reality. It will see ISKCON's coming of age as a center for learning about spiritual development. *Inside* gives us an inside look at the movement's growth over a ten-year period and the role communications has played in Srila Prabhupada's mission.

Reputation management for a *sankirtana*-friendly world requires constant strategizing and ongoing reprioritization as the journey proceeds. In fact, ICG considers itself an advisor in not only "what to say" and "how to say it," but also in "what to do." Planning is critical. "Helping ISKCON plan the preaching" has become one of ICG's most important silent mottoes.

In 1999, ICG plans to teach its first formal course in communications, in Belgium. Distance is no barrier to international teambuilding. At times it can facilitate bonds that are sometimes less easily forged in close proximity. Mukunda Goswami knows about strength in numbers, and he works to bind us together, attempting to gather those that fall, urging cooperation, always trying to create unity in diversity.

The training of those who have the aptitude and interest to work in the communications field is gathering momentum. Communications is an important and resilient resource in ISKCON. It is central to policy-making. It is preaching.

But, as Srila Prabhupada has also pointed out, in the age of Kali, the *astra* (weapon) is the usually the *shastra.* "This is the *astra.* By argument, by philosophy, by entreating, by flattering, they are giving Krishna consciousness—Advaita Prabhu, Nityananda Prabhu" (Srila Prabhupada lecture on *Srimad-Bhagavatam* 1.3.11–12, September 17, 1972, in Los Angeles).

The Golden Age is a *sankirtana*-friendly world. Let us bring whomever we know into Srila Prabhupada's ISKCON, the cloud of mercy that offers peace and hope for everyone. Hearts of stone will become temples of God. We live closer than we realize to one of history's defining moments.

Sri Sudevi-devi dasi

Foreword

I am very pleased to introduce this collection of papers from Mukunda Goswami, which provides us with a very interesting picture of the internal workings of ISKCON Communications during an important decade of the movement's development.

It is probably fair to say that the 1980s was not a good decade for ISKCON; there were just too many guru scandals and other high-profile events. Whilst for individual devotees within ISKCON, the challenge of adapting to life after Srila Prabhupada's departure was often a traumatic journey. For ISKCON to survive and develop beyond this low point, therefore, some important changes had to be made within the organization of the movement. This is in fact what happened—and the 1990s saw the movement successfully transform itself in many different ways.

What this book shows is how one such change—the development of the communications network to deal positively with the outside world of "karmis"—was an important means of presenting a much more favorable picture of ISKCON which went beyond the problems of the 1980s. But as this book shows, the development of ISKCON Communications was not intended to be (and would not have worked) as a cosmetic exercise of 'spin.' The role of ISKCON Communicators was as much a reflection of the changing attitudes of ISKCON as it was of the need to show the world a better face of the movement. And I think part of the challenge which leading figures such as Mukunda Goswami tried to achieve was also to bring the world outside ISKCON to devotees in a more comprehensible way.

Of course, there are many responses and attitudes of devotees to the world, which depend on things such as whether they are living in the temple or the community, and on how long they have been fully absorbed in their commitment to Krishna consciousness. But ISKCON is an organization, a group of people who rely on their talents, skills, and experience (albeit with the help of guidance from Krishna and His teachers). The successful management of such an organization cannot be achieved in isolation from the world, even though that world may be quite alien (and sometimes antagonistic) in many ways to the values that ISKCON devotees aspire to. Quite how to bridge that gap, between the fundamental pursuit of pure Krishna consciousness and living as an organization within an imperfect world, is something that ISKCON is always going to have to find solutions for. What is clear from this book is that for the past ten years, under the expert hands of Mukunda Goswami, leading figures in ISKCON have been trying to find some answers—to ongoing issues as well as to the specific problems that were faced in the 1990s.

As someone who has been watching with great interest the development of ISKCON in Britain—where for much of the past decade (and well before then, too) there was an ongoing legal and media battle to protect the temple at Bhaktivedanta Manor—I have found this book a fascinating read. Having some experience of the communications offices in Britain, it did not come as much of a surprise to read of the sophistication and wisdom of the public relations management of the movement. But for many I think it will be a pleasant surprise to discover that the image of ISKCON as "mind-numbed cultists" is one that now can be safely buried.

Dr. Malory Nye
Dept. of Religious Studies
University of Stirling

Introduction

This is a book about an unusual history. It spans a period of only ten years, a drop in the grand sweep of eternal time.

It has been assembled from the vantage point of an insider. From 1988 to 1998, the Hare Krishna movement was developing in ways hidden from people. The highlights of this evolution are found in the summaries written at the beginning of each chapter. Although a decade is incredibly brief, those years were greatly significant for the International Society for Krishna Consciousness (ISKCON). During that period, I was a member of the Governing Body Commission, ISKCON's ultimate managing authority.

Religions and religious movements have played key roles in the forming and unfolding of civilizations. Systems of faith start small, but their power is felt centuries later. Twenty years after its founding in 1966, ISKCON had become a fact of life. We were here to stay. In my view, our movement would influence the world.

It was in this historical context that I decided to publish the following collection of "insider" essays and editorial views, which, for a time, were strictly confidential. These were first printed in the *ISKCON Communications Briefings* (ICB) newsletter and the *Hare Krishna World* (HKW) newspaper. I have added very short introductions to each article—to help keep a perspective and to provide context; therefore, each essay can stand on its own, and one can read with profit any part of *Inside* without having to read it from beginning to end.

Articles in this book include internal advice on how to answer such questions as: "Are you a cult? Doesn't singing and dancing in public put people off, thereby defeating your purpose of winning people over to your point of view? Isn't public soliciting or begging for money annoying to the public? News reports say that Krishna leaders have been tied to murder, drug abuse, and other criminal activities—is this true?"

In fact, we had an ICB privacy policy until 1991. I thought, and most of my colleagues in ISKCON management agreed, that the ICB constituted "inside" information that could be used as propaganda against ISKCON—if it got into the wrong hands. In those days, our enemies were not just vociferous. Many engaged in head-hunting (paid kidnappings), followed by what they called de-programming. It was physical: a real and present danger.

However, even after we lifted this information ban in 1991, the newsletter usually stayed within the confines of local temples Occasionally one found its way to a bulletin board or desk in a temple's administrative offices. Most ICBs, however, wound up buried in someone's personal file. Almost no one outside ISKCON ever saw these newsletters.

Hare Krishna World is also, for the most part, an in-house publication. The editorials I wrote for HKW seldom reached anyone outside ISKCON. Still, I wrote mainly for the masses, but always from the Hare Krishna viewpoint. I commented on events of the day: the demise of Mother Teresa and of Princess Diana, euthanasia, the UN's fiftieth birthday, nuclear proliferation in India and Pakistan, Oprah Winfrey's legal battle over meat, and issues on the environment. These opinions seldom reached anyone beyond our movement. But I felt content that my editorials would present devotees with insights on how to view current events from the Krishna conscious angle of vision.

Inside is a look into how we saw things from the inside out. As ISKCON's Global Communications Minister during those ten years, I often explained in my essays how state-of-the-art public relations philosophies applied to our mission. The book reveals that many such principles have spiritual antecedents.

Many readers will be unaware that important public relations practices today are often inner directed. The philosophy of this process—often under the heading of corporate communications—is that an organization can be long-term effective only when its core and foundational values are fully solidified. I often wrote about inner communications in ISKCON, seeing that solidarity, trust, truth, and a strong central ethos were extremely important.

I always tried to put world concerns at the center. This was all the more important to me after the passing of two decades since ISKCON's inception. I realized that "thinking globally and acting locally" were central concepts. In fact, I went so far as to say in the article called "Time, Place, and Audience" (see page 99) that the thinking-globally maxim touches the very heart of what ISKCON is all about.

In my dual role as a Governing Body Commissioner and Minister of Communications, I was acutely aware of the powerful influence that communications had on management—and vice versa. This mutuality was pervasive in our movement.

For most people, the Krishnas are little more than groups of people who look a bit different, chant on street corners, or distribute religious tracts in public. But *Inside* offers a different picture. For the first time, readers can learn what the leaders of ISKCON were thinking, what they were doing, and what they were projecting.

During these ten years, ISKCON devotees sometimes found themselves working in hostile environments and had to fight hard for their basic rights. Legal and governmental battles in many countries became historical landmarks. Struggles were rallying points. Victories—even defeats—drew members closer together. Fortunately, most contests ended in triumph. Krishna was, we felt, protecting us.

In preparing this publication, it was not my intention to alter perceptions. But in re-reading the manuscript, I now believe that the contents of this book will help break down stereotypical notions about Hare Krishnas—their thought processes, their habits, and their collective worldviews. The book shows that devotees are reasonable people. In addition to their spiritual concerns, they worry as much about personal and family affairs as about social and organizational matters. And, like everyone else, they have their problems.

There is a sense that Hare Krishnas are isolationist—that they are not concerned with issues and events that affect the larger circle of humanity. Some think that devotees do not live in the "real" world—that they see everyone in terms of insiders and outsiders, friends and enemies, good and bad. This conception is uncomfortably present even within ISKCON, and therefore I address it in the ICB article entitled "Us and Them."

Sometimes people feel that devotees are mindless. But they are in fact thinkers and philosophers, even those who work in the agricultural fields on our farms. ISKCON is based on the *Bhagavad-gita,* a classic philosophical treatise that has exercised the intellects of Thoreau, Huxley, Emerson, Geothe, Oppenheimer, Einstein, and many other leading thinkers through history. Full-time members are required to learn this book's philosophy, read it and hear lectures on it regularly. They have to take examinations on its teachings. They are also expected to know how to apply the *Gita*'s knowledge in their daily lives.

How do devotees see and interact in the world? The writings in this book look at the human condition through a spiritual lens. Many of the essays document how the people of an orthodox and seemingly parochial religious movement engage the world around them. *Inside* is the story of how the Hare Krishnas have gone about establishing a universal, yet specific, spiritual culture in a secular setting.

It is often thought that religious matters belong principally to the realm of the "other world," and that God does not really figure in daily life. I think that technology, globalization, and today's unspoken educational ethos have all contributed to this widely held but rarely expressed belief. In education, postmodernism is in, values are taboo, and God has been relegated to the ash heap of irrelevancy.

In its pure form, godliness can be practical. It is as important today as it was before the Reformation, the Enlightenment, and the Industrial Revolution.

Many people in so-called developed countries have become seekers. Some have renounced standard medicines and health care, opting for natural methods. Others have turned to psychology for ultimate answers. Many have adopted alternative diets, rejected their family faiths, started reading instead of watching television, and found lower-paying jobs that give them time to pursue their personal interests.

William Van Dusen Wishard, President of Trends Research, informs us that "We're in the midst of a long-term spiritual and psychological reorientation" and that "the Divine . . . is an expression of the archetype of wholeness and completeness."*

Contrary to current streams of thought, technology and many other features of contemporary living do not have to be rejected in favor of the spiritual life. Airplanes, the Internet, telephones, automobiles, and computers can be part of godly pursuits. The arts and sciences can also be integrated into the transcendental landscape. How this is possible is explained in the pages of this book.

I hope that *Inside* will inform as well as stimulate thought. Although it was not my original intention, I also hope that this book will leave the impression that consciousness and love of God need not be an escapist, armchair philosophy, or that such thinking is impractical. It is my conviction that meditation on God can provide a foundation and an overarching principle that enables us to maneuver happily, swiftly, safely, and meaningfully through our complex world.

By way of acknowledgments, my first thanks are to Drutakarma

---

* Delivered to the Issue Management Council, Washington D.C., January 22, 1999. From *Vital Speeches of the Day*, Vol. LXV, No. 10, March 1, 1999.

dasa, whose input and editing on almost every story were extremely valuable. In many ways, he has been a mentor to me, and thus I would not have dared to finalize most of what I wrote without his remarks. His comments caused me to change many sections of what I originally drafted, and I am most grateful for his thoughtful reviews. In fact, the one story I did not write myself, "A New Direction for ISKCON Global Communications," was his composition and is so noted in the book.

Next, I would like to thank Sri Sudevi devi dasi, who wrote the Preface and conceived of this publication. She worked relentlessly on all phases of production—from editing and layout up to the production stage. In many ways, *Inside* is her book.

Without the help of many others, *Inside* would not have been. I would like to thank Srikanta for his assiduous and meticulous proofreading and editing in English and Sanskrit. Thanks also to Madri devi dasi and Pesala devi dasi for their editing comments. I offer my gratitude to the *Hare Krishna World* staff of Sarva-satya dasa and Kunti devi dasi for creating and maintaining their archive material and for offering this to me and others for research purposes. Thanks to Caitanya-lila devi dasi, who painstakingly procured photographs and furnished essential caption information. Gordon and Karmela Smetana gave me a quiet place in which to work uninterruptedly, preparing the manuscript.

Dhira Lalita devi dasi carried out important research, and Krishnananda dasa supplied vital photographs. There are many other photos in the book, and I am indebted to Devaprastha dasa, who used his scanner and e-mail facilities to copy and transmit. Grahila dasa did an excellent job creating the Index, and Krsna Priya devi dasi was immensely helpful in work connected with producing many of the ICB newsletters. Janice Wloch located important source material. Yasodamayi devi dasi was instrumental in organizing the layout of many ICB newsletters. Thanks also to Amy-Marie Khalsa, Karen Martin, and Rebecca Lucero for their invaluable transcribing work. Sudharma devi dasi assisted me on many of the ICB newsletters, providing cogent commentary and assembling articles.

Last but far from least, Alister Taylor, the CEO of Torchlight Publishing, gave me the benefit of his enthusiasm for the project. He used his expertise in presenting, packaging, and marketing a product I had no idea how to promote or sell. I am most grateful to him and his team, in particular Sujana devi dasi, who expertly steered this book through its final production phase.

Mukunda Goswami
Lord Balarama's Appearance Day
August, 1999

development, providing urgent comments and [illegible] the [illegible] last but far from least, [illegible] Zhou [illegible] gave me the benefit of his enthusiasm for the [illegible]. The [illegible] of his expertise [illegible] produced had no idea how to [illegible] and his [illegible] in particular [illegible] through to final production.

CHAPTER 1—1989

Thinking Required

In 1989, things began to thaw for devotees in the Soviet Union. Early in 1989, the first Hare Krishna restaurant opened in Leningrad (now St. Petersburg), thus beating McDonald's to the USSR. In March, fifty-nine Soviet devotees met with Indian prime minister Rajeev Gandhi in New Delhi, and Boris Yeltsin received a copy of Srila Prabhupada's *Bhagavad-gita As It Is* in September. But in October, Soviet authorities held up 191,000 books in customs for weeks. They eventually settled for "samples" of a large number of

March 29, 1989—New Delhi, India: India's Prime Minister Rajiv Gandhi (to the right of the painting) officially greets fifty-nine Hare Krishna members from the former Soviet Union, who present him with a painting of Lord Krishna. This visit signals the outbreak of religious freedom in the formerly atheistic regime.

books "for their own information." In England, ISKCON members took part in a 90-mile interfaith march during the Canterbury Festival of Faith and the Environment. A national TV network aired thirteen weeks of ISKCON's *Cooking with Kurma,* and cricket star Neil Gavaskar joined an eleven-mile march in London in support of threatened public worship at Bhaktivedanta Manor. In the United States, a punk Hare Krishna rock group, the Cro Mags, featured a painting of Lord Nrsimhadeva on their album, which included several songs about Krishna. Dozens of San Diego Krishna kids marched in an antiabortion rally, and Padayatra America officially began in Berkeley, California. The mayor of Durban, South Africa, attended the Rathayatra festival and publicly declared that the event promoted interracial understanding. Devotees held their first Rathayatra in Spain despite protests from anticult groups, and Padayatris in Guyana visited a leper colony, where they distributed *prasadam.*

BRIDGING THE GAP (YOUTH OUTREACH)

We put this article in a 1989 *ISKCON Communications Briefings* (ICB) to alert Hare Krishna boomers that a new generation, with a different style of Krishna consciousness, was springing up in their midst. They had their own vocabulary, literature, music, emblems, and "underground" status. Part of the punk scene, they were a new corps of followers, referred to as the "straight edge," denoting a lifestyle that forswore drug use, excessive recreational sex, gambling, and—for many—meat-eating. A modicum of fame attended these new followers of Krishna as some of their leaders' straight-edge recordings became popular, and a network subculture began to grow throughout the world. The Cro Mags and Shelter bands gained global popularity. Tattoos, stage dives, body piercing, slam dancing, shaven heads, racy "zines" (magazines), and many other symbols were all part of the new scene.

ISKCON Communications Briefings, October 1989

If you don't know the meaning of a large "X" on the back of

1985—USA: Tours, recordings, pamphlets, and publications give the Hare Krishna band Shelter a global following. As a straight-edge, devotee band, Shelter brings a spiritual dimension to the heavy-metal rock scene. Performing here are Raghunath dasa (singing) and Paramananda dasa (playing bass guitar).

teenagers' hands or the meaning of the words zine, crusty, pos, or bro, you may be dangerously out of touch with today's youth (see glossary at end of story).

A growing new generation of punk-oriented youth in America and Britain (the trend is said to be spreading to many other countries) are drug-free, vegetarian-oriented, averse to casual sex, and often shaven-headed. According to a recent story in British rock zine *The Pure Issue,* "They don't drink or have casual sex; they call themselves Straight Edge, and their cry is getting louder."

You may have read about Kalki Prabhu's recent benefit concert in San Ysidro, California. A leading straight-edge band called Youth of Today was featured at the concert, which Kalki organized to support his popular zine, *The Razor's Edge* (see "Dancing on the Razor's Edge," *ISKCON World Review,* Vol. 8, No.10).

After the passing of more than a generation and a half since ISKCON's inception, we tend to forget that the new generation talks differently, wears different clothes, likes different music, and thinks much differently than alternative USA cultures of the late sixties where it all began.

If the up-and-coming punk group Cro Mags sounds like people you'd rather avoid, think again. The band's members, especially lead singer Harley, openly and strongly preach Krishna-conscious philosophy and behavior in published interviews and personal one-on-one exchanges. The famous Jadurani painting of Lord Nrsimhadeva killing Hiranyakasipu is on the cover of their latest LP, *Best Wishes* (with full credits to the Bhaktivedanta Book Trust).

Just as the Mantra Rock Dance captivated the hippies of San Francisco in 1967, Kalki's program has become a fact of life for the straight-edge generation and its followers.

The following excerpt is from a report by Gunagrahi Swami on Kalki in action in Fort Worth, Texas. Kalki is part of the traveling KrishnaFest program headed by Gunagrahi dasa Goswami and Danavira dasa Vanacari.

It's 9:00 P.M. Saturday. We're at the parking lot of The Axis in Fort Worth, Texas. The club is a hangout for local youth, punks, and skinheads. We're on a mission from God.

It's our first time in Fort Worth. As we pull into the parking lot, we do a vibe check and devise a plan of action. Kalki gets out of the van and starts walking toward the crowd of fifty or sixty kids at the other end of the lot. They spot him.

Some begin chanting in a joking way, others poke fun, while others seem visibly disturbed by the oncoming intruder.

Kalki quickens his pace and walks right into the middle of the crowd. They stare at him. He stares back. No one can imagine what's going to happen next. Then Kalki breaks the chilling silence: "Hey, what bands are playing tonight?" Their jaws drop open. They can't believe it: "HE'S ONE OF US!!!"

After talking with him for a while about the hard-core scene, one of the kids notices the *Razor's Edge* magazine that Kalki just happened to be carrying under his arm.

"What's that?" they ask.

"Oh, just a little zine I put together," says Kalki nonchalantly. "Want to check it out?"

"Sure," says a boy. "Hey! Youth of Today! I know them. They're great. Hey fells! Check out this zine!"

The KrishnaFest band set up and started kirtana in the parking lot. By the end of the night, even the club owner had purchased a *Bhagavad-gita.* The kids all loved our music, the prasadam, and the books. And that Sunday, eight of them came to the Dallas temple for the feast!

Fort Worth is known in these parts as a "cow town," and it's not because they love cows. If they can take to Krishna consciousness here, they can take to it anywhere.

Straight-Edge Words, Phrases, Identification:

crusties—grubby punks who never wash or change their clothes
zine—magazine
pos—positive
bro—pal
large black "X" on the back of both hands—straight-edge fashion and identification
edge it!—a common straight edge slogan

CONSULTING AND TEAMWORK ARE KEYS TO SUCCESSFUL ISKCON MANAGEMENT

Catching many managers unaware, this short *ISKCON Communications Briefings* (ICB) story discussed a phenomenon we hoped would become an indispensable part of ISKCON. Unfortunately, it seldom got discussed in management meetings and most other important forums. The article is based on an excerpt from one of Srila Prabhupada's purports in the *Caitanya-caritamrta.* It stresses the importance of consultation. The concept of teamwork is anathema to many who say, "management by committee doesn't work," "two- and five-headed creatures don't exist," and so on. But I like to think that, in ISKCON, the days of management conducted by sheer charisma are over. This article appeals for more consultation and teamwork.

***ISKCON Communications Briefings,* October 1989**

In the purport to *Caitanya-caritamrta,* Adi-lila 1.35, Srila Prabhupada writes: "If one thinks he is above consulting with anyone else, including a spiritual master, he is at once an offender at the lotus feet of the Lord. Such an offender can never go back to Godhead."

Let's see how this instruction might translate into practical action for ISKCON managers.

Writing in *Survival on the Fast Track,* Barbara E. Kovach discusses common characteristics of managers who stand out and succeed in today's fast-paced world. They:

Develop a cadre of mentors, associates, and supporters.

Know what the hopes and dreams of colleagues are, so they can be woven into group goals.

Communicate with others to expand their knowledge and thus make better-informed decisions.

Communicate their vision of what is attainable and motivate others to work toward the goals they believe in.

Recognize that what they say influences others.

Talk about things that matter (avoid *prajalpa*).

TOWARD A CONSISTENT LIFE POLICY

"When I become a burger, I want to be washed down with Irn-Bru," says the childlike lettering, the presumed "voice" of a calf, whose innocent, five-inch-wide eyes peered out from the huge, 1998 British billboard. The advertisement was for a ginger beer pronounced "Iron Brew." Hundreds of these huge posters served to desensitize the public to the sacredness of all life and the fact that calves have a right to live out their natural lives. Don't animals have the right not to be killed by humans for food, fun, and fur?

In interesting juxtaposition to animal rights are the terms "Right to Life" and "Pro-Life," the defining phrases for the anti-abortion movement. The following perspective addresses the phenomenon that many vegetarians and animal-rights supporters widely welcome the process of abortion. We also challenge those who condemn abortion while simultaneously approving hunting and flesh-eating.

Polls show that over seventy-five percent of US citizens consider themselves "environmentalists." Current research shows that mass animal slaughter is a process that severely pollutes the environment. Yet few are aware that the meat industry harms the environment to a greater degree than most enterprises. This 1989 *ISKCON Communications Briefing* (ICB) article calls upon ISKCON to promote a "consistent life policy."

***ISKCON Communications Briefings*, December 1989**

Distributing *prasadam* en masse, networking with animal rights advocates, and recently taking part in pro-life (anti-abortion) protests in America are drawing ISKCON into the widely popular issue of protecting the earth's environment. With pollution of air, water, and soil escalating out of control, people are asking the Hare Krishnas what they're doing about it. They also inquire if we're helping to save the rain forests, forests in general, and various threatened species of animals and fish. As we delve into these issues, we discover inconsistencies among the movements dedicated to preserving various life forms.

Many save-the-earth-and-her-creatures advocates support abortion on demand. They think that killing unborn humans will thwart the "population explosion" and help maintain ecological balance. Most anti-abortion activists eat meat and remain callous to mass destruction of animals, fish, birds, and life in rain forests. Champions of animal rights are often pro-abortion and non-vegetarian and have widely varying levels of concern about the environment.

It is time for ISKCON to enter the debate armed with transcendental knowledge that true environmental consciousness means understanding that all life is sacred. Only by enlightening the public with the knowledge of *aham brahmasmi* and *ahimsa* found in Srila Prabhupada's books can a consistent life policy emerge. This field is open to great preaching opportunities.

The World Wildlife Federation (an international organization chaired by the Duke of Edinburgh) recently commissioned ISKCON's Ranchor dasa Adhikari to write a book on Hindu ecology. WWF has also contracted with him to make a research trip to India. There he'll explore the possibility of reforestation of the twelve forests of Vrindavana. This project could, in his words, "launch a major conservation project, linking one of Hinduism's most sacred sites, where trees have a very special significance as part of Krishna's lila (pastimes), to the drive for tree protection and reforestation throughout India." In conjunction with traditional Vraja-mandala *parikramas* (holy pilgrimages), pilgrims could participate in the reforestation of Vrindavana.

Saatchi and Saatchi, the world's largest advertising firm, has identified the Religion Environment Network as the most promotable of all their projects. They say they will use it as the focus for their contracted advertising campaign for WWF.

Ranchor's letterhead carries a small inscription at the bottom of the page: "This is recycled paper."

DISTINGUISH BETWEEN PR AND MARKETING

Marketing should not take precedence over communications. Counting the numbers of books sold, devotees "made," and plates of *prasadam* distributed can be deceptive. "Figures don't lie, but liars sure can figure," it is sometimes said. Without minimizing the great value of such measurement, when applied as the only yardstick of growth, numbers can be misleading. Sometimes ISKCON is perceived negatively by opinion leaders in government, science, religion, scholarship, the media, and the general public. This perception happens even in the face of large numbers of books going out. In the early days in particular, it is fair to say that large numbers of books went out at least partly because many distributors used deceitful "lines." The current Ministry of Book Distribution teaches that such deception is wrong. The preconceptions of people in general, what to speak of governments, scholars, and religionists, need to be carefully considered whenever preaching plans take place, otherwise ISKCON runs serious risks. Sacrificing our reputation and future for immediate gains is what this article was really about. ISKCON managers need to keep focused on the future and the big picture. Marketing goals tend to be immediate and bottom-line oriented; communications aims are long-term and concerned with values, aims, and reputation.

ISKCON Communications Briefings, December 1989

A panel of experts recently met to clarify the differences between public relations and marketing.

They defined marketing as: The management process whose goal is to attract and satisfy customers (or clients) on a long-term basis in order to achieve an organization's economic objectives. Its fundamental responsibility is to build and maintain a market for an organization's products or services.

They defined public relations this way: Public relations is the management process whose goal is to attain and maintain accord and positive behavior among social groupings on which an organization depends in order to achieve its mission. Its fundamental responsibility is to build and maintain a hospitable environment for an organization.

In ISKCON the marketing aspect may take the form of distributing books, convincing people to join the *ashram* or congregation, bringing many people to a special event, or promoting business for a restaurant. But the public relations aspect takes into account our total image in the wider community.

For example, if devotees promote a restaurant by massive leafleting of homes, they may spark a lot of new business. But if many residents are annoyed with the paper on their doors and floating around the neighborhood, the long-term effect could hurt the restaurant's reputation and its business.

Another scenario might be a hard-sell campaign to quickly move as many potential devotees into the *ashram* as soon as possible in order to facilitate various temple projects. While such efforts might indeed fill up the *ashram*, low-quality recruits could reduce morale, lower the standard of purity, and taint the temple's spiritual atmosphere. Thus, temple projects could suffer rather than improve.

Therefore, careful attention should be given not just to immediate marketing goals but also to long-term effects and the larger community of "outsiders." We can examine our own history to discover many instances in which short-term marketing strategies that ignored essential public relations principles have harmed our preaching efforts in the long run.

CHAPTER 2—1990

Marshalling Resources

Baba Madhava dasa, considered a Vaishnava saint, bequeathed on his passing on March 27, 1990, Vrinda Kund (a sacred lake) and its adjacent Vrinda Devi temple to ISKCON. This became the first Vrindavana-area temple to be willed or donated to ISKCON. During the summer, a devotee theater and dance troupe from Manipura toured the world, playing at major venues such as New York's Lincoln Center. A German court in Schenenfeld determined that

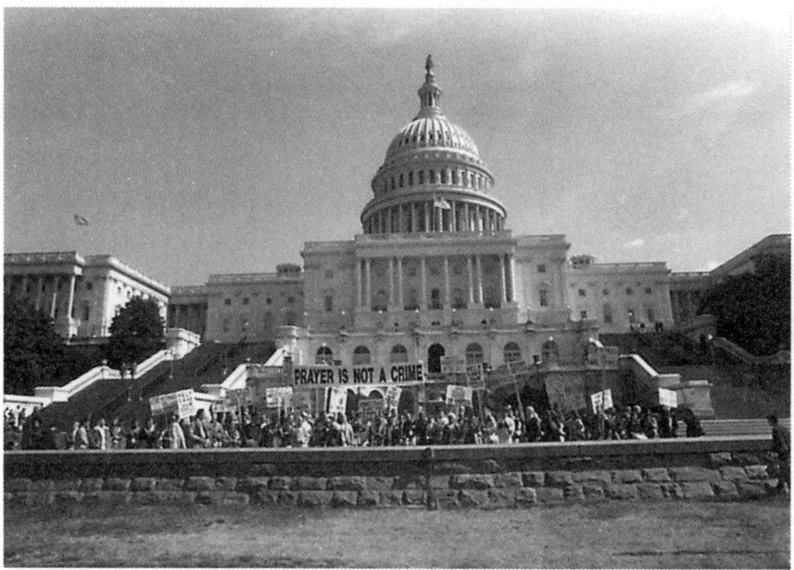

April, 1990—Washington, D.C., USA: "Prayer is not a crime" becomes the national slogan to fight charges against ISKCON brought by teenager Robin George. During a 24-hour protest vigil held around the world, devotees show solidarity at the US Capitol.

ISKCON was a bona fide religious organization and officially allowed its members to distribute books. In Czechoslovakia and Romania, devotees established many home programs and Hare Krishna Food for Life centers. Days after his release from prison, South African devotees presented Dr. Nelson Mandela a set of Srila Prabhupada's books in Johannesburg. In March, the British government ban on visitors coming to Bhaktivedanta Manor spurred member protest and the start of the Hare Krishna Temple Defense Movement. At an interfaith meeting in Dallas, devotees gave Chinese Protestant Bishop K. H. Ting a Chinese-language edition of *Bhagavad-gita As It Is.* ISKCON's Bhaktivedanta Institute hosted a conference called Consciousness Within Science, in San Francisco. In Washington, D.C., the US Supreme Court overruled brainwashing charges in the Georges' multimillion-dollar lawsuit against

March 28, 1990—Calcutta, India: Yasser Arafat, chairman of the Palestinian Liberation Organization, is greeted by Calcutta devotees, who present him with Srila Prabhupada's *Bhagavad-gita As It Is.* The PLO leader promises to read it. ISKCON's Airavata dasa and others continued organizing and participating in interfaith meetings with Islamic leaders as late as 1999.

ISKCON. When Indian devotees gave Yasser Arafat a copy of *Bhagavad-gita As It Is* in Calcutta, the Palestinian leader praised the book.

HOW TO PREPARE AND SEND OUT A NEWS RELEASE

These days, no matter how good you are, no one will know or care, unless you know how to promote yourself. For ISKCON there are few better and less-expensive ways to do this than to use the media. This article teaches a skill. Although the impressions the media give us tend to be fleeting and superficial, constant repetition of good news is remembered by readers, listeners, and watchers. Writing and sending news releases is not difficult. In fact, it's really easy. This hands-on ICB instructional article told readers how to do it. Media releases should be fun. They should also be novel, give the media a peek behind the scenes, and have an angle or news hook that gives newspapers, magazines, radio, and television something their audiences want.

ISKCON AND THE MEDIA

***ISKCON Communications Briefings,* February/March 1990**

In *ISKCON Communications Briefings,* August 1989, we recommended that ISKCON adopt a bold, assertive attitude toward the media.

We urged leadership to "see every contact or potential contact with the media as a great opportunity to reach thousands and sometimes millions of people."

The most basic and widely used tool for achieving media attention and placement is still the good old news release.

The term "news release" is generally favored over "press release," as the latter implies exclusion of the electronic media—radio, television, and now the Internet.

A well-written, intelligently conceived, and systematically distributed news release often results in interviews and coverage.

When devotees include worthy photographs, properly captioned, and other graphics with the release, chances of placement are usually increased.

For example, ISKCON news releases announcing protests, such as the ones we staged throughout the world to help free the Soviet Hare Krishnas, resulted in substantial media coverage.

Also, when we've included attractive photographs with news releases announcing major festivals or events, we typically achieve good articles and photos in the media.

News releases that announce news conferences (not "press conferences") or give a position statement (such as ISKCON's response to a news story linking it with New Vrindavana) are less likely to attract the media's attention. News conferences are not events in and of themselves.

The first question to ask before sending out a news release is "Is it news?" or "Who cares?" Think like a reporter looking for news before deciding on a news release and while preparing it.

The more your release reads like a news story, the greater its chances of being read completely and used.

If the news release relates to an event or situation previously reported or in the news, it's usually a good idea to include a copy of the most recent newspaper stories on the subject. If you have a newspaper clipping from any of the newspapers to whom you're sending the release, be sure to include that clipping with the news release going to that newspaper.

In our next issue of *ISKCON Communications Briefings,* we'll tell you how to use, prepare, and send photographs with your release and how best to distribute releases and photographs to the media.

Here are some of the basics for pulling together a professional news release. (For more detailed information and examples of types of news releases used by ISKCON, I strongly recommend you purchase *Seven Ways to Preach Through Writing,* by Drutakarma dasa.)

Include the name of an ISKCON contact person—usually the public relations person—with day, evening, and weekend phone numbers. News doesn't keep "banker's hours." Reporters may need comments at 11:00 PM for a morning story.

Use ISKCON news release letterhead if you have it, or use ISKCON letterhead with the words NEWS RELEASE in large bold letters just under the printed heading. If you're releasing news from a non-ISKCON entity such as BBT, BI, or KrishnaFest, use their letterhead. This makes it clear to the media exactly who is sending it to them.

Use one side of a sheet of 8½" by 11" or A4 white paper. Good quality photocopies are fine, since most editors assume you're attempting multiple placements. If the release has been specially prepared for one editor, note it on the release.

Put a release date on your news release. This tells the reporter or editor when you're requesting the story be used. Or simply type in FOR IMMEDIATE RELEASE. But in all cases make sure to include the date (with the year) when the release was issued.

Leave adequate margins so editors can make notes. Some public relations experts begin their stories about half-way down the first page to give editors extra space at the top.

Consider providing a capsule summary of the release as a descriptive title or headline above the story.

Double-space the release.

Type "more" at the bottom of each page (if the story contains more than one page) except for the final page. Some PR people don't break paragraphs between pages, starting each page with a new paragraph. Others think it's better to break them, as it leads the reader more compellingly to the following page.

Add a slug, a one- or two-word capsule of the story that editors will use to identify pages of the release should they become separated, to the upper-left-hand corner of the second and following pages. Below the slug, indicate the release page number.

Mark the end of the release on the final page with traditional symbols: center either a ### or a -30-.

Limit each paragraph to two or three short sentences. Many

paragraphs—especially the first, called the lead paragraph—may contain only one sentence. Ideally it should be newsy, relevant, entertaining, and give readers a behind-the-scenes look.

Limit the size of your release to one or two pages. Supplementary or background information can be included in the same package as separate, related items.

Don't staple the pages. Paper clips are okay.

October 13, 1991—USA: (Above) The Manipuri troupe performance includes acrobatic drumming and martial-arts demonstrations.

October 13, 1991—Houston, USA: (Right) "Culture speaks a universal language," says ISKCON's Bhakti-svarupa Damodara, organizer of the Manipuri Dance Troupe's tour of campuses and concert halls in 32 North American cities. In Houston, young members depict the colorful Rasa Lila Dance of Radha and Krishna. Manipur is a state in northeast India, all of whose citizens are devotees of Krishna, the Supreme Personality of Godhead. Manipur has remained a Vaishnava state since Chaitanya Mahaprabhu's followers visited in the 18th century.

A POWERFUL POTENTIAL

As early as 1990, ICB cited a potentially brilliant future for ISKCON temples: congregational development. Being with people and doing meaningful things with them is one of the highest forms of human enjoyment. Teaching and setting a personal example for others in their own homes benefits everyone involved, and it's enjoyable because it's preaching. Also, such visits can put core devotees in touch with the current of the world without them becoming victimized by newspapers and television. ISKCON members can teach people how to practice Krishna consciousness in their own homes. With such personal treatment, families who host such visits come to identify with ISKCON and gradually begin to assist in devotional service, seeing such activity as the high point in their lives. Read this ICB article and find out how we accurately predicted future trends.

ISKCON Communications Briefings, June/July, 1990

The line between "inside devotees" and "outside devotees" is blurring. Thousands of initiated devotees now live outside temple precincts. Many hold jobs—some with influential positions in society—and spend most of their time away from the temple environment.

Congregational members are performing devotional service and making financial contributions to ISKCON temples and projects.

In order to help provide American temples with solid financial support systems and to free temple devotees for preaching and book distribution, the North American GBC has been promoting congregational development.

Congregational membership includes Nama Hatta programs, regular temple visitors, the Indian community, FOLK members, life members, and anyone else who professes Hare Krishna as the primary spiritual inspiration in his or her life.

In many regions outside India, Indian congregational support has been an essential element in temple life. This is true of New

York, Toronto, Chicago, Houston, London, Durban, Nairobi, and Trinidad.

Financial support from the Hindu community has provided most of the funding to date for the ISKCON vs. George campaign. Srila Prabhupada gave specific instructions to support Bhaktivedanta Manor with donations from the Indian community. In a letter dated October 1975 to Kartikeya Mahadeva, Srila Prabhupada writes, "In India especially people are religiously inclined. They like to live in village and also like to love Lord Rama, Lord Krishna. This idealism is running through their blood and veins."

Mr. Shrikumar Poddar, a key advisor to many ISKCON projects, including *Back to Godhead* magazine, spoke at a recent North American GBC meeting in Detroit. He presented a simple formula for developing the congregation and obtaining financial support from it. Mr. Poddar advised that each temple maintain a monthly newsletter to all its contributors and potential contributors. He also recommended that a detailed financial statement be mailed out at least quarterly and that temple management view all of its congregation as potential devotees.

The experience of temple presidents has shown that increased dissemination of temple news and financial information to the congregation better enables temple devotees to reach out and engage these members. In turn, this engagement ignites or fans their enthusiasm and inspires greater participation.

America's *Chronicle of Philanthropy* recently published this statement from management expert Peter Drucker: "Non-profit groups that have succeeded haven't said, 'We want your money; we do good.' They say, 'You're a member, we do things for you.'" One professional in the field of non-profit support made this observation: "Too many non-profit organizations say, 'Our heart is pure and our mission good, and don't ask if we really make a difference.'"

Development of an active, vibrant congregation is not the answer to achieving all of ISKCON's goals or curing all of its problems, but with determination and good planning, a fired-up congregation can be one of the temple's greatest resources.

Some have suggested that emphasis on congregational preaching will detract from the spiritual purity of the movement's inner core. A solid inner core of devotees, however, serves as inspiration to the congregation. Enlivened congregational members feel inspired to serve Srila Prabhupada's movement by facilitating the spiritual education and preaching activities of a temple's full-time devotees.

In temples where full-time devotee staffs are short, congregational members can furnish funds and services. They perform secretarial and bookkeeping functions, help maintain the physical plant, make their homes available in the evenings for preaching programs, and provide donations of all sorts of goods, from *bhoga* to office furniture.

Funding from congregations can help relieve temple devotees from the financial burden of maintenance and give them time to preach and distribute books. This is particularly helpful where temples are short-staffed.

A properly situated congregation can also free devotees to extend preaching activities to a variety of groups, including schools, youth clubs, Nama Hatta and Indian community evening programs, service clubs, Scout groups, retirement homes, rehabilitation programs, prisons, New-Age organizations, animal-rights groups, vegetarian societies, churches, and temples.

Experience has shown that a percentage of congregational members become devotees. For example, many members of the Indian community who began as life members became initiated devotees. Subsequently, they influenced their family members and close friends to join ISKCON and, in turn, many of these new recruits accepted initiation.

Our congregations are attracted by dedicated, hard-working groups of temple devotees, by "the opulence of renunciation." Undoubtedly, a prime motivation for an enthusiastic, productive congregation is the temple devotees' spiritual purity.

Almost all churches, synagogues, mosques, and temples throughout the world are easily supported by their congregations. Even so, none of them has a core group with the spiritual purity and mood of renunciation found in ISKCON's Vaishnava temple devotees. When the right organizational principles are applied, there's an enormous potential for this kind of preaching in Srila Prabhupada's movement.

July 11, 1991—New York, USA: Devotees chant on New York's Brooklyn Bridge on the 25th anniversary of ISKCON's founding. They had obtained a 10-year lease on April 1, 1991, on the original ISKCON premises, located at 26 Second Avenue in Manhattan, New York City.

OUR BEST FOOT FORWARD

The use of engaging melodies, enchanting music, expert singing, charming choreography, gorgeous costumes, and excellent sound systems can bring a new dimension to *hari-nama* parties. When these elements are expertly put in place, the cultural position of Krishna consciousness is more easily established. In carefully planning *hari-nama* parties we can literally follow in the footsteps of His Holiness Indradyumna Swami. His publics are not only entertained but are exposed to the traditions, history, and philosophy of Krishna consciousness. They always want to know more. This can be especially true when handouts explain the history of *hari-nama.* Attractive chanting parties can become an integral part of almost any culture of the world. In many places on earth they have become an indispensable part of the local scene. The following ICB article is based on a suggestion by His Holiness Kavicandra Swami.

***ISKCON Communications Briefings,* September/October 1990**

Srila Prabhupada gave great emphasis to distributing three features of Krishna's mercy: his books, the holy name through *hari-nama sankirtana,* and *prasadam.*

ISKCON has excelled admirably throughout the world in book distribution, with the printing and distribution of millions of books in dozens of languages. *Prasadam* distribution has been a pervasive, ever-increasing phenomenon at Sunday feasts, festivals, Hare Krishna Food for Life programs, restaurants, cooking classes, congregational and FOLK programs, conferences and seminars, and in dozens of other preaching areas.

ISKCON's daily or weekly *hari-nama sankirtana* in many parts of the world, however, has not seemed to have kept pace with the constant expansion of book and *prasadam* distribution. The numbers of devotees who participate in *hari-nama,* and the quality of most of the parties, needs addressing.

Why is *hari-nama* so important?

The image of an organization is not artificially created by media exposure, advertising, or slick marketing procedures. Ultimately, the reputation of an organization is the sum total of its personal contacts with members of the public. Literally tens of thousands of people—and often hundreds of thousands—will hear or see an ISKCON *hari-nama* party in a single day or evening. From a worldwide perspective, *hari-nama* presents a unique opportunity to broadcast the holy name to millions of people each month or week of the year.

Why is the quality of our *hari-nama* parties so important?

First, it makes a big difference when many devotees join the party. When the public sees many devotees participating, the people get a sense of our movement's strength and endurance. And when devotees dress nicely, sing and play instruments in a coordinated, pleasing way, and dance rhythmically and gracefully, both observers and devotees become spiritually enlivened.

Srila Prabhupada, who taught us how to glorify the Lord through chanting, dancing, singing, and playing musical instruments, greatly appreciated *kirtanas* in the style and mode of our disciplic succession.

We can imagine how beautifully the *kirtana* singers and dancers must have sounded when Lord Chaitanya was present.

In *Caitanya-caritamrta,* Madhya-lila, Chapter 13, verses 33–48 speak of the ordered manner in which *sankirtana* parties were arranged for the Puri Rathayatra festivals that took place in Sri Chaitanya Mahaprabhu's presence. Each party was assigned someone to lead, others to respond, others to dance, and two *mridanga* players to keep the beat.

When Srila Prabhupada first arrived in England in 1969, he gave personal instructions on where *mridanga* players should be situated for certain types of *kirtana,* how instruments should be played, and how in Lord Chaitanya's time instruments were played softly while accompanying the lead singer and louder for the chorus, back and forth. He also gave choreography instructions for the Conway Hall programs in which he participated.

While ecstasy cannot be controlled, it can be intensely felt by both devotees and the conditioned souls when the chanting, dancing, and playing of musical instruments on *hari-nama* are well coordinated.

Cleanliness, proper attire, "orchestration," even choreography —all have their place in Lord Chaitanya's movement. *Hari-nama* parties need not be massive to make a good impression, but since millions of people see them every year, more frequent and better-organized ones will have a greater impact. And *hari-nama* parties do affect the way people perceive the Hare Krishna movement. They can help develop positive attitudes.

ISKCON is more famous for chanting Hare Krishna than anything else. Chanting in public is something to be proud of, and it's time to revive, emphasize, and upgrade this vital element of preaching throughout the Krishna consciousness movement.

EVALUATE YOUR AUDIENCE

There's no better way to discover how people perceive ISKCON than to ask them. Communications in ISKCON is about changing people's attitudes and perceptions. It is most difficult to know if this has been accomplished unless we can learn how to evaluate. Customarily, communications specialists conduct surveys directly before and right after public relations campaigns. Unfortunately, systematic surveys are usually expensive operations. But simpler forms of evaluation are possible and can be effective. One way this kind of evaluation is achieved is through questionnaires. A sample of just such a set of questions and how they were used in a US high school classroom forms the basis of this 1990 ICB story.

ISKCON Communications Briefings, September/October 1990

An important element often missing in many communications or public relations programs is evaluation after the event. Evaluation is usually the final phase of the research-planning-implementation-evaluation public relations cycle. By helping to better understand a particular audience's reaction, evaluation can provide helpful information when one formulates future programs for that audience.

As an experiment, ISKCON Communications designed a tentative questionnaire for nondevotee schoolchildren in the 14–18 age group. Devotees used it in classroom programs given during school hours. Students were usually given the questionnaire at the end of an hour-long presentation, sometimes including the slide show "Meet the Hare Krishnas." Before the lecture, the devotees obtained permission from teachers to administer the survey.

At the end of the class, devotees handed out two sheets, each containing about five or six questions. These gave the students a chance to make meaningful comments.

We found students quite willing to take a few minutes at the end of the talk to write their impressions of various parts of the presentation and to answer questions about Krishna consciousness in general.

You can use this survey designed for the 14–18 age group (or devise your own) in order to (1) gauge the response of young people to the Krishna consciousness movement; (2) learn about any concerns they might have; (3) determine what relevance Krishna consciousness might have to social issues of concern to young people; (4) help design future presentations.

Following is a partial list of questions asked in the survey. Each survey contained a preface inviting them to write additional remarks in the ample space under each question:

Has today's presentation deepened your understanding of the Krishna consciousness movement?

What was the most interesting part of the presentation?

"A vegetarian lifestyle can greatly affect a person's life—physically, mentally, and spiritually." How do you feel about this statement?

Have you ever visited a Hare Krishna temple or read any Hare Krishna literature? If yes, please specify which one(s).

Do you think there should be laws preventing Hare Krishna devotees from selling their literature in airports?

Have you ever contemplated a "consistent pro-life policy," which would afford protection for the unborn human child (prohibit abortion), as well as for animals and for the trees and other plants in rain forests?

Has today's presentation made you feel you want to learn more about the Hare Krishnas? If yes, what specifically would you like to learn, and how would you consider going about this?

List the parts of the presentation which annoyed or troubled you (say what was weak, what you disliked or didn't agree with, and what could have been done better).

Some results: About 60% of the American high school pupils questioned said that they found the Hare Krishna Food for Life program the "most interesting" part of the presentation. More than 70% found the presentation as a whole "interesting" and felt they wanted to know more about the movement. A majority said they remembered the words of the *maha-mantra* more than anything else in the presentation. Over 90% said "no" to laws that would prevent Hare Krishna devotees from selling literature in airports. About two-thirds said they found the entire presentation "very informative" and interesting. Generally, no more than 5% had visited a temple. A majority in most schools agreed with legalized abortion.

We also redesigned the original questionnaire to produce a second one containing only five questions, some of which combined queries on the first questionnaire.

CHAPTER 3—1991

Spirit Matters

This year millions of Australians, via television, saw and heard the Hare Krishnas' chanting party in Brisbane's Lion's Parade, and actress Hayley Mills opened the city's first Food for Life program with police inspector Dick Condor. Padayatra-affiliated devotees visited the mayors of forty cities in New Zealand as the walking parade toured the country. Globally, ISKCON's Governing Body Commission began a network of social services through its Health and Welfare Action Committee, formed in 1990. Sons and daughters of initiated disciples, sometimes known as "second generation devotees," held an annual reunion in Los Angeles in July. After considerable religious violence in the region, Hindus and Muslims marched and sang together in Hyderabad's first full-scale Rathayatra festival. In St. Petersburg (formerly Leningrad), several rooms in the Russian Museum of Ethnography exhibited Hare Krishna art and culture during thirty days in July. President Borja of Ecuador praised the Hare Krishna Food for Life program. For the first time in Rio de Janeiro, Rathayatra took place—along Ipanema Beach. The Reverend Jesse Jackson visited ISKCON Detroit and hugged Lekhasravanti-devi dasi, proclaiming her father (the late Walter Reuther) to be his hero. In March, former ISKCON leader Kirtanaananda was convicted of racketeering.

PEOPLE WANT TO KNOW—DO WE CARE?

"You talk about the environment, but I don't see you doing anything about it." This is the message that many environmentalists gave to ISKCON temples, especially when they saw the widespread use of nonbiodegradable materials during public festivals. Here is a case where actions speak louder than words. It's one thing to preach about how the simplicity and austerity of a Krishna consciousness lifestyle can positively impact the environment. However, if our actions are not consistent with these teachings, we are perceived as hypocrites. This 1991 ICB article explains how a guest at a Hare Krishna Sunday Feast stimulated enough concern about "hands-on" action to change a temple's buying patterns. This in turn inspired the North American ISKCON Governing Body Commission to pass a resolution banning the use of Styrofoam cups and plates, along with nonbiodegradable detergents and soaps.

***ISKCON Communications Briefings*, July/August 1991**

On May 4, 1991, the North American GBC banned Styrofoam use in temples, along with nonbiodegradable detergents and soaps. The resolution also directs each temple to use recycled paper wherever possible and to take up recycling programs in the disposal of garbage.

This resolution (voted on by the North American GBC and temple presidents), although jurisdictional only in North America (and enforceable maybe nowhere), is almost revolutionary for ISKCON. Rarely does the GBC attempt policies with this powerful an impact on temples' economic independence.

This exceptional move signals sensitivity on the part of ISKCON leadership toward public concerns about the environment (see enclosed pamphlet: "Save Earth Now—Krishna Consciousness and the Environment").

Environmental quality has become the most important single worldwide issue of the day, and public opinion experts say this will continue, probably through the remainder of the decade.

If ISKCON follows the GBC resolution, this will help demonstrate to a public generally misinformed of Krishna consciousness that devotees care about the quality of life on our planet.

Okay, you might say, but we have a pamphlet on the environment, and we're putting a book out about our perspective on the environment (the BBT book with a proposed title the same as the pamphlet is scheduled for printing at the end of this year), and our philosophy is that Krishna consciousness in and of itself is the highest welfare work. Why endeavor extraneously, worrying about garbage disposal, Styrofoam, and recycled paper?

August 30, 1991—Berlin, Germany: Rock star Boy George performs with Hare Krishnas on stage at the International Radio and TV Fair, seen by fifteen million viewers. Devotees accompany George as he sings his hit tune *Bow Down, Mister.* The song includes the group refrain, "Hare Krishna, Hare Krishna, Krishna Krishna, Hare Hare; Hare Rama, Hare Rama, Rama Rama, Hare Hare." Flower petals rain down on the chanters at the finale.

Just after a recent lecture in the New York temple by Romapada Swami, a guest challengingly asked why the temple used cups and plates made of Styrofoam, whose manufacture is widely thought to erode the earth's ozone layer and add to nonbiodegradable waste.

After explaining that it was probably because Styrofoam costs less, the guest volunteered to help find inexpensive alternatives to Styrofoam. Romapada Maharaja feels that the implementation of certain environmentally conscious habits is a great and important challenge for ISKCON. He fears that after publishing tracts and a book on the environment, we might be regarded as hypocrites if we don't clean up our environmental act.

It's essential to provide the philosophical basis for creating a purer world, but, as Prabhupada said many times, "practice is better than precept."

Part of an excellent communications program these days is the capability to make appropriate changes in our personal and collective behavior to meet current preaching needs. Instead of contradicting or compromising our Vaishnava principles, appropriate changes will support them.

A commitment to renounce Styrofoam, use recycled paper, and manage waste responsibly would be a great place to start.

NOW WE'RE NO LONGER CONFIDENTIAL

Halfway through 1991, we decided that *ISKCON Communications Briefings* should no longer be confidential. After all, we weren't revealing any deep, dark secrets. Mostly ICB talked about communications philosophies and techniques that could work with many organizations. We thought it was time the communications component come of age and be included as an essential element of management, leadership, and preaching. We even started punching holes in the ICB papers so that ISKCON leaders could keep ICBs in a notebook. Thus, temples and individuals could have a notebook or manual to deal with all types of communications. "All types" includes crisis communications and the planning of preaching activities. We wanted it known that the communications component should never be left out. By the way, we decided to discontinue ICB at the end of 1997 and put all the ICBs to date in a single book. We did this because we felt that we should be teaching and training ISKCONites to put ICB to work; we felt that there should be a systematic way to impart this knowledge to others. In one sense, we found that we had been getting ahead of ourselves. We realized that it is wiser to teach what we had been writing about instead of simply publishing and "presenting new ideas."

ISKCON Communications Briefings, July/August 1991

Starting with this issue of *ISKCON Communications Briefings,* which includes an article on "two-way symmetrical communication," we've decided to emphasize the "how-to" aspect of communications.

Although we've been recommending that all subscribers keep

each ICB in a notebook for reference, we've learned that many devotees who would benefit from ICB never see it.

So, we're switching our "Confidential" label on every page to "Please Post," so that ICB can be used increasingly as a practical manual for proactive public relations. So we ask you to please post ICB prominently on your devotee bulletin board.

We're committed to providing you with state-of-the-art public relations theory and practice, including important ISKCON case histories, quotes from Srila Prabhupada, fax listings, and special tips, all directed toward helping you to better propagate Srila Prabhupada's mission.

PLEASE USE ICB DURING ISTAGHOSTIS. In 1966 Srila Prabhupada implemented the system of a weekly *istaghosti* for all ISKCON temples. His instruction was that the first part of the *istaghosti* be used for philosophical discussion and the second part for practical matters. We're firmly convinced that ICB will give philosophically based, practical perspectives on many phases of preaching.

If you read aloud relevant sections of the current ICBs during your regular *istaghosti* meetings, we're convinced that many devotees who could not have taken advantage of ICB will find opportunities to expand the preaching in your region. We receive several new subscriptions each month, attesting to the fact that devotees increasingly depend on ICB for information. Also, please make your binder of ICBs readily available for devotees to review, so that they can avail themselves of back issues. Some may even wish to subscribe separately.

ICB WILL BECOME YOUR CRISIS COMMUNICATIONS MANUAL. In future issues, ICB will more systematically address how to act in a crisis situation. By keeping each ICB in a binder, you will be compiling your ISKCON crisis communications manual. "Crisis communications" is not a system of management that operates in an ongoing crisis situation. It's a method for dealing responsibly and effectively with a situation that's so exceptional that it warrants being called a crisis.

In general, ICB will be your proactive, positive PR manual, but crisis communications planning, strategies, and techniques will play a regular role. In this way you will soon be as prepared as possible for each and every crisis.

If you'd like us to address any specific crisis or types of crises, please write to us about this. We want your input. Maybe we'll publish one of your stories on how you handled a crisis, or address a possible future crisis you've alerted us about.

CHAPTER 4—1992

A Post-Secular World?

The year's most striking event was the July Hare Krishna Gauranga Bhajan Band performance in Moscow's Olympic Stadium, where devotees chanted with 35,000 newly-liberated Russians. Earlier, the ISKCON Christchurch Hare Krishna Food for Life program had received a major grant from the country's gaming commission. In late summer, Catholic priests in Poland stood by reverentially as Indradyumna Swami delivered a sermon to a packed church. In war-torn Soviet Georgia, devotees began a Hare Krishna Food for Life program, feeding hundreds every day, and in September, Advaita Candra dasa and Bhakti Charu Swami saved ISKCON France's New Mayapura rural community from seizure by creditors. A second generation of ISKCON devotees started a program called Project Future Hope. They organized apprenticeship programs, which later

August, 1992—Krokowa, Poland: A local Catholic priest poses in his Krokowa church with Polish devotees. At the priest's request, Indradyumna Swami (to the priest's left) speaks to an assembly of 500 parishioners. Polski national television had previously aired a 40-minute special called *Preacher of Bhagavad-gita,* featuring Indradyumna Swami. Krishnas are widely known in Poland.

led to the formation of the ISKCON Youth Ministry, headed by Manu dasa.

LOOKING AHEAD: SYMBOLS AND SLOGANS

Semiotics has now become a serious sociological study of signs and symbols. It's a communications language that includes gesture, symbols, and clothing. It underscores the fact that logos and slogans are important. They can also be fun, beautiful, and evocative. Good ones are always memorable. On today's information highway, we tend to retain only the simplest and shortest of messages—like the hundreds of billboards one passes on typical US highways. The year 1992 marked the fourth year of a decade-long odyssey, the search for an ISKCON logo. An early logo idea mentioned in the ICB article below was the image of the Divine Couple. This was ultimately put aside in favor of a design that combined a lotus, tilaka, and peacock. Many had objected that images of Deities might be easily defaced. The final design—that combining lotus, tilaka, and peacock—was used as the Centennial logo and now, slightly altered, has become the official logo of ISKCON. We hope it will become as popular as the words "Hare Krishna!"

ISKCON Communications Briefings, March/April, 1992

As we look toward ISKCON's next quarter century and beyond, we'll be thinking more about slogans, logos, mission statements, symbology, organizational and cultural identification, reputation, "specific messages," preaching to target audiences, and official position statements (like the one on Hinduism published this year as a GBC resolution).

Srila Prabhupada often said we should present Krishna consciousness as a cultural, scientific movement and not necessarily as a religion. One of hundreds of examples can be found in a Melbourne conversation of April 22, 1976: "So this Krishna consciousness movement is a scientific movement; it is not a religious faith . . . it is not like that. It is a science to understand your real identification."

When His Divine Grace Srila Prabhupada ordered the North American BBT to pay for the printing and distribution of 270,000 copies of a 12-page, full-color booklet entitled *The Krishna Consciousness Movement Is Authorized,* he approved a statement inside that designated ISKCON as "a cultural movement."

Following in this vein and drawing on various other published statements by Srila Prabhupada, we often suggest that ISKCON communications specialists refer to ISKCON as "a cultural movement for the re-spiritualization of humanity." This can be considered a "position statement." Srila Prabhupada also gave us other slogans, such as "simple living and high thinking" (for devotees and the public) and "Books are the basis, preaching is the essence, purity is the force, and utility is the principle."

ISKCON is in search of a standardized worldwide logo. The ISKCON Communications Ministry (IC), having been assigned the task of producing one for GBC approval, presented a first draft of such a logo to the international GBC body this year at the annual Mayapura meeting. IC was then given the go-ahead to pursue this design and to finalize it for acceptance as soon as possible.

The logo involves an image of Radha-Krishna and the word ISKCON. The figures, drawn by Jadurani and developed further for logo design by Locan Prabhu, are based on the original ISKCON letterhead, which Srila Prabhupada personally designed. The logo will have hundreds of applications, such as letterheads, business cards, jewelry, paperweights, pens, clothing, key rings, decals, membership cards, lapel pins, watches, flags and banners, hats, balloons, laser displays, posters, neon signs, book covers, buttons, incense packets, shopping bags, plaques, signs, and vehicles.

Such a logo could be combined with a slogan. For example, we might visualize the Radha-Krishna logo printed on the side of a large, cloth shopping bag together with a prominent slogan such as "Hare Krishna—A More Natural Way of Life."

Some ISKCON slogans currently in wide use include "Feeding the Hungry Worldwide" (Food for Life), and "Krishna Prasad for

Everyone" (Food for Life, India). Another slogan, less publicized but widely known in some circles, is "The Kitchen Religion."

Slogans and symbols, maxims and mottoes, if misused or overused, can trivialize the profound philosophy and contemplative spiritual practices of Krishna consciousness. But as we move into the '90s, an era of "information overload," devotees will increasingly seek recognition as solvers of real-life problems, and we're almost sure to find that these concise and focused means of identification will play a far greater role in our ISKCON of the future.

TIPS FOR VIDEOGRAPHERS

If the United States and many other countries are becoming nations of "couch potatoes," we've all the more reasons to take video seriously, even though it's one of maya's favorite weapons. Along with face-to-face discussions, video—like it or not—is today's most comprehensive form of communication. A magazine like *Back to Godhead* or a newspaper like *Hare Krishna World* will typically include 30–80 images (color or black and white); but a single *Hare Krishna Today* (HKT) video show will always comprise more than 250 images, all in color, all moving, and all with sound—sometimes four layers of it (voice-over, ambiance, sound effects, and music). Apart from direct personal discussion, there is no better way to show the miraculous advance of Srila Prabhupada's movement than through video. I recommend you show everybody HKT, for starters. The following "tips," excerpted from an ICB issue, take you behind-the-scenes, or literally behind the camera. This article gives you an inside glimpse of what the editors of HKT expect their videographers around the world to do.

ISKCON Communications Briefings, March/April 1992

With *Hare Krishna Today,* ISKCON's video newsletter soon to be sent around the world, the ISKCON videographer's role will assume a new prominence. Some general suggestions from the experts can be of great help.

Make sure you understand lighting for video shooting. Buy a book on the subject if you need to, or consult experienced television cameramen in your locality. Even outdoor scenes in bright sunlight often require extra lighting. Poor lighting can ruin your tape of a good event or interview. When you're starting out, play back what you shoot on a VCR and monitor, to better understand how the final product will come across. This will tell you how well your lighting worked.

Make sure the sound quality, especially for interviews and messages, will be good enough for viewers to understand what you want them to understand. If you're conducting an interview, this is especially important. As you shoot, use headphones to continually monitor the sound. Check your sound quality by playing your tape back on the VCR when you begin, in order to see how the final product will come across. You may need to use a lavaliere microphone for interviews. This is a very small microphone—the kind often seen on television programs—that clips onto the speaker's clothing, somewhere just below the neck. Your camera will have an input jack for such a microphone. The microphones on some cameras are good enough to make lavaliere microphones unnecessary for most situations.

If you're covering an event, try to interview a key person, such as the organizer, the planner, the person who inspired it, master of ceremonies, the temple president, or, for a third-party perspective, participants or festival-goers. Move in close and get them to explain what was behind the event: the inspiration, foundation, and the scriptural basis. If the subject is an observer or outside participant, try to get him or her to say what it feels like to be there and how he or she is benefiting from the event.

For events, be sure to procure and scan all relevant newspaper and magazine coverage, showing the front-page banner (logo or masthead) and date, the section, the headline, and a slow scan of the entire article, including all used photographs. All this can be edited and used in the video newsletter and other video presentations.

Also for an event, you may use your VCR to tape news broadcasts reporting it. This material can then be edited and used in the video newsletter. But first check your local laws governing this practice.

HINDU COMMUNITIES STRENGTHEN ISKCON

"Are you Hindu?" This often-asked question to devotees was sometimes greeted with the scornful cry "Who cares?" But we have learned to care. ISKCON communications leaders, including me, grappled with this question and finally, together with several other ISKCON leaders, fashioned a position statement on ISKCON vis-a-vis Hinduism. ISKCON's international Governing Body Commission officially accepted this declaration in 1992. Already it is somewhat out of date, and a new, updated position is being formulated (as of July 1998). Even after the position paper was well

May 29, 1981—Preston, England: At the opening of the Preston Hindu Temple Community Center, Prince Charles, wearing a Krishna garland, leafs through a copy of the Srila Prabhupada *Lilamrta* by Satsvarupa Goswami, the authorized biography of Srila Prabhupada, as Krishnananda explains the meaning of the book and its effect on the world.

established, contradictory evidence saying, for example, that ISKCON has "nothing to do with Hinduism" found its way onto ISKCON's official web sites. ISKCON Communications effected its removal. If ISKCON had chosen to officially opt out of the Hindu culture, "legions of scholars in the future," says Julius Lipner, published author, professor and a curriculum director at Cambridge University, "would refer to ISKCON as the Hindu group that didn't call themselves Hindu." The following ICB article includes an explanation of why we are concerned about this aspect of our identity and re-prints the 1992 officially accepted "position paper" on ISKCON vis-a-vis Hinduism.

***ISKCON Communications Briefings*, March/April 1992**

Outside India, communities of Indian nationals have consistently patronized ISKCON temples. In England and South Africa these communities have played key roles in supporting and developing ISKCON. Now, in the United States, the movement is increasingly focusing on this sector of its congregation.

This new focus arises mostly out of the formation of the ISKCON Foundation, headed by Ambarisa and Naveen Krishna Prabhus. The Foundation's initial objective is to actively involve Indian communities on many levels. During the course of the Foundation's initial development, Naveen Krishna discovered that members of the American branch of the Vishva Hindu Parishad were interested in attending meetings of ISKCON administrators.

As an initial step in this direction, several leaders from the VHP (US) were invited to and attended a meeting of a group of ISKCON Foundation trustees, including Ambarisa, Naveen Krsna, Sridhar, Ravindra Svarupa, and Mukunda Goswami. Among the VHP leaders were Dr. Babu Susheelan (Vice-President), Dr. Shia Subramanya (Director of Western Operations), and Ramesh Gandhi.

The two-hour session was most valuable in developing a deeper understanding of ISKCON's relationship with Hindu communities in America. ISKCON and the VHP agreed to meet again when the Foundation has its next meeting in Los Angeles. The question of ISKCON's relationship with the Hindu community was raised and discussed at some length. VHP members seemed quite satisfied with ISKCON members' explanation of ISKCON's position vis-a-vis Hinduism. ISKCON members also mentioned that a proposal would be voted on at the annual Mayapur GBC meeting in 1992 officially articulating ISKCON's relationship with Hinduism. Mukunda Goswami read the draft of this proposal. It was voted on, and the resulting resolution, now part of ISKCON policy, reads as follows:

Whereas ISKCON sometimes characterizes itself as alternatively Hindu and non-Hindu, often apparently according to convenience;

Whereas ISKCON is under increasing pressure lately from some friendly Hindu organizations to interact with them on specific issues or at certain times; and

Whereas ISKCON members, even its leaders sometimes, when confronted with the questions of ISKCON's relationship with Hinduism, give contradictory statements and answers; be it resolved that the GBC adopt the following official position statement on ISKCON's relationship with Hinduism:

"The International Society for Krishna Consciousness (ISKCON), also known as the Hare Krishna movement, was founded by His Divine Grace A.C. Bhaktivedanta Swami Prabhupada. ISKCON follows the teachings of the *Vedas* and the Vedic scriptures, including the *Bhagavad-gita* and the *Bhagavat Purana;* it teaches and practices Vaishnavism, or devotion to God in the supreme personal aspect of Radha-Krishna.

"ISKCON receives these teachings through the preceptorial line known as the Brahma-Madhva-Gaudiya *sampradaya.* This well-established traditional line descends through the respected teacher Sri Chaitanya Mahaprabhu (AD 1486-1534), a full incarnation of Sri Krishna, whose philosophy and practices unify the teachings of all four major Vaishnava *acharyas:* Sri Madhvacharya,

Sri Ramanujacharya, Sri Vishnuswami, and Sri Nimbarkacharya.

"ISKCON embraces the chanting of the holy name of Krishna as a primary practice and accepts the concepts of transmigration, karma, vegetarianism (*ahimsa*), worship of the Deity (Sri Vigraha), and the preceptor-disciple (*guru-siksa*) relationship. Initiated members vow to refrain from gambling, illicit sex, intoxicants (including coffee, tea, and cigarettes), and nonvegetarian food.

"In this way ISKCON faithfully continues the core traditions of the Hindu faith. ISKCON's teachings are nonsectarian and nondenominational, for they are not limited to any particular historical religion. That principle, called *sanatana-dharma* in Sanskrit, denotes the natural and eternal activity of all living beings—loving devotional service to the one Supreme Personality of Godhead."

ISKCON Communications will provide two final forms of this statement—one with consistent, correct diacritics (for internal and scholarly use) and another with phonetic spelling for public use.

TARGETS, MESSAGES, AND METHODS

This article takes you inside the communications system. You'll discover how publics are influenced to change the way they think about or behave toward a particular group. The public relations tricks of yore, like Edgar Bernay's "engineering of consent," have given way to ethical and systematic processes for advancing ideologies, services, or products. If you're interested in how ISKCON communications works, this article will help you understand the whole process. You can apply many of these communications principles in your own life, regardless of your status or stature. The "inside story" is that the media are made up of people like you and me. People are dependent on relationships. ISKCON communications teaches devotees to learn techniques, but to focus on relationships. Read, learn, and enjoy.

ISKCON Communications Briefings, May/June 1992

Excellent communications in today's world seek not just to

change an organization's reputation but to change society. American communications scholar Rakow has gone so far as to write that "Symmetrical P.R. cannot function without a major change in US culture and political structures."

This view has some merit from ISKCON's perspective, as ISKCON's message ultimately involves the implantation of an entire culture, a spiritual civilization, in a godless world.

State-of-the-art communications is a carefully planned and structured process whose goal is not merely to change perceptions or even attitudes, but to change behavior. More to the point, an organization's communications efforts are successful when it is able to change the way people behave toward the organization.

In ISKCON we should not be satisfied with measuring our preaching success only by counting numbers: books distributed, temples opened, plates served, devotees made, projects started, *hari-nama* occurrences, and visitors to the temples. Of course, we will continue to use and broadcast the numbers because they are certainly indicators, dramatic and persuasive evidence, of growth, maturity, and success. If we add quality to quantity, though, we'll realize even greater quantity, with the added benefit of a positive change in behavior.

Behavior change in this case means: people who buy books, read their contents more thoroughly and apply it to their daily lives; new temples are widely supported by local communities; *prasadam* eaters adopt Krishna-conscious philosophies and practices; new devotees become exemplary in character, behavior, and preaching; new projects involve many community members; *hari-nama* parties are increasingly attractive; specific messages are imparted and elicit perceptions of a deep culture; temple visitors eagerly participate in the community's devotional activities.

The application of tested communications methods for changing the way people behave toward ISKCON involves employing an established system of planning in which one decides which target publics (social groupings) we want to speak to, what messages we want to communicate to each public, and how we want to communicate those messages.

In North America, a national communications team has begun just such a process, in association with the ISKCON Foundation, and is engaging leaders throughout the continent. It's important to note that this particular application is being conducted for ISKCON of North America and is related to a major fundraising campaign. Thus, it is not universally appropriate as a communications technique. Nonetheless, many parts of it, and its general principle, may be applied more broadly.

To start the process, our team, including the Foundation and communications counsel, identified ISKCON's publics and listed them in priority, starting with the most important, as follows:

Devotees
- A. Core
- B. Congregational
- C. Youth

Donors (prospective)
Indian communities
- A. Indian media
- B. Youth

Media (Western)
Special interest groups
(such as those who protect
religious freedom)
Alternative media
Local communities
Academia
Government
Youth/high-schools/colleges

The next step was to analyze each of these targets, one by one, asking the following seven questions: (1) How are we perceived? (2)

How do we want to be perceived? (3) What behaviors do we want? (4) What messages will best facilitate these behaviors? (5) What are the obstacles to achieving these behaviors? (6) What programs do we currently offer to deliver these messages? (7) What strategies will achieve the desired behavior?

Following is one abbreviated example of this analysis, using "congregational devotees" (point "B" under "Devotees," above). "Congregational devotees" in this particular instance refers to initiated devotees who do not live in the temple and do not work full time for the temple. This is only a summary—the full analysis is seven pages long.

1. How are we perceived?
   - Being dedicated and sincere
   - Having suffered a lot (due to Prabhupada's disappearance, court cases, our own mistakes, etc.)
   - Not well-managed
2. How do we want to be perceived?
   - Possessing saintly qualities
   - Imbibing the spirit of cooperation
   - Well-managed
3. What behaviors do we want?
   - Add Krishna consciousness to their lives and make spiritual advancement.
   - Integrally associate and participate with the devotee community.
   - Be involved in the development of their devotional communities and take responsibility for many activities, especially for those that are congregationally based (i.e., advisory boards, festivals and their planning, consultations, devotional services according to their propensities, etc.).
4. What messages will best facilitate these behaviors?
   - ISKCON leadership is undergoing systematic training and education.

- Lord Chaitanya's movement is a congregational movement in which many of His followers lived outside temple grounds. Being a congregational devotee is not qualitatively lower than being a temple devotee. It is healthy to be an upstanding member of the community, and we feel it is advantageous for the congregation to utilize the world in Krishna's service and dovetail their propensities accordingly.

5. What are the obstacles to achieving these behaviors?
   - Logistics
     A. Apparent shortage of money and manpower
     B. Inadequate databases and office equipment
     C. Lack of training facilities
   - Attitudes
   - Lack of understanding
6. What programs do we currently offer to deliver these messages?
   - Publications
   - Advisory board and planning committees
   - Posting of minutes of temple community and congregation board meetings
7. What strategies will achieve the desired behavior?
   - Supply information and success stories to the ISKCON leaders.
   - Encourage networking within the congregation.
   - Establish lifelong goals for congregational involvement.
   - Cultivate a genuine appreciation of the congregational contribution.
   - Cultivate key relationships.
8. The Action Plan. This usually involves identifying the action steps, people responsible for each step, and starting and completion dates. And the execution of the plan requires a good manager.

To conclude, we return to our philosophical basis. As is the case with the computers, cars, airplanes, printing presses, and telephones so many of us use, these systems are of no value without linkage to Krishna consciousness. However, when the process is combined with specific actions and goals in Krishna consciousness, it becomes an integral part of *yukta vairagya* (proper renunciation), engaging material energy in the Lord's service. Like other techniques, such as those we use in distributing books and building temples, state-of-the-art communications can be an important instrument for establishing the Krishna-conscious culture in a materialistic world.

PARADIGM SHIFTS NEEDED: SOUTH SEA COMMUNICATIONS COMMITTEE

Like many other ICB articles in this book, this item chronicles a piece of ISKCON history. The South Seas meeting was historic. The coming together of twenty devotees from Australia and New Zealand helped propel communications concepts into the foreground. Jaya Sila's video presentation of "paradigm paralysis" helped us realize that change is not a bad thing as long as Krishna consciousness philosophy remains intact. In Australia, where ISKCON is generally held in high regard, devotees like Priyavrata (of Food for Life) commented that the ANZ conference was "absolutely essential for the health of ISKCON." Devotees at the conference came to understand that we could ruin even an excellent reputation if we do not adopt a proactive attitude in communications.

ISKCON Communications Briefings, July/August 1992

The South Seas Communications Committee, ISKCON's fourth and most-recently-formed continental communications committee, held its first conference from May 25 to May 27 at the New Govardhana farm near Murwillumbah, Australia. The purpose of this panel and others around the world is to serve the movement by developing Communications philosophy and practice in regions where ISKCON is active.

Twenty devotees from Australia and New Zealand participated. Specialists made presentations on media relations (Taittireya dasi, former journalist), fundraising (Sridhara Swami), Food for Life (Priyavrata dasa, Australian FFL director), congregational preaching (Stava Priya dasa), and preparing for the future (Jaya Sila dasa, president of ISKCON Auckland).

Committee members agreed to ask the Zonal Council to approve the group's recommended duties for communications officers at each temple. They also resolved to ask the Australian Zonal Council about Food for Life fund-raising methods and the use of those funds. The results of the Zonal Council meeting were not available in time to include in this newsletter.

One of the most stimulating presentations and discussions dealt with "paradigm shifts." Presenter Jaya Sila used a video by futurist Joel A. Barker to underscore one of his themes: that our work habits, even in *bhakti-yoga,* can create "paradigm paralysis," resistance to progressive preaching ideas. In discussions, a consensus emerged that ISKCON can be seen as presenting a major paradigm change—from material thinking to spiritual thinking.

The group also concluded that good ideas or practices could be accepted from nondevotee sources, as long as the essential philosophy and practices of Krishna consciousness were not compromised in the process. We discussed being able to change strategies according to conditions, as in "utility is the principle," while recognizing limitations on freedom to change, based on "purity is the force." On this topic, the committee acknowledged that Prabhupada had some ideas that ran contrary to the Gaudiya Math of his day and had the courage to effect a paradigm shift. He thus succeeded in the global preaching mission, an area where his Godbrothers had failed.

Along parallel lines, an accord was reached on the practice of taking ideas from professionals. The history of consulting with experts in the South Seas region had roots in Srila Prabhupada's instructions and actions, and this could be substantiated by citations from his writings and recorded talks. Coincidentally, this same subject arose at the third European communications conference, held in Belgium (Radhadesh) from June 19 to June 21, especially during

Rohininandana dasa's presentation on counseling, called Caring for Preachers.

The Melbourne temple president, Aniruddha dasa, was elected chairman of the South Seas Communications Committee, and Suci Rani dasi was elected secretary-treasurer.

"There was a definite sense that new directions and possibilities for preaching in the zone have been opened up by the establishment of this ISKCON Communications Committee," said Suci Rani after the conference. "I hope that this will help to unify the efforts of devotees who are working in similar ways in different parts of the zone and also to establish a more clearly defined set of goals to communicate to all the devotees in our temples."

Priyavrata provided another assessment: "The Communications conference was absolutely essential for the health of ISKCON. Now I can understand the real purport of Srila Prabhupada's request that we cooperate. We can only begin to cooperate when we learn to communicate."

The committee will meet again in December just before the next zonal council meeting. Both bodies will be at New Govardhana, and as with the May meeting, Communications proposals will be put before the Zonal Council.

In addition to the South Seas, continental communications committees are now operational in India, Europe (East and West), and North America. South America and Asia await the formation of such councils. It is still not clear whether the C.I.S. (the former Soviet Union) and its main breakaway independent states (Latvia, Estonia, and Lithuania) will join the European or Asian committee. Soon, when committees in all world regions are operating, IC will convene a world communications congress, inviting committee members from around the world for a week-long conference.

EIGHT WAYS IC CONTRIBUTES TO THE ISKCON "BOTTOM LINE"

The following ICB perspective presents eight reasons why

reputation management is crucial to ISKCON. This article, in my view, is fundamental to understanding why we must follow systematic communications principles. Identifying trends and opportunities, tuning in to the public relations body of knowledge, improving relationships, planning for crises, being socially responsible and ethical, motivating participation, assisting the process of change, motivating the preaching spirit, and building reputation are all part of the communications process. As you read this article, you may well question some of your own personal systems of values, ethics, and guiding principles.

1982—Washington, D.C.: A three-chariot Hare Krishna Rathayatra (cart parade) festival takes place on the Washington, D.C., Mall. The hand-pulled chariots stop before the US Capitol. *The Washington Post* took many photographs of the chariots at the Capitol, like the one pictured here.

***ISKCON Communications Briefings,* July/August 1992**

How often do we hear the infamous query, "Exactly how does communications help ISKCON?"

There are many ways ISKCON Communications specialists serve ISKCON. The following list is not comprehensive, but it mentions many of the most important ways the communications function contributes to ISKCON's "bottom line"—preaching.

• Builds reputations, establishes friendships, helps identify specific audiences, produces publications. RESULTS: Paves the way or contributes directly to fund-raising, book sales, devotee-making.

• Motivates preaching through *Hare Krishna World* (HKW) or HKW seminars, conferences, teaching, presentations at GBC, zonal, and regional councils, and at TP meetings. RESULTS: Raises morale, develops teamwork, brings a sense of unity and "big ISKCON" consciousness.

• Identifies trends and issues and anticipates changes in laws, social and political trends, policies, and legal structures that have direct positive or negative effects on preaching. RESULTS: More opportunities to preach due to favorable laws and trends; avoidance and prevention of problems before they occur due to unfavorable legal, social, or political trends in governments, "established" religions, and the media, to name a few.

• Identifies opportunities through knowing important external and internal audiences, such as Indian communities (outside of India), peace groups, environmental organizations, animal rights and vegetarian societies, government-sponsored festivals, parades, and other events in which ISKCON can participate. RESULTS: More exposure, especially for *hari-nama.* Higher visibility and possible new markets for books and *prasadam.* Drawing wider community support by establishing ISKCON's position on issues such as animal rights, the environment, drug abuse, ethnic and national conflicts, vegetarianism, hunger, economics, rural life, social organization, and education.

• Plans for crises: preparation of written plans showing how to respond to or how to prevent disasters or attacks. Development of third-party assistance and endorsement by individuals and organizations, networking and condition-building. RESULTS: Expert handling of problems by being prepared in advance for all such possibilities. The best result of managing a crisis is to turn it into a positive event that improves ISKCON's reputation.

• Develops a body of knowledge and resource base for senior managers. RESULTS: Assisting managers on a regular basis in making realistic and enlightened decisions.

• Assists the process of change. Research on internal and external changes needed in preaching, goals, plans, strategies, execution, and evaluation. RESULTS: Easier implementation of new or different preaching plans and techniques so as to help achieve better qualitative and quantitative results.
• Sharpens focus on social responsibility and ethics. Helps in developing codes of ethics for internal and external behavior. RESULTS: Stronger devotee communities and improved public reputation in local and worldwide communities, leading to greater facilitation of all preaching programs.

DO WE REALLY NEED THE MEDIA? (PART I)

At almost any time of day, you can be sure that hundreds of millions of people are glued to their television sets, taking in glamor, humor, amusement, sports, adventure, culture, finance, nature, news, and millions of ads. Television has become the true "opiate of the masses." This degree of penetration is enough to turn any thinking person off television. For starters, most people think that television news is too intrusive on peoples' lives, invading "private space" like never before. But for spreading Krishna consciousness, we need the media. Ultimately, "the media" consists of people who are not terribly different from you and me. They are intrinsically not our "enemies."

May, 1983—London, England: ISKCON's Bhakti-lata-devi dasi garlands Queen Elizabeth II at the Great Children's Party in London, as a security guard observes the exchange. International newsmen, photographers, police, and onlookers converge on the scene.

But like the mind, anyone can become our best friend or the worst enemy, depending on how we relate with him or her. In any case, the media is an "active public," one which is constantly reporting on us (whether we like it or not) and constantly shaping peoples' opinions. When we look up long enough from our personal needs to understand the urgent organizational needs of ISKCON, it's easy to realize why we need the media and that its members can be our best friends.

***ISKCON Communications Briefings*, November/December 1992**

The question is sometimes raised, "Do we really need the media?"

Even in the face of sustained media persecution of the past in countries such as Germany, the former Soviet Union, and Argentina, Krishna consciousness has survived and even thrived. Did it really matter that the media were persecuting us? And if it did matter, how much? Some communications savants suggest that far too many organizations depend on the media more than necessary. There are even some scholars who say that communications should depend on the media very little, if at all.

Such theories hold that an organization should concentrate on its most supportive publics and build its reputation upon them (this generally excludes the media). This will allow an organization to flourish even in the face of adverse media attitudes that foster bad coverage.

The supportive publics for ISKCON usually fall into categories like book customers (those who have already bought books), restaurant customers, devotees, congregational members (devotees and nondevotees), Indian communities, devotee youth, Indian youth, schools, and special interest groups.

At the same time, however, most communications scholars admit that an organization should master the art of media relations, even if the media play a minor role in an organization's total communications functions. This theory holds that the media are not exactly a public but a conduit for the masses. A public, strictly speaking, is a precisely defined segment or subset of the mass public.

But for ISKCON, in contrast to the majority of other organizations, the media themselves need to be accepted as a public. Even the most media-wary communications specialists agree that ISKCON should consider the media not only a public, but an active public. Active publics are defined as "groups which can do great good or harm to an organization."

ISKCON almost always attracts media attention, even when devotees steer away from it. In areas where ISKCON members have made little or no attempt at media relations, media coverage has gone on, but unfortunately, in most such cases, coverage has tended to take on a life of its own. Such representation is often oblivious of what ISKCON is really all about.

Therefore, whenever and wherever devotees have tried to cut their losses by ignoring or avoiding the media, sometimes stumbling through media interviews because they haven't learned basic media skills, ISKCON's reputation has suffered.

Many precedents for developing media relations exist in our *sampradaya.* For openers, examples from the lives of Bhaktivinoda Thakur and Srila Prabhupada indicate that ISKCON should seriously strive for excellent media relations. Although it's absolutely necessary for ISKCON to focus on specific target publics, this article will deal with the media as a public.

In 1871, after the famous eighteen-day Orissan trial of the infamous Attibari Bisakisen, the yogi was convicted of multiple offenses. The Thakur sentenced him to eighteen months of hard labor. Soon after his incarceration Bisakisen died in prison. But Bhaktivinoda Thakura foresaw potential dangers coming from Bisakisen's fifteen thousand Attibari followers.

He decided to issue a comprehensive warning to the Orissan public. So he wrote a 630-word letter to *Progress,* a prominent newspaper in Cuttack. His scholarly letter described all of the debauched practices of the Attibari cult and ended with the following statement: "With all attempts for improvement, Orissa will never rise till these wicked and designing members of the Attibari class are converted into 'Honest Citizens.' "

Bhaktivinoda Thakura also wrote a lengthy newspaper article that was published in what is still Bengal's leading newspaper, the *Amrita Bazaar Patrika.* In this article, the Thakura enjoined readers to support his mission to build a temple at the newly-discovered birth site of Sri Chaitanya Mahaprabhu. From this incident, it appears that Bhaktivinoda Thakura was fully aware of how to utilize an important media organ to fulfill one of his most cherished goals —establishing the correct birth site of Sri Chaitanya Mahaprabhu.

In part two of "Do We Really Need the Media?" we shall explore Srila Prabhupada's relationship with the mass media.

BECOME A SPIRITUAL RESOURCE

It's easy to forget that Srila Prabhupada said Krishna consciousness is meant to "solve all problems of the world." The phrase is a repeated theme throughout his teachings. The steps are first to identify the problems, then learn who's working to solve them and, finally, to show how one can see them from a spiritual or Krishna conscious perspective. I argued in a 1996 *Hare Krishna World* editorial that Srila Prabhupada had an agenda for social change. He sometimes even addressed financial, social, and political issues. Examples: Mauritius was too dependent on its sugar crops; thousands of square miles of arable lands were fallow and unused in the USA; abortion was commonplace; the former USSR and the USA both had nuclear bombs at the ready; education was substandard; so-called independence had not brought genuine progress to India. As one television station manager advised, "You ISKCON people have to be in the media people's little black books; you have to be their contacts; they need to keep your phone numbers close to their chests. You need to be experts in your field, people with answers." And isn't that exactly how we move from irrelevant to relevant?

***ISKCON Communications Briefings,* November/December 1992**

Changing the way people behave toward ISKCON. That's what it's all about, cutting-edge communications, that is.

And what better way to do it than to become a spiritual resource? Can ISKCON be the group that social reformers, psychologists, politicians, doctors, scientists, and religionists turn to for answers to problems they encounter?

In a small way it happens every day in the course of our teaching Krishna consciousness. People have problems. And in dealing with people in the process of becoming devotees or otherwise involved in the Krishna consciousness movement, we often need to counsel them on how to solve their personal problems using Krishna consciousness philosophy.

It also happens on a larger scale. For example, during 1983, in Sweden, Vegavan and Ajit Prabhus started a popular call-in radio program. They became widely known among Swedish listeners for having unique and practical answers to callers' many problems. Some even called in to say that Vegavan's perspectives were the only ones that gave "real" solutions.

In recent times, the media and government have sought solutions or answers from ISKCON on issues of the day:

ITEM: One year ago the Mayor of Philadelphia personally asked Devi Deva to take over operations of a 40,000-square-foot, four-story building in the center of the city to shelter and feed homeless US war veterans. Devi Deva accepted the offer.

ITEM: Bombay's 1 August, 1992 Weekend Observer, the largest weekly newspaper in the city, published a 6,000-word picture article entitled "Material Problems, Spiritual Solutions." The interview-style story articulated Gopal Krsna Goswami's spiritual answers to India's economic problems.

ITEM: Detroit's largest newspaper approached Bhusaya dasa, director of the Bhaktivedanta Cultural Center, about a claim by medical science that it would one day extend the human life span to 400 years. The Sunday, September 13 issue of *The Detroit Free Press* identified Bhusaya as a member of the International Society for Krishna Consciousness and quoted his response.

ITEM: November 12, 1992: a radio program in Athens asked ISKCON to take part in a discussion about a major issue in Greece—whether the dead should be burned or buried. The Orthodox Church is known to be opposed to cremation, but burial space in Greece is scarce.

In Philadelphia, ISKCON has gotten deeply involved in the issues of hunger, homelessness, and rehabilitation. Bombay ISKCON has taken up the cause of reviving Vedic culture, and Detroit devotees have been actively involved in urban renewal and cultural renovation. Tackling social problems in these cities has gained for devotees a deeper appreciation from the public, so much so that politicians and journalists have sought out devotees for their opinions (including solutions) on current issues.

By comparison, Athens is a relatively undeveloped field, and the request for a radio appearance probably stems from the media's desire to present an opinion opposed to that of the Orthodox Church on the issue of human burial. Nonetheless, it's an example of the many opportunities that await us if we are willing and able (taking into consideration the social, political, religious, and racial situation of each region) to get involved in issues of the day, in order to show that Krishna consciousness does in fact offer genuine solutions. The request from a radio show in Athens clearly shows that there's an opening for our point of view, even in situations where our reputation is far from established.

In the March/April issue of ICB, 1992, we cited references from Srila Prabhupada's books and conversations indicating that "Krishna consciousness could solve all problems of the world." Our ongoing research has discovered further references supporting this point, three more in the *Srimad-Bhagavatam* and twelve more in Srila Prabhupada's lectures, letters, and conversations.

It seems clear that ISKCON can be recognized as a spiritual resource for the betterment of society and that ISKCON should consider such recognition as a goal and strategy in spreading Krishna consciousness.

CHAPTER 5—1993

Walking Our Talk

The largest judgment ever against ISKCON—originally US$32 million—was finally settled out of court in May for an undisclosed amount, after a fifteen-year legal battle. The case went all the way to the US Supreme Court. I refer to this case and what we learned from it in Chapter 9, in the ICB essay entitled "Managing Conflict" (page 227). During the summer, India's President Shankar

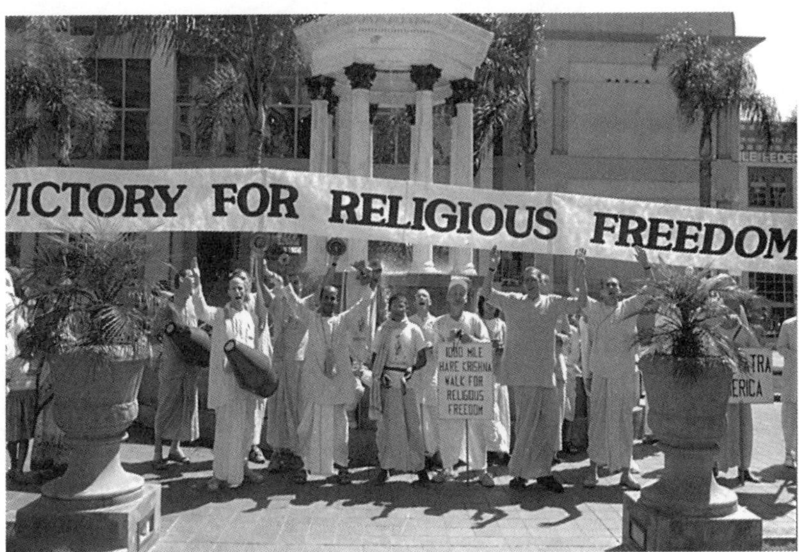

August, 1989—San Diego, USA: A California Court of Appeals throws out charges of "brainwashing" against the International Society for Krishna Consciousness. Taking the media by surprise, members celebrate this partial victory hours after the verdict is rendered at Horton Plaza, near the city's Federal Court House. The legal battle continues 4 more years. The initial judgment against ISKCON in 1983 had been for US$32 million. (See page 229.)

May, 1993—New Delhi, India: India's President Shankar Dayal Sharma (right) appreciates an architectural portrayal of ISKCON's Glory of India Vedic Cultural Center project, headed by Gopal Krishna Goswami (left). The 7-acre site, near New Delhi's Nehru Place, promises to house a temple, guest rooms, a cultural center, a multimedia show, audio-animated robots, and a restaurant. (See Glory of India story on page 244.)

Dayal Sharma met with Gopal Krishna Goswami and recognized the importance of ISKCON's Glory of India project in Delhi. In South Africa, President F. W. de Klerk publicly praised ISKCON for promoting peace and harmony as he officially inaugurated the movement's annual Rathayatra festival in Durban.

DO WE REALLY NEED THE MEDIA? (PART II)

Peppered with examples from Srila Prabhupada's own life, this ICB continuation article gives dramatic evidence of the central role the media can play in the process of propagating Krishna consciousness. Communications experts at Nuffer, Smith and Tucker have said that at this stage of our movement's growth, up to forty percent of our outreach should be directed toward the media. It is fascinating to see how Srila Prabhupada dealt with even tabloid newspapers like *Blitz* in India because of their enormous influence. He exhibited both proactive and reactive communications methodologies. The same basic principles of media relations are as relevant today as they were when Srila Prabhupada was personally teaching us.

ISKCON Communications Briefings, January/February 1993

Srila Prabhupada appreciated both proactive and reactive media relations. One of many early incidents showing how much he valued proactive media relations occurred in 1968. He was in America when an Associated Press story published in a local newspaper came to his attention. He was struck by the headline "Krishna Chant Startles London." Originally published in the *Times of London,* the article respectfully described activities of ISKCON's early missionaries to England. Prabhupada carried the clipping with him as he traveled around America and often quoted from it as evidence that Krishna consciousness had made an impact on one of the world's largest cities.

July, 1972—London, England: London's *Daily Telegraph* publishes this photograph, including a caption with the lead-in, "A Rival for Nelson." The Hare Krishna Rathayatra festival paraded from Hyde Park Speakers Corner to Trafalgar Square, London's famous landmark. The colorful Rathayatra canopy appears to challenge the national monument of Admiral Nelson, a gray statue atop the 185-foot column.

In 1973, the *Guardian,* also one of England's major newspapers, published a large picture making ISKCON's Rathayatra Chariot—parked during the festival next to the famous Nelson Column in Trafalgar Square—appear to be almost as tall as the 185-foot-high column. A headline over the caption read, "A Rival for Nelson." Srila Prabhupada quoted this caption frequently as an indication of ISKCON's strength in England. Since Admiral Horatio Nelson was one of England's most celebrated colonizers, the photograph must have had great symbolic significance for Srila Prabhupada, who had lived under British rule for most of his life.

"We are stronger than the British Empire," he said in 1976, referring to the photograph. "Simply by Rathayatra we are conquering. And actually that is being done." Three years later he still talked about this photograph.

Other instances show how Srila Prabhupada handled the reactive side of media relations. He was acutely aware of the importance of media relations. In Volume 2, No. 1 of this newsletter, an article entitled "Don't Stand Idly By" quotes Prabhupada saying, "We should demand at least equal time from the press to explain the entire situation clearly, and when necessary we should file suit against such newspapers in that things are not distorted." (Letter to Yasomatinandana, May 26, 1976)

On August 21, 1976, Srila Prabhupada had a lengthy discussion with his leading disciples about a defamatory newspaper article that appeared in a Bombay tabloid called *Blitz.* Srila Prabhupada ordered that ISKCON sue the paper for libel, particularly for its headline "The Ungodly Face of Krishna Cult." Devotees contacted *Blitz* about their intentions, and high-level discussions with Srila Prabhupada about the story continued intermittently for nearly a month.

At one point Srila Prabhupada learned that *Blitz* had published a statement favorable to ISKCON by the endowments minister of Andhra Pradesh. The minister said that Indians "owed a great debt of gratitude" to Srila Prabhupada for reminding them of the great treasure they had in their own culture. On hearing this, Prabhupada called off the lawsuit and expressed his satisfaction with Gopal Krsna Maharaja's explanation that ISKCON would be getting regular reportage from *Blitz*. On the basis of such future articles, he concluded that a letter would suffice to correct the misrepresentation in the first article.

Prabhupada had reacted to the first article by instructing devotees to file suit, but when he learned that a proactive effort to publish the endowments minister's statement was successful, he immediately shifted gears, approving of an ongoing relationship with the tabloid instead of a lawsuit. This willingness to develop relations with *Blitz* is of special interest because this tabloid, like many of its kind, isn't highly regarded by the intelligentsia. Nonetheless, Srila Prabhupada took its reporting seriously because of the extensive mass readership it enjoyed.

In ISKCON, not everyone can be a communications or media specialist, but it's important that almost all devotees have at least a basic understanding of how the media work. ISKCON seminars about basic media principles in relation to ISKCON preaching have proven effective. Occasional *istaghosti* forums for discussing basic media understanding and how good relations can enhance the preaching are also beneficial.

Seasoned communications specialists who have worked with ISKCON and analyzed its situation tend to conclude that between twenty-five and forty percent (depending on global location) of ISKCON communications work should be in the realm of media relations. A big part of this skill is educating all devotees about ISKCON's relation with the media.

The key to success in media relations lies in learning media skills. These are taught at the VIHE [Vrindavana Institute of Higher Education] in Vrindavana by Mukunda Goswami as part of a course in communications and by Saunaka Rsi dasa, Anuttama dasa, and others at regional communications conferences and seminars held in various parts of the world. Check the upcoming conferences and seminars in your area so that you can take advantage of this training. Devotees who receive this training can gradually train others.

DO WE REALLY NEED THE MEDIA? (PART III)

Colorful examples from Australia show how the proactive approach with the media has kept ISKCON's national reputation in good health. This reputational state of well-being began with a 1980 telephone call to the Sydney temple from Australia's most-watched public affairs program, *60 Minutes.* The producers had seen a recent picture of two Hare Krishna children on the cover of *Life* magazine. The charming photographs of the girls with *tilaka* and saris inspired them to want to do a story on the Hare Krishna children of Australia. At that time most of Australia's Hare Krishna youngsters were domiciled in a *gurukula* at the movement's thousand-acre New Govardhana farm near Murwillumbah. After some tough face-to-face wrangling, with an ISKCON attorney present, *60 Minutes* producers agreed to let ISKCON have the final editorial approval over the show—an unheard-of concession from a television news producer. From that point on, media relations and reportage were all upbeat. The movement's reputation in Australia changed almost overnight from nonexistent to extremely positive.

ISKCON Communications Briefings, March/April 1993

Although the media tend to create only fleeting impressions, positive or negative, a sustained pattern of biased media coverage—positive or negative—tends to create more lasting impressions, even though these impressions are not nearly as deep as those formed by personal contacts. History has shown that media coverage can in fact make a noticeable difference in ISKCON's reputation. A case in point is the Australian *yatra.*

When Krishna consciousness began there, devotees were subject to persecution from the public and the media as well. Devotees in *hari-nama* parties were routinely arrested and ordered to pay hundreds of dollars in fines for "obstructing the footpaths." Several times devotees were physically attacked and property was destroyed. To sum up, ISKCON members were under great suspicion by the public and the media.

However, in 1980, when *60 Minutes,* Australia's most popular public affairs television program, aired "The Children of Krishna," ISKCON's reputation changed literally overnight. The reporter and producer became enchanted with the Krishna kids at New Govardhan, ISKCON's 1000-acre farm near Murwillumbah, and broadcast a favorable report.

Because most Australians were ignorant of ISKCON, their minds changed quickly from suspicion to admiration; such is the power of the media. The reporting and the attractiveness of the children and the community itself created a positive impression that every devotee in Australia became aware of almost immediately.

Fortunately, the leadership of the Australian *yatra* understood that this windfall could disappear almost as quickly as it appeared. They decided to take advantage of their new-found reputation and made plans to publicize all their major events—and even create a few new ones—so that the media awareness of ISKCON would continue to be positive.

Within two years of the *60 Minutes* broadcast, Australian devotees produced two colorful magazines and paid many Australian newspapers to insert them in their editions on a particular day. One of the magazines carried the story of the wedding of Ambarisa dasa and Svaha devi dasi. Amazingly, and beyond even the expectations of the devotees there, several local and national television news programs carried the Hare Krishna magazine insert as a lead news story. This news led to devotees appearing on television and radio talk shows in different parts of the country.

The magazine "insert" thus kept the waves of positive publicity, that started with the *60 Minutes* broadcast, rolling on. Subsequently, devotees followed up with a national bus tour, including a *hari-nama* party and book distribution party, which visited literally every city and town in the entire country. Later, a similar bus tour

1986—Gold Coast, Australia: At EMI studios in Springbook, Australia, Prahlada dasa (at the microphone) and the Australian Krishna kids sing Hari Bandhu's arrangement of "Dear Mr. Gorbachev, Please Let Our Friends Go."

of the country promoted the cause of the oppressed Soviet Hare Krishnas, culminating in a popular record sung by twelve-year-old Prahlada dasa, "Mr. Gorbachev, Set Them Free." The media broadly covered this Soviet campaign, characterizing Australian devotees as fighting for the rights of their brethren and even the people in general in the totalitarian USSR.

Since the liberation of the Soviet devotees, ISKCON Australia's external communications have continued to build ISKCON's reputation, primarily through *prasadam* distribution in the form of Food for Life. Devotees' free *prasadam* distribution and budget restaurants in Melbourne and Perth have become famous. As this newsletter goes to press, *60 Minutes* of Australia is producing a follow-up to the 1980 "Children of Krishna" show that will let viewers see where the kids are now, thirteen years later. Aniruddha dasa, Melbourne temple president, is optimistic about the final product:

"It will be a balanced piece and will help enhance people's understanding of us here."

ISKCON experienced a similar situation in Italy, although the movement didn't suffer from much persecution at the start. Through the excellent public relations practiced by Gaura Krsna dasa, the Hare Krishnas still enjoy a good reputation in Italy, and this has been due almost entirely to ISKCON's excellent media relations in this 83% Catholic country.

By contrast, the British yatra started off in 1969 with a big hit record, *Hare Krishna Mantra.* It reached the top ten all over Europe. However, because the neophyte devotees of the British *yatra* were not quick enough to develop media skills in the large, complex, multi-ethnic British society, their good reputation faded over the

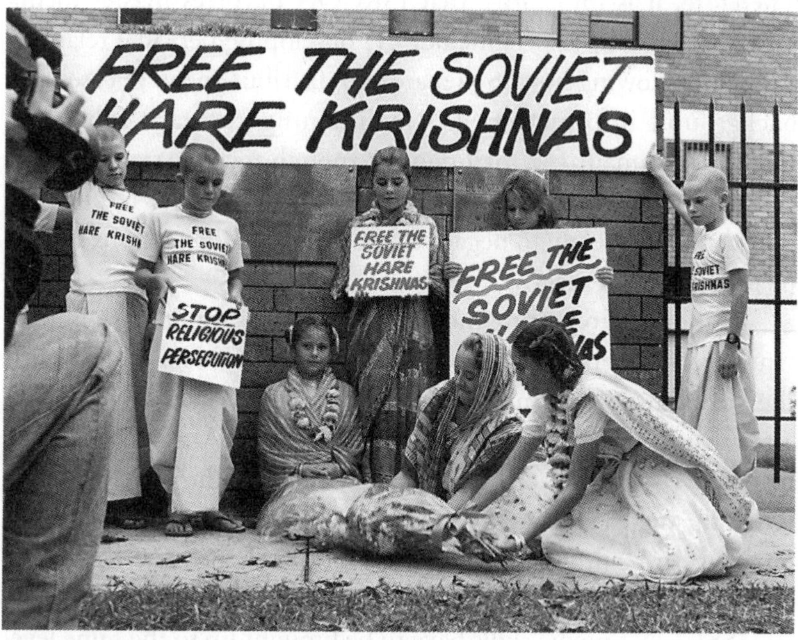

May 20, 1986—Sydney, Australia: Australian Hare Krishna children protest outside the Soviet consulate in Sydney about confinement and mistreatment of devotees in jails, psycho-prisons, and labor camps—all part of the Soviet Union's policy to repress religious activity. Some Krishna members, including an infant, died in captivity. On the same day, devotees held protests in front of Soviet embassies, high commissions, and consulates worldwide. (See "Do We Really Need the Media?" in ICB, March /April, 1993.)

ensuing years. As in America, the British public tends to accept and tolerate ISKCON, but, as polls in Britain show, 98% do not understand us—our philosophy or goals.

But since the mid-'80s, ISKCON's reputation in England has improved somewhat. This is because British devotees, led in the communications field principally by Akhandadhi dasa, have developed a high level of expertise in media relations. Their efforts have centered on stopping the government from curtailing mass visitation to Bhaktivedanta Manor, which the media now regard as the country's largest Hindu pilgrimage site.

One has to define people in the media as an "active public," first because they never sit still, and second because they report on ISKCON whether or not ISKCON chooses to interact with them. Therefore, it is imperative that ISKCON devotees master media skills. These skills always include (1) developing personal relationships; (2) knowing how to prepare and distribute news releases and background information; (3) maintaining constant follow-up through the mail; (4) maintaining enough awareness of current events to relate ISKCON's relevance to the media; (5) responding quickly and correctly to negative reporting. Media relations should be proactive, not reactive.

In addition to honing media skills to precision, it's also important to remember that as an organization ISKCON has to deal with the media more than most organizations, because we are by nature attractive to the media, especially to television. Attractiveness can be positive, negative, or many shades between. The basic principle is that the media are drawn toward us because of our "differentness," our powerful cultural presence, and ultimately because Krishna is all-attractive.

ISKCON's media skills have to be brought up to the same level as the experts'. We needn't reinvent the wheel. The knowledge of media relations already exists. We have to learn it and dovetail it in Krishna's service.

The offices of IC Global, IC North America, and IC Europe

have begun producing manuals on this topic and are providing training. One of IC's goals is to see that at least one devotee in each ISKCON center knows the basics of media relations.

THE SEVEN DEADLY SINS OF MEDIA RELATIONS

Has a reporter ever asked you a question you didn't know the answer to, and you pretended you knew and faked your way through the interview? Did you ever tell a reporter, "No comment"? Did you ever tell a news investigator something "off the record" because you didn't want him or her to make it public? If you answered "yes" to any of these questions, you were wrong. The media could approach anyone, including yourself, so don't think it will never happen to you. Because of ISKCON's rapid growth and far-ranging scope, an individual's knowledge of the movement is sometimes at odds with the movement's official views. (What you're reading right now was written in 1998.) It's important to be informed, but if you're not, don't be afraid to say, "I don't know" and promise you'll get, or do your best to get, the information the media seek. And get back to them, even if you can't find the answer. The following ICB article was written in 1993.

ISKCON Communications Briefings, May/June 1993

Although the media is not the only target public that ISKCON Communications experts deal with, it is one we cannot avoid. The following are among the most common flaws in media relations.

Lack of subject knowledge. You must know thoroughly what you are promoting. That is to say, you should have a list of specific messages and facts you want to get across. Details are important. If it is a festival like Rathayatra, for example, what exactly does Rathayatra signify? Good reporters usually want to know. If they do not want to know but you tell them or give it to them in writing anyway, there is a good chance they will report on it.

Lack of planning. Make sure you have thought long and hard about any promotions or other contact with the media. For example, reporters do not usually work on weekends. Are you taking this into account? Have you given enough notice? Is there a budget for your media work, and is it sufficient? A budget that ends up being too small to accomplish what you plan to do will hurt your credibility within ISKCON, and it may make it impossible to complete your task at hand. Are you prepared for media follow-up to an event? This can go on for days or more afterward (radio or television interviews, talk shows, and magazine stories), and this may require more time, organization, and budgeting. Make sure you work out in advance how much everything will cost. Initial planning should be done in consultation with ISKCON leaders and organizers in the area of your event.

Poor internal communications. All the devotees who might be approached, interviewed, photographed, or involved in any way with the media of an ISKCON media event should know the nature of the media coverage being sought and how to respond if approached. Communication specialists should keep all organizers and leaders closely informed before, during, and after an event. In most cases, at least one of these devotees will be part of the event. The media must have one interviewee. Such spokespersons should be briefed just before the event.

Ignorance of journalism or broadcasting. You should have both a basic understanding of the kind of writing and language used by the media and an understanding of what their work environment and schedules are like. News releases should be journalistically well written and in the style of newspaper news. All the main facts have to appear, and they must be accurate. If you can arrange to spend even a very little bit of time among reporters, editors, producers, and cameramen, you can ask them questions and get answers about their craft and their personal approach to their jobs.

Lack of persuasiveness. To convince a reporter to take up a Krishna conscious story, you need to establish a working relationship. The relationship should be based on what reporters need and want. It can help to know something about their personal lives. Approaching a particular reporter with this understanding will help you convince him or her that Krishna consciousness is worth reporting on. In effect, you are selling an idea. The better you understand your buyer, the easier it will be to sell your story.

Poor writing skills. The more you practice writing clearly, the more persuasive you will become. Even Srila Prabhupada used to ask his early disciples to write something, at least about their realizations of Krishna consciousness, every day. Bhurijana Prabhu's book, *The Art of Writing,* and Drutakarma Prabhu's *Seven Ways to Preach Through Writing* can greatly help you with writing. If you study writing and practice even a little every day, you will greatly sharpen your skills. As you put ideas on paper, your ability to write convincingly and compellingly will increase.

Using depersonalized or "overprofessionalized" methods. Sending out a release to dozens or hundreds of unnamed media contacts (such as to "news director" or "city desk editor") tends to be less effective than a personalized model. The former is sometimes referred to as the "shotgun" approach. Sending personally addressed packages to fewer contacts usually proves more effective, especially over the long term. If you can include personal letters or short, handwritten notes, all the better. Super-glossy, full-color media kits are expensive and can even be counterproductive. Use a personal approach as often as possible.

PERCEPTION, CREDIBILITY MUSTS

It's one thing to always do things right. But in this day and age, it's not enough. One must be seen to be doing things right. Right or wrong, people today judge us by how we dress, what kind of car we drive, how we speak, and how we behave. That is the fate of everyone, especially public figures. And anyone in ISKCON, whether in Vaishnava dress or not, is a kind of public figure. We are known as spiritual people, those who embrace a spiritual lifestyle. So, I argue in this ICB article, we had better be ready to act the part. We should act, dress, and speak in a way that people cannot find fault in us. This essay explains how perception and reality are inextricably related. A leader in the communications field is known for saying, "Perception is reality," shortened from, "What people perceive a situation to be is the real reality, because that determines how they will respond to it." I also explain how actions must be louder than words.

ISKCON Communications Briefings, May/June1993

In 1971 Philip Lesley, head of the Philip Lesley public relations firm in Chicago and prolific public relations author, wrote, "What people perceive a situation to be is the real reality, because that determines how they will respond to it." He later shortened his premise to the oversimplified version, "Perception is reality."

Although this communications axiom is severely flawed in many ways, especially in terms of ultimate knowledge, it has gone a long way in helping us understand how people perceive institutions and events as well as the facts. Therefore it is a critical determinant of how people react and respond to communications messages.

The purpose of communications in ISKCON is to change people's perceptions and behavior toward the Krishna consciousness movement. Changing people's perceptions can change behavior, but only if two conditions exist:

The actions of an organization or person must be seen as consistent with what is being said. If one says Krishna consciousness is enjoyable, a feast or a festival is proof.

Actions must be substantive, consistent, and in people's interest, rather than manipulative or solely in the organization's interest. It is one thing to say our books are the basis of ultimate knowledge and perfect peace of mind, but these facts need to be demonstrated. Showing this by one's personal example can make such pronouncements believable.

People are increasingly skeptical, so credibility is becoming more important. When credibility exists, ISKCON can much more easily gain acceptance for its philosophy, products, services, policies, and role in the public arena.

Credibility is like a reputation for virtue: It can be lost in a moment and can take decades to regain. In some regions, devotees still receive adverse public reactions for immature, abrasive, or dishonest actions that occurred many years ago.

Today, when dishonest actions occur, although they happen rarely compared with the past, the result is still worse than stubbing a toe; it is like breaking both legs—it leaves you without a leg to stand on. This is so partly because skepticism is not only insidious but contagious.

Further, if a favorable perception is created and then found to be exaggerated or deceptive, the credibility of the source will be damaged. Unfulfilled expectations can be more damaging than lack of expectations. Critically honest presentations can be devoid of hyperbole and still be positive.

In fact, if the human element of imperfection is admitted on a personal basis, this can enhance credibility. After all, in the "clearing stage" of Krishna consciousness, many flaws are necessarily present. Srila Prabhupada once said, "I am not perfect, but because I am receiving knowledge from the supreme perfect, therefore whatever I say, it is perfect." (*Conversations with Srila Prabhupada,* Vol. 6, p. 297.) In this and in other situations where circumstances dictated it, Srila Prabhupada declared himself to be "imperfect" or "came down," as we say, to the *madhyam-adhikari* platform.

If a number of favorable perceptions are later dashed, the damage to credibility will increase geometrically. The metaphor of the black spot on the white tablecloth is well known to us.

The loss of credibility that results from a negative incident will at first be greatest among those directly affected. But when a significant number are affected, they spread their negativism to others. Statistics compiled by business researchers in the USA show that each dissatisfied customer tells an average of more than ten others, who in turn tell at least one other person. So in the universe of the displeased patrons, one equals twenty.

If a number of favorable perceptions are created and prove sound but are interspersed with perceptions that are negative, the latter will be remembered longer and have greater impact.

People must feel they are being talked with rather than at. Excellent communication always employs the two-way principle.

New devotees and younger people are more likely at first to accept a promise of future performance. But these audiences will be quicker to lose respect and withdraw trust if a positive perception turns out to be baseless.

The effect of both positive and negative impacts will be greatest on those who are most perceptive—usually the most important people.

A NEW DIRECTION FOR ISKCON GLOBAL COMMUNICATIONS

Surprising many devotees, Drutakarma argues in this ICB article that "we shall have to become expert in making the right enemies." Is this a violation of the "Don't see in terms of friends and enemies" warning? Read on. "Hate the sin, not the sinner," says Jesus Christ. If the sin is the concept that God doesn't exist and that all existence, including consciousness, can be explained in terms of electromagnetic forces, the sin may rightly be called "mechanism." Mechanism is certainly a form of *maya* and one of Kali Yuga's principal weapons. One of ISKCON's missions is to expose the "unreality industry," the sinful manifestations of science, psychology, religion, philosophy, *apasampradayas,* and current political corruption.

ISKCON Communications Briefings, July/August 1993

For many years, ISKCON's relations with the academic community, religionists, the media, the entertainment industry, politicians, and other elites have emphasized careful cultivation with the view to obtaining endorsements. Although this will certainly continue, an expanding, self-confident ISKCON of the future will also be developing the mood of challenge and confrontation. Just as we have become experts in making the right friends, we shall have to become expert in making the right enemies.

In other words, we must learn to carefully target persons and groups holding ideas that pose obstacles to the path of spiritual progress in Krishna consciousness for the people in general.

This will require new attitudes. It is certainly no news to ISKCON members that Srila Prabhupada adopted a very challenging attitude toward materialistic scientists, impersonalists, bogus yogis and meditators, cheating politicians, sectarian religionists, and other "rascals." What is news to many is the suggestion that we ourselves should take up the challenging mood.

One common reaction to such a proposal is, "Prabhupada could do it but we cannot. He was pure. Therefore, when he challenged someone, that person could understand and accept it. Also, Prabhupada was elderly. If we young neophytes try to adopt the challenging mood, it is just a manifestation of our false ego, our tendency to feel superior and propensity to become angry at others."

But sometimes Srila Prabhupada ordered his young and neophyte disciples to take up the mood of challenge, and he was very happy when they did so. In 1969, when Govinda Ḍasi publicly challenged some bogus spiritualists in Hawaii, Srila Prabhupada wrote to Goursundara Dasa on July 13: "I was so much pleased with Govinda Dasi and with you also when I heard about her spirited preaching. . . . I am always thinking of Govinda Dasi. Although she is young and delicate, almost always suffering from some ailment, still she is so sincere, devoted and spirited preacher that I have named her Heroine Govinda Dasi."

As ISKCON preachers become more mature, expert, and experienced, individually and collectively, they will be able to better carry out Srila Prabhupada's instructions, following in his footsteps. In coming years, we expect to see many more heroines and heroes stepping forward to take up the task of challenging the targets that Srila Prabhupada identified—not just in a *Bhagavatam* class but in the public arena.

ISKCON Communications specialists and leaders will become increasingly involved in developing realistic strategies for aggressive issue-oriented preaching in various areas. The goal will be to transform ISKCON's image from a tiny, besieged religious organization in constant need of help and protection to a strong, vital, spiritual movement that is actively identifying and combating those who are exploiting and misleading the public.

The first and most obvious target is the materialistic scientist. This group was certainly number one on Srila Prabhupada's "bad list."

How does this challenge fit into ISKCON Communications' policies and program? The mission statement for ISKCON developed by ISKCON Communications says that the Hare Krishna movement is dedicated to solving the world's material and spiritual problems. These problems include crime, drug abuse, and violence, as well as others. Also in the list of problems is "the materialistic worldview" of modern science. The importance of challenging this worldview cannot be overestimated—almost all of the other problems listed can be traced to this one.

In future issues of ICB we shall be exploring how ISKCON Communications specialists can help carry forward the mood of challenge in the scientific arena and in other spheres.

TO SUE OR NOT TO SUE

Rupanuga dasa, Tosan Krishna, our lawyer, and I didn't just drop in to NBC Television Network headquarters at Rockefeller Tower on a casual visit. We had a purpose. Sitting around the table with us in their well-appointed forty-fifth-floor conference room were NBC's National Director of Public Affairs and two of the network's top lawyers. Between heavy questions and deep thought, I snatched glances through panoramic windows at the dizzying New York skyline. My ISKCON colleagues and I had decided to do battle over a very negative piece shown throughout the US during a January, 1978 national NBC news telecast. NBC "reported" on the opening of our fabled temple in Juhu, Mumbai. Our strategy was to play "legal hardball" and possibly to accept a nonfinancial settlement based on NBC's commitment to present a piece of equal time and prominence on national television. Situations like this arise from time to time, but lawsuits can be avoided if positive, proactive, and ongoing programs with the media are in place. This ICB article discusses the fine line we have sometimes had to walk between filing lawsuits, playing the game of brinkmanship, and actually suing.

ISKCON Communications Briefings, July/August 1993

In our April/May 1989 ICB, our lead article quotes Srila Prabhupada as saying, "Why should we sit idly by and allow the press to unfairly take advantage of such a situation to misrepresent the Hare Krishna movement? . . .We should demand at least equal time from the press to explain the entire situation clearly, and when necessary we should file suit against such newspapers in that things are not distorted."

The key phrase here is "when necessary."

Excellent communications means excellent media relations, in which lawsuits are a last resort. Sometimes they are necessary, especially when all appropriate attempts to develop friendly relations and to correct wrongdoings fail. A recent court decision against the media in Budapest was a victory for ISKCON.

More often ISKCON has used the threat of a lawsuit as a means to negotiate for a positive story or a meeting of the minds of opposing parties as to how ISKCON should be presented by the media.

For example, IC director Mukunda Goswami and other members of the GBC in 1978 "negotiated" a favorable news story with NBC, at the time one of the three major USA television networks. A meeting took place with ISKCON's lawyers and NBC's top legal counsel present. Also at the bargaining table that day at NBC corporate headquarters in New York was the network's national director of public affairs.

NBC had aired a humiliating story about ISKCON's Bombay temple in Juhu. ISKCON looked like it was simply pumping money into the project, leaving local people unimpressed. None of this was true. The NBC producer made the devotees look foolish and fanatical and the Bombayite observers to be totally apathetic.

At the NBC headquarters conference table, in an atmosphere heavy with the threat of litigation, NBC agreed to air a positive piece of equal duration, which it did, in place of dueling with ISKCON before a jury.

After the agreement, correspondence, mailings about ISKCON's activities, and several telephone calls to the network's PA director ensued. A resulting network broadcast about ISKCON's "Palace of Gold" in West Virginia was acceptable to ISKCON because (1) NBC's respectful coverage neutralized the negative broadcast by about 50%; (2) a leading programming director and decision-maker at NBC had developed respect for ISKCON; and (3) a working relationship had developed with a high-ranking representative of the network.

Good media relations generally avoid lawsuits with the media by establishing good relations and intelligent means of educating the media in an ongoing fashion.

As argued in the May/June ICB, positive messages communicated day-in and day-out should be in place before any crisis hits. In this way, many a crisis can turn into a non-crisis.

Some organizations, even in the upper echelons of the corporate world, have resolutely avoided the media. Such corporations see the media as unremitting enemies. Mobil Oil adopted a policy of running ads in the form of essays that routinely criticized the media as "anti-business." Another company that has a reputation for an adversarial relationship with the media is General Motors, one of the world's largest auto-makers.

In March of this year, GM negotiated an out-of-court settlement with NBC after suing the television network for millions of dollars. NBC agreed to make a retraction and apology. During the course of the litigation, NBC fired some of its top officials. The network admitted that, to sensationalize a potentially dangerous defect, it had rigged a GM pick-up truck with explosives, videotaped a staged explosion, and run it on the evening news. GM manufacturing defects had in fact caused fires in many models of these trucks, generating some lawsuits. Some NBC reporters had decided to stage an explosion to dramatize the danger.

Because a lawsuit can magnify and expand an unfair accusation, many organizations never sue the media. In the GM case only a small audience saw the November 1992 TV program. It can be argued that any measurable impact soon went away. But after GM sued, the film clip of the exploding truck was run and rerun, and print media gave high visibility coverage for several days. All this new coverage had to begin by repeating the accusation about fuel tanks on GM pickups.

Did GM think that an NBC apology would drown out the accusations that were to be repeated in the news again and again as the many lawsuits against GM came to court for trials and appeals? Also, feature writers, researchers, and others had been made aware of a hot topic.

According to one theory, if an issue involves personal danger, then the more the issue is discussed, the more people will adopt the attitude that best protects them—i.e., GM fuel tanks may be dangerous. Facts have little to do with it.

Memory science says that in six months details fall away and one or two major points linger. Basic psychology suggests one point, which would be that GM designed some fuel tanks that were dangerous.

Behaviorally, that's the only memory people can act on: they can avoid GM products, or at least pick-ups. Assume the other thing remembered, which seems likely, is that TV rigged a story. What can anyone do about that, besides distrust TV or journalists—which most already do? What publics did GM really care about in this case? Truck buyers? Owners of pick-up trucks with the defective tanks? All auto buyers? Government regulators and those who influence them? Future judges and juries on such suits? The overall public?

The answer is found by rating the list by ability to behave in a way that could harm GM coupled with the opportunity to do so. Worrying about damage to overall reputations is fruitless. Every auto-maker has had recalls and suits (or so it seems), and this is just the latest. Also, this incident is but one of a multitude of personally felt elements that make up a reputation. If I own a GM product that has served me well, this incident does not affect me. It seems GM's main target was the media, and to teach them a lesson, they sued. In this particular case, they may have succeeded.

Some people may feel that the public and business have been bullied by the media so long that they fear to challenge, oppose, or fight back. GM's action might therefore influence some people to buy a GM product, if only to offer token support to a company not afraid to act, that is willing to challenge the media in what some think is the only place there is hope of redress—the courts.

A recent ISKCON case supports this view. In the wake of a US Supreme Court decision banning collecting monies for books in US airports, ISKCON Los Angeles took its case before the Los Angeles City Council. ISKCON's purpose was to establish its right to distribute books and collect money in the Los Angeles airport. To almost everyone's amazement, ISKCON won, and today devotees distribute and receive contributions for books in one of the world's largest airports. Although this was not a media case or court battle, the incident demonstrates that to fight for one's rights in public forums is sometimes the right course.

NEIGHBORS: A TARGET AUDIENCE?

It may seem too close to home for some, but neighbors can make or break you. I wrote this ICB article long before England's Department of the Environment gave an unequivocal "yes" to public worship at Bhaktivedanta Manor in May of 1996. That official declaration came after ten years of battling the UK government, local and central. In the process, devotees had to buy land and pay legal fees, all of which amounted to millions of pounds, and on top of all that, ISKCON had to duel internally with those who opposed fighting the government. Stories in other countries, now well rooted in ISKCON's history, tell of the importance of good relations with neighbors. How many of your temple's neighbors do you know? How many ISKCON temples are considered part of their neighborhood or community? Is that important to devotees? In this article I argue that community relations are not only important, but they can cause you great harm or give help beyond your dreams. In homes it is considered uncivilized to ignore our parents and siblings; it is equally reprehensible from a communications point of view to pretend our neighbors don't exist. Preaching means reaching out to everyone, and our neighbors, as this piece shows, can help or hurt, depending on how we relate to them.

***ISKCON Communications Briefings*, November/December 1993**

Aristotle wrote, "Man is a political animal." And politics take place in the context of community.

For most people, identifying with their city or nation is not as important as being part of a smaller community like a church or temple, volunteer or interest group, or neighborhood organization.

Krishna consciousness centers—urban, suburban, or rural—are communities within communities. These centers tend to be viewed as alien by the larger communities that surround them. This has often led to problems. For example, neighbors have influenced local governments to enforce zoning restrictions that limit the number of worshipers and residents. Conversely, when devotees have succeeded in integrating their Krishna communities with "host" communities, they tend to be able to conduct their preaching with little or no interference from the neighborhood. Some even get various kinds of support from neighbors. This can make a significant difference.

If devotees become experts at local community relations, they will be much better equipped to deal with larger or more distant communities. Also, goodwill built up locally can easily be exported and built upon. Poor community relations at home can have a widespread negative effect on all preaching.

Community relations should not be viewed as an outside activity to be left to a few specialists. Like it or not, we are neighbors to others. The ISKCON centers in Detroit, Dallas, and Kiev (Ukraine) provide some instructive cases of excellent relations.

Over ten years ago, devotees in Detroit purchased several houses opposite the temple and renovated them. This was viewed by local government and neighborhood associations as first-class community service. The area was blighted and by most accounts a slum. It is now becoming "gentrified," with condominiums and other new developments proliferating. But ISKCON was there first, improving the neighborhood. This widely recognized neighborhood improvement is one of the key reasons for ISKCON's good reputation in Detroit.

Again, over ten years ago, the devotees at the temple in East Dallas, a poverty pocket of the city, thought of abandoning that location for a more prosperous one. But presiding Deity Kalachandji wasn't going anywhere. Devotees dug in, bought houses near the temple, and started renovating them. They also turned a schoolhouse into a beautiful temple room, built up an attractive and popular restaurant, and managed all operations carefully and with great concern for the "host" community.

Today the Dallas temple has one of the best reputations of any ISKCON center in the USA. This temple also enjoys widespread support from the Indian community, attributable in no small measure to the good local reputation ISKCON Dallas has achieved over the years.

In Ukraine, where economic turmoil has become commonplace, government corruption is widespread. This conservative country, although officially democratic, is ruled by the same people who ran it when the Ukraine was part of the USSR.

In the capital city of Kiev, devotees have constructed five floors of a projected seven-story building, which will comprise a temple, community hall, restaurant, and living facilities for men and women. The construction site is in the middle of a suburban residential area. Each floor is approximately 3,000 square feet—not small by ISKCON standards. According to regional secretary Acyuta dasa, it is virtually impossible to get permits to build anything without paying exorbitant bribes. And even then, progress can be agonizingly slow.

The Kiev devotees found themselves with no permission to build, even though they did have all the funds and building materials on hand to complete the entire structure. So they decided to begin an intensive Hare Krishna Food for Life program among all their would-be neighbors, promising to make this a lifelong program.

Local officials tried to pressure the neighbors to petition against the devotees, but to no avail. In fact, the neighbors insisted that ISKCON's plan move forward unobstructed. Acyuta is convinced that without their Food for Life community relations program, they would have had no chance to build an ISKCON center. Their neighbors are both protective and supportive of their ongoing presence in the neighborhood.

Many other ISKCON centers, far too numerous to mention, have been successful with community relations. This list includes Melbourne, Bangalore, Hong Kong, Toronto, Durban, Dubey (Radhadesh, Belgium) and Waldkirchen (ISKCON's farm in Germany).

Now let's consider examples of how poor community relations can cause problems. One of ISKCON's greatest political battlefronts has been Bhaktivedanta Manor, where the local council's interpretation and enforcement of a planning law could stop tens of thousands of people from visiting the Manor, their place of worship for the past twenty years. When the Manor was first acquired in 1973, Srila Prabhupada tried to appease the neighbors, some of the most inimical of whom came to his room to discuss the matter. The outcome was inconclusive. Prabhupada encouraged one of his disciples, Bhadra Krsna, to remain active and make friends in the local village, Letchmore Heath.

Letchmore Heath has about a hundred residents, many of whom have opposed ISKCON's presence from the very start. Although the number of people deeply opposed to ISKCON dwindled to only a few, the local council (and the central government that presided over the hearings) had supported the enforcement notice to restrict the Manor to a "theological college" zoning rule, limiting visitation to almost nothing. Even though the devotees and Prabhupada himself engaged in ongoing attempts to improve relations with the neighbors, the tide had not yet turned in the devotees' favor.

There is still hope that the European Court of Human Rights will support ISKCON's appeal and that a back access road to the Manor, circumventing Letchmore Heath altogether, may be a solution. In any case, ISKCON owns the seventeen-acre estate and will stay, regardless of zoning problems. Ultimately, it may prove possible to retain the Manor's present status as an unrestricted, full-scale temple open to visitors 365 days a year.

In Copenhagen, neighbors were so determined to stop public meetings at the ISKCON house in suburban Copenhagen that devotees finally moved to a much bigger facility in the country. They maintain a recently established and successful restaurant in central Copenhagen, and thus recruiting continues.

These situations attest to the difficulties ISKCON can encounter in community relations. Such problems should be studies to learn the dos and don'ts of community relations.

In America and Canada, city government officials have on several occasions tried to restrict or stop the operations of ISKCON public dining halls (which the public usually refers to as "restaurants"). Under American law, a church, mosque, temple, or synagogue can serve meals to the public and receive a donation. Since governments can interpret this gray area of the law as a ban on "restaurants" in ISKCON temples, devotees have had to preach to officials about the benefits ISKCON provides for the community, especially in relation to its prasadam distribution. In almost all cases in North America, ISKCON has prevailed in its legal efforts to operate public eateries. Victory is often won only after temples with restaurants have exchanged documents, won endorsements, and gone through court proceedings, all showing that ISKCON renders an important service to the community.

ISKCON's reputation with and impact on the local community are key factors that devotees have had to address. Almost every temple has experienced difficulties with neighbors for a variety of reasons: the volume of *kirtanas,* the unattractive look of a temple building or grounds, smells of cooking, old cars on the premises, picking neighbors' flowers, rude or inconsiderate devotees, *hari-nama* parties in the neighborhood, parking and congestion from many visitors, etc. Some complaints are justified and some are not, but almost every temple has experienced at least some opposition from neighbors.

The best way to deal with this opposition is to meet it, understand its cause, and deal with it squarely and maturely. Meeting with neighbors individually is always beneficial, especially when devotees take it upon themselves to go door to door introducing themselves and inviting neighbors to visit the temple. If a married couple does this, it's often more effective. Devotees can also attend neighborhood council meetings and take part regularly in certain neighborhood functions or festivals.

The key is to be perceived as an active member of the local community. This requires ongoing relationships, and prasadam distribution can play an important role here.

It's even beneficial to ask neighbors what they would like to see us do. Although we might not be able to meet all their desires, we can nonetheless learn something about their mentality so as to better plan how to dovetail our Krishna consciousness outreach to enlighten and satisfy them.

The following is a suggested survey to find out about devotee awareness of neighbors.

SURVEY: The aim of this questionnaire is to help the ISKCON GBC Body and the Global Centennial Committee to determine the level and quality of the relationship between ISKCON temples and the local communities. The information gathered will provide a basis for future community relations programs. Future surveys will be taken from members of local communities.

"Local community" refers to residences and businesses within a quarter-mile radius of the temple.

1. How would you rate the way your local community regards the devotees at your temple, on a scale of 1 to 10, with 1 being the best?
2. Can you name any local community projects devotees are involved with?
3. How many people resident or in business in the local community do you know personally?
4. How many local residences or businesses have you personally visited for social purposes (indirect preaching)?
5. Are you aware of any negativity or hostility toward the devotees from the local community? If so, please specify.
6. Do you think greater involvement in community affairs, individually or collectively, would benefit preaching? (Yes or no.) If yes, please specify.
7. What do you think could enhance the relationships between devotees and the local community?
8. On a scale of 1 to 10, how important would you say it is for the devotees to have good relations with the local community (businesses and residences)?
9. How many people in the local community do you know who have visited the temple, and how often do they come?
10. Do you personally feel uncomfortable or apprehensive because of a lack of good relations with the local community?

CHAPTER 6—1994

PR Versus Reputation

After a successful global campaign masterminded by Saunaka Rsi Prabhu, the Hungarian government, in March, gave ISKCON full rights to practice its religion in eastern Europe's most powerful and influential country. In Uganda, ISKCON-BBT produced Srila Prabhupada's books in the Luganda language. Meanwhile, devotees demonstrated at Armenian embassies throughout the world, protesting against violence toward ISKCON members in

1996—Vrndavana, India: After crisscrossing the Indian subcontinent several times on foot, the ISKCON Padayatra, or "walking parade" (ox-cart included), headed by Lokanatha Swami, crosses the sacred Yamuna River on an ancient-looking boat. Personnel changes occur regularly to keep this austere and vital program going.

that country. In England, thirty-six thousand marchers walked to the Houses of Parliament to protest a government ban of public worship at Bhaktivedanta Manor. Soon afterward, the Manor won a temporary stay. Devotee "kirtanaeers", headed by Gunagrahi Das Goswami, held dance contests all summer in front of the most frequently visited US museum, the Smithsonian Air and Space Museum in Washington, D.C. In September, Padayatra, the worldwide "walking parade," headed by Lokanatha Swami (I call it "ISKCON in microcosm" because it includes book distribution, chanting of the *maha-mantra* and dancing, *prasadam,* "simple living and high thinking," dramas, and close association with devotees), celebrated its tenth year of continuous walking in India. South Africa's new President, Nelson Mandela, visited ISKCON's Durban temple in November.

REPUTATION MANAGEMENT

How can I think there is a mirror or video camera trained on me with monitor always in full view? That's a kind of meditation. To see myself as others see me and to hear myself as others hear me is to begin to understand what organizational reputation is all about. If you have ever seen yourself on video—walking, talking, listening, relaxing, or playing a dramatic role—you know that you are seen differently from what you think you look like. Lord Ramachandra and other *rajarshis* would sometimes disguise themselves and walk among their subjects to hear what they were saying, particularly about their country's leaders. As potential leaders of society, it is important to know how we—as a society—are perceived by our own members. If our individual or group practices conflict with our precepts, we will be known as pretenders. As early as 1966, Srila Prabhupada typed out the twenty-six qualifications of a devotee, beginning with "doesn't quarrel with anyone," to help us to realize that, in addition to fully comprehending the philosophy and history of Krishna consciousness, our personal behavior would be germane to the success of ISKCON.

"Increase. That will depend on your character, behavior, preaching" (Srila Prabhupada conversation, April 10, 1977, Bombay).

***ISKCON Communications Briefings,* March/April 1994**

Did we forget something? While increasing the numbers of temples, devotees, books, life members, festivals, and *prasadam* meals all over the world, did we leave something behind?

Could it have been our reputation—that evasive force which so often seems to move on its own, bringing happiness and distress, causing ISKCON to be honored and damned, welcomed and banned?

Reputation is mentioned in the *Caitanya-caritamrta* (Madhya-lila 4.147) in relation to Madhavendra Puri. There it is said, "Reputation brought by love of Godhead is so sublime that it goes along with the devotee, as if following him." In the purport Srila Prabhupada continues, "When a person, out of humility, does not desire fame, people generally think him quite humble and consequently give him all kinds of fame." In a published radio interview with Newton Minnow, Prabhupada said of devotees that they are such perfect gentlemen that "no one can find any fault in them."

To Srila Prabhupada, enhancing ISKCON's reputation was important enough for him to have based many management decisions on it. He wanted his followers to establish an excellent reputation for his mission.

Here is a brief sampling of some of his published statements about reputation.

"If required, we shall appoint professional man and keep everything very vigilant; things are going. Otherwise, once bad reputation—finished, so much attempt" (room conversation in Mayapur on February 28, 1977, regarding the Bombay restaurant).

"So our program, if it is kept pure according to my many instructions, will give you the deserved reputation of being the topmost members of the society" (letter to Jagadisa, November 17, 1970).

"The program in India should be done in consultation with all. We have now got our reputation and we must do everything very carefully to keep it" (letter to Madhavananda, August 26, 1972).

"The incident in Germany has caused havoc all over the world. It is hampering our reputation everywhere. I do not want this record distribution to continue. It must be stopped immediately" (letter to Brahmananda on January 7, 1970).

"By unfair and slanderous newspaper and television propaganda, they have ruined our reputation and turned the general public against our movement. We cannot sit down and be idle" (letter to all ISKCON temple presidents, dated February 6, 1975).

"If someone feels cheated by our men because they are using dubious methods of distribution and collecting money, our purity may be doubted and reputation spoiled" (letter to Kirtanaanda, October 15, 1976).

ISKCON GBC resolutions also reflect the seriousness with which ISKCON leadership has maintained the Society's reputation after Srila Prabhupada's departure. For example, the 1988 global GBC resolution on the suspension of a GBC member reads in part: "The Body may suspend a member when there is sufficient reason to believe that continuation of his status as a member in good standing is injurious to ISKCON or its good name."

A North American GBC resolution passed that "it is the duty of every GBC representative, temple president, and other ISKCON leader to insure that they personally act according to the highest standards of ethical, moral, and legal behavior. They shall also insure that all ISKCON members under their charge, and the ISKCON corporations they oversee, act according to the highest ethical, moral, and legal standards."

COMMUNICATIONS MANUAL FOR ISKCON READY NOW

It took two years to complete, but it's all part of the process—the *ISKCON Communications Manual,* that is. It has become of utmost importance for me to render into writing the body of communications knowledge (and skills) I have learned, developed, and created over the years. This putting-to-paper process is consistent with my personal mission statement, which in part reads as follows: "I will teach one or more persons as much as possible of what I have learned, realized, and believe in regarding the effective realization and spreading of Krishna consciousness, so that whatever my contribution to society and the disciplic succession may be, it may not be lost but will continue through the agency of other devotees after I leave my body. I will produce and develop teaching materials (including written manuals and instructions, video and audiovisual presentations like CD-ROMs and so forth) as necessary to help achieve this." This 1994 ICB article gives an overview of the manual. Principles and values, woven throughout, are close to being timeless. I am convinced, therefore, that this manual will continue to be relevant, valuable, and useful for many years to come.

ISKCON Communications Briefings, September/October 1994

The 412-page *ISKCON Communications Manual* (ICM), subtitled "How to Start Your Own Communications Program," is now in print and available worldwide.

ICM is a compilation of ISKCON Communications knowledge accumulated since the ISKCON Ministry of Communications began in 1976.

We highly recommend this manual for use in your ISKCON Communications programs. To give you a better picture of its nature and contents, we have excerpted a section that gives an overview of the manual.

Overview of the *ISKCON Communications Manual* (from the introduction):

This manual will teach you how to communicate essential messages to specific groups of people.

It is important to realize that in many, if not most, cases, you are communicating Krishna consciousness to specific individuals or groups of people more than to the general masses. The main publics or "targets" are the media; religions and interfaith groups; academia (higher education); schools (lower education); government; local communities (neighbors); interest groups (includes vegetarians, environmentalists, religious freedom and yoga societies); Indian community (in countries other than India); active adversaries; youth; devotees; devotee youth; parents of devotees; congregation or members.

It may appear that in the case of book and *prasadam* distribution, segmentation of the mass audience does not exist. Well, it does, and it also does not. Srila Prabhupada told us to distribute books and *prasadam* without discrimination. And do that we must.

But it is easy to understand that while distributing books, we routinely speak in a different way to each individual we approach. This is necessary in order to sell the book. We dovetail our preaching to best accommodate the particular person, place, and circumstance. In this way, we automatically preach to each individual in a unique way. This is an unconscious segmenting of the audience.

Also, methods of *prasadam* distribution range widely in ISKCON, from upscale restaurants to feeding derelicts. The methods and nature of the *prasadam* and distribution vary according to time, place, and circumstance. In this way, we segment the audience that receives *prasadam.*

The ICM will teach you how to establish a good reputation for ISKCON by effectively communicating key messages to your various key publics in an ongoing and effective fashion.

Part I mainly explains how to develop behavioral analyses and action plans for each public. Combined together, these two components make up your total communications plan for each of the fourteen different publics described in Part I.

Part II gives much more detailed information about each public and how to properly relate to them, based on years of ICG experience. Thus, Part II enhances your ability to implement the total communications plan described in Part I.

Part III provides you with further resources for communications plans. These include a Hare Krishna Food for Life presentation, an IC essay on Padayatra, and information about LINK and COM communications systems. The Food for Life sections in Part III can help you immensely with key publics such as the media, government, religions, academia, and local communities. This section gives you some simple, easily actionable ideas about *prasādam* distribution in the Hare Krishna Food for Life style. It will inspire and equip you with practical guidance on how to use Food for Life to enhance ISKCON's reputation. You will discover that Hare Krishna Food for Life is especially helpful with the media and the government.

Another program discussed in Part III is Padayatra. The establishment, organization, and promotion of a Padayatra can in many ways help you make your communications plans and achieve your communications goals. In one sense, Padayatra is the complete Krishna consciousness preaching program, because it includes *hari-nama sankirtana,* book distribution, *prasadam* distribution, and the promotion of "simple living and high thinking." Although the organization of Padayatra does not come under the aegis of ICG, we have found that it is one of the best ways to communicate ISKCON's essential messages. When making your behavioral analyses and action plans of this manual, remember to incorporate Padayatra.

Part IV (Appendix) provides further resources and information about reference materials. Some reference materials exist in full in Part IV (Appendix). Others are only referred to and given in part, and these may be acquired as needed from ICG or other sources.

You can purchase an IC Manual now by sending a check or money order for US $50.00, to ISKCON Communications, 10310 Oaklyn Drive, Potomac, MD 20854, USA. (US funds only).

LORD CHAITANYA PERFECTED PR POWER

Obviously, Lord Chaitanya didn't have to put a "spin" on anything, but His inner teachings did give knowledge of how to propagate Krishna consciousness in today's world. Much of what we can learn from Him is consistent with cutting-edge twentieth century communications principles. Even the San Francisco Ballet Company once sent their own troupe members to dance on the crowded central streets of that city to boost a flagging ballet fund, and they were hugely successful. I have no doubt that the ad agent got the idea from the Hare Krishna *hari-nama* parties. In this ICB story, I point to a model used by modern communications specialists and then show how Sri Chaitanya Mahaprabhu—without access to this model—expertly fulfilled all of its components. The article also explains how Srila Prabhupada, a full-fledged follower of Lord Chaitanya, embraced the same principles Lord Chaitanya exercised, and was an expert twentieth-century communications specialist and marketer in his own right.

ISKCON Communications Briefings, November/December 1994

We accept wholeheartedly that Lord Chaitanya preached the Absolute Truth. And because His method of delivering this Truth is also absolute, there is something to learn in analyzing certain aspects of the Lord's methodology in reaching out so successfully to both the classes and the masses.

Lord Chaitanya exhorts, "I order every man within this universe to accept this Krishna consciousness movement and distribute it everywhere" (Cc Adi 9.36)—a tall order, to be sure, and one demanding major change.

And yet we discover in the pages of *Caitanya-caritamrta* that Mahaprabhu's entire life was a demonstration—not just a demand—of exactly how to adopt this order and put it into practice. Therefore, His desire was fulfilled by appropriate words and actions carefully tailored to the people of His time.

He capitalized on the public's need to gain spiritual credits for honoring saints, their concern with making spiritual advancement, and their natural interest in His beauty, His singing and dancing, and His arranging an easy access to transcendental experience.

Lord Chaitanya was believable. He was able to effect social change by showing how simple it was to chant and dance and that anyone anywhere could do so, regardless of social differences (*kiba vipra, kiba nyasi* . . .) (Cc Madhya-lila 8.28). The symptoms of happiness appearing on the faces of His devotees showed an immediate, practical, and easily attainable benefit.

The Lord also spoke extensively on the benefits of pure devotional service and the dangers of avoiding it. And because He induced thousands of people to chant, dance, and partake of *prasadam* with Him, He directly helped almost everyone He came in touch with to practice the system of *bhakti.*

Lord Chaitanya's ability to influence people is reflected in modern communications appeals that contain some of the same elements the Lord applied in His preaching.

For example, one contemporary pattern for excellent communications is based on four points:

1. The communication addresses a public need, concern, or interest.
2. The desired behavior clearly presents believable solutions.
3. One clearly presents the benefits of acting and the consequences of inaction.
4. One has helped the individual rehearse the desired behavior.

It so happens that Lord Chaitanya's way of spreading Krishna consciousness resembles this latter-day system, coined as the behavioral framework by public relations author and practitioner Kerry Tucker. Sri Chaitanya radically changes not only attitude but the behavior of millions of people, thus proving Himself to be, among other things, of course, a consummate public relations authority.

He could also be described as a master of spiritual marketing. In the *Caitanya-caritamrta* (Madhya-lila 19.114 purport), Srila Prabhupada writes, "The Lord again comes as Sri Chaitanya Mahaprabhu to induce people to take to Krishna consciousness. The Lord also empowers a special devotee to teach people their constitutional position." Prabhupada himself was certainly one such devotee.

Today this empowered teaching takes many forms that did not exist during Mahaprabhu's time, such as printing and distributing millions of books and broadcasting Krishna consciousness through mass-media outlets.

Srila Prabhupada, a dedicated follower of Lord Chaitanya, may also be regarded as a marketing maestro. In addition, he was also a management and literary genius, but our focus here is specifically how he found consent among thousands of people to radically change their behavior, and we can study this success through analysis.

We can see Srila Prabhupada's marketing mastery at work by remembering the small book he brought with him on the ship Jaladuta—a book he named *Easy Journey to Other Planets.* Armed with this publication, which acted as a major wedge of his spiritual foray into the West, Srila Prabhupada took advantage of the needs, interests, and concerns of mid-sixties Americans.

Naming the book in such a way, Srila Prabhupada was addressing a prominent need. Russian scientists had successfully launched a space satellite (Sputnik), and the United States felt a great need to be involved as a leading world power in the space race. People had become greatly interested and fascinated with the wonders of space technology, and Americans were concerned not to be left out of these dazzling advances. Seen from the perspective of the behavioral framework, Srila Prabhupada was addressing the needs, concerns, and interests of the Western world.

Secondly, he presented the desired behavior in a believable fashion by being an *acharya.* In other words, he constantly taught by example through his chanting, dancing, and studying *Srimad-Bhagavatam.* As to the third principle, Srila Prabhupada incessantly taught about the benefits of Krishna consciousness as well as the damages of avoiding it (*prema bhakti jaha hoite avidya vinasa jate*).

Because he chanted, danced, and discussed philosophy constantly, often in large groups, Lord Chaitanya regularly trained and rehearsed thousands in the process of engaging in the practices of *bhakti-yoga,* thus fulfilling number four, above.

Contemporary communications (public relations) specialists have taken great pains to show how these principles apply in the modern context, and we can take advantage of them to help in our work of effectively carrying out Lord Chaitanya's mission and His methods. As the ideal preacher of Krishna consciousness, He was the consummate ideal public relations personality for Kali Yuga.

These four points provide a useful model for writing news releases, obtaining endorsements for opinion leaders, writing ISKCON news, speaking to audiences, and writing for newspapers and other public forums. It can also be applied to one-on-one meetings and a multitude of other preaching situations.

Excellent communications these days means more than altering attitudes; it means changing the way people behave toward an organization.

LET'S BOLSTER OUR FUTURE GENERATIONS—NOW!

This brief editorial was a lead-in to Manu's opinion piece on the future generation of ISKCON. I have become something of an advocate for creating systems whereby the children of the sixties and seventies, whose parents were initiated devotees, want to be a part of ISKCON in the way Srila Prabhupada had hoped. The responsibility lies with the parents and the ISKCON organization to fill in whatever may be missing in order to create a "youth-friendly" environment for Generation X. Manu, a contemporary child of this generation, is dedicated to making things work for the young people of ISKCON. I wrote the following editorial to call attention to his opinion piece, which recommends that second-generation youth involvement become a top priority for ISKCON.

Hare Krishna World, November/December 1994

Manu dasa knows ISKCON education because he went through it as a student and has served as an ISKCON elementary school teacher. Currently, he serves on the ISKCON North American Board of Education and dedicates his spare time to Project Future Hope, a seed program aimed at bringing ISKCON closer to Srila Prabhupada's vision of secondary education, which he called Varnasrama College.

There are few higher priorities in present-day ISKCON than that of shoring up and expanding its educational system for youngsters. How can we respect ourselves or achieve credibility when our Society does not make sufficient sacrifices for the future of its next generation?

There have been heroic efforts on the parts of handfuls of devotees, but that is not enough. Relegating to them the monumental task of education is one reason why some sincere teachers have left their posts, exhausted and discouraged, and why parents have felt forced to put their kids in public school—they simply were not able to be the sole financial sources for *gurukula.*

Educating children is a shared responsibility. Even our *sannyasi* members, who have renounced family life for themselves, want to see Krishna's children protected and educated. Srila Prabhupada stated in many letters to his leading disciples that ISKCON's *gurukula* is the most important preaching field.

In many ways, our children are the future of our movement. Manu suggests actions that any of us can take to help make that future successful.

CHAPTER 7—1995

Relevance

Devotees spent months collecting water from 1,008 sacred sites in India, preparing for Srila Prabhupada's 1996 Centennial celebrations. In this chapter, I call attention to this amazing feat in a *Hare Krishna World* editorial entitled, "Take a Deep Breath—Let the Centennial Begin!" In May, Balabhadra and his wife Chaya, directors of the International Society for Cow Protection (ISCOWP), met and talked shop with Michael Fox, a vice-president of the Humane Society of the United States. Opinion leaders throughout

February, 1995—Grozney, Chechnya: Local Food for Life director Sukhananda dasa walks the bombed-out streets of Grozney, Chechnya, in what little remains of this southern Russian city, fingering his beads and reciting the *maha-mantra.* In *The New York Times,* Michael Specter's feature story explains how the elderly citizens of Grozney see devotees of Krishna as saints because of their selfless and liberal distribution of nutritious foodstuffs during the crisis.

the world praised Hare Krishna Food for Life for its work in Bosnia-Herzagovina. Michael Specter, writing for *The New York Times,* said that stranded Chechnyans regarded *prasadam*-distributing devotees there as "saints." In November, a group of scholars met in Detroit to assess the impact of Srila Prabhupada's books on the world.

ISKCON'S AGENDA FOR SOCIAL CHANGE

Change the world? That's a tall order. First we have to change ourselves, many say. In this *Hare Krishna World* (the newly-minted name for the *ISKCON World Review*) editorial—the first such editorial in this book—I contend that Srila Prabhupada didn't want us to completely change ourselves before starting the process for changing the world. During his time on earth, he set in motion many programs geared to effect major societal change. He went to great lengths to insure that his devotees would remain fixed in the philosophy and practices of his Krishna consciousness movement, but at the same time, he expected us to help make this a better world to live in. In the editorial I used examples from Srila Prabhupada's life and from Vaishnava teachings and history to help readers focus on Srila Prabhupada's expansive vision for preaching Krishna consciousness. This editorial generated considerable controversy. One reader wrote in to say that all we need do is chant, read, and worship the Deity. We were getting ahead of ourselves by promoting social change. Another, however, wrote in supporting the case of spiritual social change. *Hare Krishna World* printed both reader comments.

Hare Krishna World, January/February 1995

ISKCON devotees have tended to relegate themselves to the realm of irrelevance. This is not acceptable for a society which Srila Prabhupada specifically designated as a "movement" to establish a spiritual civilization throughout the world—or, in his words, to "respiritualize human society." Movements are supposed to bring about visible social change. Clearly that is what Prabhupada wanted.

In some of his earliest writings, appearing in the India-based biweekly *Back to Godhead* magazine, Srila Prabhupada wrote or edited articles entitled, "Mr. Churchill's Humane World," "Mr. Bernard Shaw's Wishful Desire," "Philosophical Problems With Society Awareness," "Human Welfare Activities" and "Nationalism and Pure Consciousness." As their titles indicate, these articles were topical, addressing vital interests, needs and concerns of the day.

Srila Prabhupada laid great stress on the distribution of his many books of spiritual knowledge. And yet he asked that money from sales of these be used liberally to fund the Bhaktivedanta Institute (BI), ISKCON's science arm. It was Srila Prabhupada's ardent desire to discredit the theory of evolution and eventually establish the Vedic version of creationism. He wanted to expose the cheating, atheistic elements of modern science.

"Realization," according to Srila Prabhupada, is presenting spiritual subject matters in an "interesting manner for the understanding of the audience" (*Srimad-Bhagavatam* 1.4.1. purport). We might recall that when Srila Prabhupada traveled from India to America for the first time, he brought with him one of his books, entitled *Easy Journey to Other Planets.* In the beginning he addressed the ambition that Russians and Americans had at that time—to be the first nation to "conquer" space.

Part of the reason we resist efforts to achieve major social change is that many of us are convinced that Krishna consciousness automatically solves all problems. Another reason is our concern with contamination from materialistic influences. These apprehensions are supported by the fact that some devotees' spiritual commitments have been lost to material attractions. No doubt, as Lord Brahma warns, there is danger at every step in the material world.

But Srila Prabhupada sought to minimize outreach risks by establishing vows at initiation (no intoxication, meat-eating, gambling, or illicit sex, and chanting a fixed number of *mantras* daily), accompanied by an array of other activities. These included many devotional principles and practices such as book and *prasadam* distribution, public chanting, Deity worship in the temple and at home, study of scripture, adoption of essential Vedic rituals, development of Vedic devotional culture (Vaishnava art, music, song, dance, and architecture), cow protection, and urban and rural community development.

Srila Prabhupada himself took great risks to effect transcendental social change, and he expected his followers to do likewise. In *Caitanya-caritamrta* he writes, "How Sri Krishna Chaitanya Mahaprabhu was always thinking about the deliverance of the fallen souls is shown by the statement *e duhkha apara* ('It is My great unhappiness')" (Cc Antya 5.1, purport). This was the mood of compassion (and subsequent action) Srila Prabhupada conclusively established as coming from his spiritual predecessors for thousands of years. He not only translated scripture but also relentlessly pushed almost to his last breath for the creation of a powerful spiritual movement that would change the world. In *Srimad-Bhagavatam* he speaks of his desire to "convert this hell of pandemonium [the material world] to the transcendental abode of the Lord" (*Srimad-Bhagavatam* 1.5.36 purport).

Hare Krishna devotees have many things to say about many issues: abortion, animal rights, nationalism, family values, education, food production and distribution, the flaws of mechanistic science, pollution and the environment, religious freedom, overpopulation, hyper-industrialization, crime, mental stress, and disease, to name only a few. We can see that the solutions are all based on individual sense control and the philosophy that this is God's world and that we are all His servants.

Devotees are not meant to live in ivory chambers, shrinking back from the world and devoting themselves solely to the attainment of other-worldly salvation. We have to show the public that we can benefit their lives, individually and collectively. If someone asks, "What's in it for me?"—we'd better have plausible answers.

In what little time that remains of the twentieth century, we might ask ourselves: What exactly does the Hare Krishna Movement have to offer?

PUTTING OUR ENVIRONMENTAL HOUSE IN ORDER

"A grounded tanker spills millions of gallons of oil into Alaskan waters; a nuclear reactor explodes, poisoning the Ukrainian countryside; a chemical plant in India spews poison gas, killing hundreds of poor people living nearby." That's how Drutakarma and I began the pamphlet *Krishna Consciousness and the Environment.* We can all see that our air is full of smoke and smog, most of our water is unfit to drink, much of the food we buy is tainted, and our lands are burdened with trash and toxic waste. The motivating force behind the following *Hare Krishna World* editorial was to raise ISKCON members' awareness of "the environment." As devotees, we know that much environmental degradation comes from mountains of waste, which comes from excessive buying, which comes from greed, which comes from a lack of spirituality. But we sometimes forget

May 27, 1995—West Virginia, USA: Fourth-generation Montana cattle rancher Howard Lyman (hands in pockets) meets with members of the International Society for Cow Protection (ISCOWP) at the Hare Krishna's New Vrindavana rural community. The world's leading spokesperson for vegetarianism, Howard was global chairman of the World Vegetarian Union and head of the "Eating with Conscience" campaign, sponsored by the Humane Society of the United States. He has spoken at several ISKCON centers, and his publication *Mad Cowboy* was published by Scribners in 1998.

the many practical day-to-day things that show we really care about our environment. In this editorial I promote our book *Divine Nature* and re-print word-for-word the 1995 GBC resolution on the environment, authored by Drutakarma and myself.

***Hare Krishna World*, March/April 1995**

Respect and concern for all living things, an imperative for devotees of Krishna, is often taken for granted, even forgotten altogether. By scriptural definition, we Vaishnavas are deeply aware of the entrapped situation of all living entities. Yet we tend to think that our commitment to "the highest welfare work" enables us to act automatically in the best interests of the earth and its ecology.

We sometimes recall with amusement that a hunter, after conversion to Vaishnavism, danced around ants to avoid stepping on them.

Srila Prabhupada has told us on several occasions that trees feel pain when cut and that Sir Jagadish Candra Bose had proved this with a machine. In the *Srimad-Bhagavatam* (7.2.12 purport), he writes, "The cutting of trees simply to manufacture paper for the publication of unwanted literature is the greatest sinful act."

People no longer care for their environment, and everyone knows we have poisoned our planet, possibly beyond repair. Surprisingly, many people, especially in affluent nations, think they are environmentally aware. For instance, one poll revealed that eighty-five percent of United States citizens considered themselves to be "environmentalists."

In response to this belief and to drive home the importance of spiritual environmentalism among Hare Krishna devotees, Drutakarma dasa and Mukunda Goswami have written *Divine Nature: A Spiritual Perspective on the Environmental Crisis.* The book was published this month by the Bhaktivedanta Book Trust.

The writers also wrote ISKCON's official position statement on the environment, which was passed this year as a resolution by ISKCON's global Governing Body Commission (GBC).

Because environmental concerns are too often neglected in our personal lives, and serious and ecological reform in ISKCON needs to take place, *Hare Krishna World* is publishing in this editorial the full text of the GBC resolution on the environment.

Simple acts such as shopping with cloth bags instead of accepting paper or plastic bags from markets, separating garbage for recycling, conserving electricity, reducing the use of petroleum-driven vehicles, and hundreds of other commonsense practices can make a big difference. Using cow dung and its by-products for fertilizer, cooking, cleansing, flooring, heating, and lighting in rural communities is another way of demonstrating that Krishna consciousness has practical solutions to many environmental problems. We recommend that you read *Divine Nature* for more details on how you can become more environmentally aware—spiritually.

Here is the full text of the resolution passed this year by the GBC:

That the following statement is accepted as ISKCON's position statement on the environment:

Fostering a more simple and natural way of life is one of the founding principles of the International Society for Krishna Consciousness. The members of the Society are therefore committed to helping solve the planet's environmental problems. These include water pollution, air pollution, toxic waste, nuclear and chemical accidents, destruction of wildlife, and desertification.

While appreciating the good intentions of those working to solve these problems by individual and group efforts of a material nature, we believe the environmental crisis is ultimately a spiritual one requiring a spiritual solution.

The environmental crisis is a product of a society that has become severely dependent upon destructive industrial technology. This dependency is rooted in reductionist science, which has removed God and the soul from the forefront of human concern. When people forget that nature is the property of God, they are driven to exploit it unlimitedly for their own material gratification.

Scholars of the International Society for Krishna Consciousness are therefore introducing an alternative culture based on the Vedic teachings of ancient India. This philosophical system acknowledges the fundamental reality of a nonmaterial conscious self, or soul, present in each individual. All souls have their source in a Supreme Conscious Self, God. Nature also emanates from God as a perfectly balanced system capable of sustaining all living things. When humans fail to properly understand their total identity as body-mind-soul and the connection of nature with God, the system becomes unbalanced.

Ultimately, we would like to see society move toward a more natural economy, in which people are not dependent upon the present environmentally destructive system. They would instead live in smaller, self-sufficient economic units, based on simple living and high thinking. These villages, towns, and small cities would provide for basic needs locally and offer secure lifetime employment.

To this end ISKCON is gradually developing rural communities all over the world and a town for 20,000 in Mayapura, India.

To reduce the urge to excessively exploit and consume material resources, ISKCON teaches people methods for experiencing nonmaterial happiness from the soul. Chief among these is the time-honored practice of Hare Krishna *mantra* meditation. Without elevating desires from material to spiritual, the basic impetus toward environmentally destructive behavior will remain intact.

We recognize the major detrimental effect the meat industry, particularly the cattle industry, has on the environment. ISKCON's model programs for protecting cows and using bulls for transport and agriculture, based on the Vedic spiritual teachings, are thus environmentally beneficial. Such programs are now operating in ISKCON rural communities around the world. The spiritual vegetarian diet followed by ISKCON members saves scarce resources and has a far less negative impact on the environment than a meat-based diet. Since its founding in 1966, ISKCON has provided over 900 million vegetarian meals through its restaurants, temples and Food for Life program (for the homeless, hungry, or disadvantaged). The Society has also sold over 10 million vegetarian cookbooks.

While working to make this world a better place, ISKCON also encourages people to understand their identity as spirit souls and return to the spiritual world, which is the natural environment of the soul.

Without doubt the philosophical basis of ISKCON members' world view is that the spiritual world is the only true and natural environment for the soul. While universally agreeing to this, we may continue to forget that a more fully realized understanding occurs when we simultaneously do the many seemingly mundane (environmentally friendly) things that aim "to make this world a better place."

Books and position statements on the environment can easily become long-standing, empty expressions that belie a lack of full commitment and understanding about ISKCON's relationship with the environment. As the adage goes, actions speak louder than words.

VIOLENCE AND VALUES IN AMERICA

How do I cope with life? Most human beings ask themselves this question at one stage or another. But "coping capability," what some call peace and happiness, is all too often made possible by little more than Disney-esque fantasies, childish worlds of illusion, comprising fairy tales, fast cars, theme parks, computer games, television, parties, fast foods, and intoxication. Such happiness is, unfortunately, only skin-deep. Despite all these pleasure-filled escapades, statistical research suggests that humanity suffers from severe social disorders. In the US alone, in 1997, people under nineteen committed 3,200 murders with guns. Seven out of ten men in the US who earn $70,000 or more per year admitted to cheating on their wives. One in five earning $50,000 or more per year confessed to having had sex with at least six co-workers. In an attempt to deal with problems like this, people form interest groups and cry out for "values" and "decency" in television, advertising, and the Internet. Unfortunately, however, we have turned morality into a private, relative affair. This HKW editorial recommends that people in the US examine the absolute principles of morality and values found in standard books of spiritual truth, particularly the *Bhagavad-gita* and *Srimad-Bhagavatam.*

Hare Krishna World, May/June 1995

The United States—a superpower in terms of armaments, entertainment, communications, and technology—influences behavior patterns throughout the world. Therefore, we thought it timely to focus on two emerging and related American trends: growing concerns with violence and values.

Terrorism, like many other social evils, is essentially a spiritual problem. The evildoers see their adversaries as soulless entities. Notions of the human family and universal kinship among all people have no meaning for the terrorist. Americans were traumatized when a bomb recently killed 168 federal employees and many of their children, destroying a government office building in Oklahoma in the deadliest terrorist event in US history. A widely publicized possible motive for this mass killing was hatred for the US Bureau of Alcohol, Tobacco, and Firearms agents' handling of a siege one year ago in Waco, Texas. The Waco incident resulted in the death of 85 people (including 25 children) belonging to the Branch Davidians, a little-known religious sect. The rights and wrongs of the government's action is a hotly debated topic. It became the subject of an official hearing by the US Department of Justice to take place on an unspecified date.

Whether the target be a "reckless government" or an "evil cult," people throughout the country have been shocked by senseless displays of hatred against real or imagined enemies. The horrific face of terrorism, brought home so dramatically in Oklahoma, has left many Americans groping for answers, reasons, and meaning.

But as the scornful cry "enough" echoes from coast to coast, an equally strident demand has begun to ring through the concrete corridors of US cities. It is a demand for "values" and "morality." William Bennett's *Book of Values* has become a surprise best-seller. The fiction, *Celestine Prophecy,* about a quest for ultimate spiritual evolution, became a best seller last year. *A Moral Sense* by James Q. Wilson, and *The Dream and the Nightmare* by Myron Magnet are two other popular books that plead a case for morality in America.

Even a person as immersed in worldly affairs as Robert Bartley, editor of *The Wall Street Journal,* calls for a moral consensus, "one to which philosophers and lawmakers and judges can repair. A foundation, that is, for saying that some things are right and others wrong. . . . If we are to deal with the issues of crime, welfare, violence, abortion, and so on, we need to recover a sense of shared morality. As a society, we need to start developing, to start looking for, a new establishment to lead us." (*The Wall Street Journal,* 26 May, 1995).

But who will lead people out of violence and toward morality? What institution or individual is qualified? More to the point, what is meant by morality and how can common standards be discovered, established, and applied?

Current ideals of morality are rarely broad, holistic, consistent, or interdependent enough to make a difference. Many look for answers in religion and churches, while others hope to legislate morality through political processes. Still others join action or interest groups that advocate, for example, "decency in the media," "schools with values," and "ethics in business." But as Mr. Bartley indicates, a broadly shared sense of moral values has yet to be found.

Indeed, a moral consensus is hard to find when animal rightists support abortion, pro-life proponents wear fur, major sports tournaments are blanketed with beer and cigarette ads, environmentalists eat meat, parents who want their children to be "good" let them watch television indiscriminately, and promoters of peace insist on the right to bear firearms.

To remedy these and numerous other conflicts, many are desperately seeking value systems that reconcile modern life's myriad contradictions. What they don't know is that such values have to be rooted in spirituality and must discourage human beings from dominating and exploiting both each other and nonhuman species as well.

Spirituality is the fountainhead of all religion, values, ethics, and moral principles. But today's morality is generally misconceived. It attaches to the widespread belief that morality is an individual, relative affair. This view dictates that each of us has to establish his or her own moral code to live by—"I'm a good person, honest, faithful to my spouse, and doing the best I can." But this is proving to be disastrously inadequate.

Vedic knowledge, India's sacred Sanskrit texts, especially *Bhagavad-gita* and *Srimad-Bhagavatam,* are an important, longstanding source of spiritual knowledge. These ancient works deal with sustainable spiritual values that can help us distinguish right from wrong, even in complex situations.

Such standards posit that we are all essentially spiritual beings, that our bodies are different from our true selves (souls), and that our souls and those of all other beings have a personal relationship with the Supreme Soul, or God. This understanding leads to awareness that kinship exists between everything that is alive, just as siblings feel bonded because of common parentage. An early result of such understanding is a dramatic reduction of purposeless violence to all living entities.

Another spiritual principle is that human enjoyment, propriety, and even compassion have limitations, but that these qualities are infinitely present in God and truly saintly persons. We ordinary humans have to know our limits, how we are all related to God, and where to draw the line. Acquisition of spiritual wisdom and learning to enjoy nonmaterial pleasures such as yoga, meditation, and chanting generate a sense of voluntary restraint on worldly pleasure and false egotism and bring a sense of peace.

Although many are turning to conventional religion with renewed optimism, answers found there are often incomplete. Universal spiritual principles, on the other hand, transcend sectarian allegiances to denominational doctrines. The *Bhagavad-gita* advises that one "abandon all varieties of religion" and surrender unto God (*Bhagavad-gita,* 18.66).

Vedic literature argues that as nonmaterial beings living under karmic law, we have no right to take the lives of other living creatures—other than in exceptional cases—because we are all related.

Spiritual practices also help us reduce material greed, develop tolerance and compassion, discover practical moral standards, and develop a sense of relatedness to all other beings. When these practices are followed, the tendency towards violence, crime, abortion, and intoxication is greatly reduced. Discovery of happiness within overrides the more conventional approach of seeking all pleasures outside of our inner selves.

Bhagavad-gita and *Srimad-Bhagavatam* should be our guidebooks for improving the quality of life. They present a basis for broad values and a morality universal enough to help America unravel its present moral enigma.

With spirituality, answers do not come instantly, because they are not of the band-aid, quick-fix variety. Nor will such answers solve all problems immediately. They are long-term and sustainable. Vedic knowledge gives us a solid foundation upon which to proceed; it shows the way forward. Most importantly, it gives us and future generations a value system that works.

THE UN'S 50TH BIRTHDAY GIFT: A WORLD AT WAR

In 1995, fifty years after the formation of the United Nations, war had become a way of life for millions of people. More national conflicts than ever before in human history were scourging the earth. The following editorial highlights this irony. Twenty-one years after the UN's formation, Srila Prabhupada understood people's growing dissatisfaction with the institution. Acting on this discontent, he led a small group of devotees to the UN Secretariat building in New York City and began chanting the Hare Krishna *maha*-mantra with them. While some chanted, others handed out the "peace formula," which expounded on the *Bhagavad-gita* verse in which Lord Krishna claims to be the Proprietor of all lands. At that time, during the late sixties, millions of young people were openly angry about the US involvement in Vietnam, and their quest for "peace" found a ready partnership in Srila Prabhupada's performance outside the UN Secretariat that September morning in 1966.

***Hare Krishna World,* July/August 1995**

Although the United Nations has gathered and spent vast amounts of human resources and money, at the year of its fiftieth anniversary, it has yet to achieve its goal. This is further proof that the world cannot unite under a secular banner. The ever-growing array of flags flying outside the UN headquarters in New York City is sad testimony to a planet flooded with strife. Events of the past fifty years have all but destroyed hopes for a "new world order."

Recently governments have killed UN peacekeeping forces and defiled UN "safe" areas with wanton violence. France's seemingly unchallengeable commitment to test nuclear bombs in Tahiti makes the UN seem utterly helpless in stopping one of the most globally destructive programs a government can execute.

Although peace treaties have been signed and anarchists arrested, statistical data shows that terrorism and the number of armed conflicts in the world have escalated steadily during the past fifty years. US President Harry Truman's hopeful pronouncement in 1945 of an "end to all war" sounds more remote than ever.

Some political analysts warn that the world is becoming more divided. Yugoslavia and the former Soviet Union have broken up into competing nations. Racial, religious, and ethnic clashes are growing, even in countries known for traditions of tolerance and peaceful coexistence.

The *Isopanisad* informs that under universal law no one has the right to accept as one's own any part of the world beyond his or her designated quota. According to these teachings, everything belongs to God. Those who take more than their rightful share are thieves under universal law, and *karma* invariably catches up with the offenders, sometimes in the form of war. Only when God is widely recognized as the central figure and proprietor of the universe can all people live on earth compatibly. The essence of this knowledge needs to be incorporated into the United Nations charter.

Most armed struggles are based on vying for lands people mistakenly identify with, due to their ethnic or national background. But, according to the *Bhagavad-gita,* the best-known Vedic text, no people are the actual owners of any region of the world. Falsely identifying with tracts of land is at the heart of most violent struggles in the world. This misconception repeatedly frustrates humanity's many well-meaning efforts to achieve peace. Sovereignty that ignores the Supreme Sovereign is a great burden for society, one that has uselessly led—and will continue to lead—millions of people to their deaths.

Transcendentalists, particularly Vaishnavas, unceasingly work for the peace and happiness of others by striving for global cooperation. In a spiritual sense, living beings—though always individual personalities—constitutionally live in a state of spiritual harmony and unity, because Krishna is at the center of their consciousness. However, contact with the material world has polluted our original consciousness, which recognizes God as the Supreme Proprietor. This ignorance gives way to the philosophy of individual, family, communal, state and, ultimately, national jurisdiction, creating irreconcilable disputes even over trifling and insignificant matters.

Although human beings can never live in a state of complete peace and harmony within this material world, the masses can feel protected and secure under a God-conscious government.

In 1966, Srila Prabhupada wrote the seven purposes of the International Society for Krishna Consciousness. The first one reads,

"To systematically propagate spiritual knowledge to society at large and to educate all peoples in the techniques of spiritual life in order to check the imbalance of values in life and to achieve real unity and peace in the world."

In that same summer he led eight fledgling devotees to the United Nations General Assembly Hall in New York. There he conducted a protest that consisted of chanting *Hare Krishna Hare Krishna Krishna Krishna Hare Hare, Hare Rama Hare Rama Rama Rama Hare Hare* and handing out a leaflet called "The Peace Formula." Based on the *Bhagavad-gita* verse (5.29) in which Lord Krishna declares Himself the Supreme Proprietor, Srila Prabhupada's paper urged the people of the world and the United Nations to give up temporal notions of peace, to establish a God-centered society, and thus obtain permanent unity and happiness.

WOMEN'S CONFERENCE SKIPS CRITICAL PERSPECTIVE

The formation of a global ISKCON Women's Ministry demonstrates that ISKCON has grasped the nature of a persistent social problem that troubles US society. The issue of women's rights and the feminist movement have entered ISKCON in a way that traditionalists sometimes find disquieting. These concerns test our understanding of both the philosophy and culture of Krishna consciousness. Within ISKCON, there has been a lack of full realization, or so it seems, of the meaning, "I am not this body." I wrote this editorial to show how even major global conferences on women's rights, because they lack the understanding that *aham brahmasmi* (I am spirit), achieve far too little. There is a tendency to equate "reproductive rights" (read "abortion rights") with "women's rights." As I state in this 1995 *Hare Krishna World* editorial, "Krishna consciousness is the necessary starting point of any discussion on women's rights and must be at the foundation of any plan for changing the inequities in modern society." In other words, "Let's get off the bodily platform."

Hare Krishna World, July/August 1995

Women from around the world gathered in Beijing, China, last month, at the United Nations Fourth World Conference on Women, seeking a philosophical consensus on which to build a program for improving the lives of half the world's population. In spite of decades of activism, struggle, and change, conference organizers maintain that huge numbers of the world's women remain impoverished, disenfranchised, and barred from the education and legal rights that could materially improve their lives.

But the conference, the largest formal gathering of women ever, exposed deep disagreements among women of various nations about what actions the international community should take toward improving women's lives. The conference passed a voluminous Program of Action, which includes, among other things, a concept of a woman's unqualified right to control her sexuality. This resolution has generally been interpreted in the "developed" countries to include a woman's absolute authority to terminate her pregnancy. A record forty-three nations, and the Catholic Holy See, filed formal objections to the document.

At issue, according to the Holy See delegation's leader, Mary Ann Glendon, is a concern that the document may be embodied in the UN's Universal Declaration of Human Rights. Ms. Glendon identified those human-rights principles as: the recognition that human rights are grounded in the equal dignity of all men and women; that the family is entitled to special protection by society and the state; that men and women have the right to religious freedom, either alone or in community with others; that parents have rights and responsibilities; and that motherhood and childhood are entitled to special care and assistance.

Ms. Glendon charges that a minority coalition, led by the European Union, sought to impose its own political agenda on the world's women by placing its radical stance on reproductive issues before a more reasoned platform that would protect the rights of women in the context of family and motherhood.

Ultimately, the ideological conflicts at the conference as well as the oppression of women in general could be resolved through solutions based on Vedic philosophy. Oppression of women stems from the conviction prevailing in the material world that "I am this body" as opposed to the Vedic ideal of seeing all living entities with "equal vision."

Trapped in bodily consciousness, the individual soul makes unreasonable distinctions between living entities and asserts an unfounded right to control or oppress others. According to Vedic teaching, it is the desire to be the controller, to rule or dominate others, that causes us to take birth in the material world, identifying ourselves as American, Indian, Russian, black, white, or female. Small wonder, then, that this ignorance is manifest in laws and social conventions that abuse women economically, politically, and personally.

The *Bhagavad-gita* teaches how our goal is for no one to make distinctions based on bodily identification, seeing that all souls are God's beloved children. When we recognize the Supreme Soul, Krishna, as the ultimate controller and proprietor of all living beings, we lose the impulse to impose false sovereignty over others.

In order to achieve this ideal, in Krishna conscious society, males are taught to regard women as "mother," so that they do not see them as objects of gratification to be exploited. Instead, they see every female devotee as someone to be treated honorably, conscious that this is a sacred soul and, thus, a respected child of God.

Vedic society provides for women to have rights and security. The home is traditionally their autonomous domain. They own wealth. They are protected by their fathers in youth, their husbands in maturity, and their children in widowhood and old age. Marriage partners are selected and chosen with care, because good marriages and proper child-rearing are considered sacred values. As long as God consciousness is the core of the family's consciousness, divorce becomes unnecessary. Krishna (God) is present in His holy name, in the temples, in the scriptures, in the instructions of the spiritual master, and in the hearts of His devotees, to guide them in their relationships.

Service to God in the family strengthens the fabric of society, greatly reducing marital estrangement and adultery. With love, spiritually grounded parents teach their children to live according to higher principles. These and other practices of Vedic society are taught in the Krishna consciousness movement. Within the context of Srila Prabhupada's vision for a more God-conscious world, they facilitate spiritual development. There is, of course, a need to ensure that these higher principles are dovetailed into the globally diverse cultures of ISKCON members, with respect and sensitivity. What works for a traditional family in India won't necessarily work for a devotee business woman in New York.

Unsuccessful family relationships foster alienation of children. Disaffected children often turn to lives of depravity and crime, adding significantly to society's burden. "From degradation of womanhood . . ." the *Bhagavad-gita* teaches, comes "unwanted progeny" who cause "hellish life." Degradation of womanhood directly relates to degradation of manhood. One gender tries to exploit the other to fulfill personal desires instead of the desires of God.

The UN conference's nonbinding Program of Action, while a valuable starting place for political discussion, is no substitute for the change in consciousness that is needed before women's rights can be properly addressed.

Krishna consciousness is the necessary starting point of any discussion on women's rights and must be at the foundation of any plan for changing the inequities in modern society.

TAKE A DEEP BREATH—LET THE CENTENNIAL BEGIN!

It was an event that happened only once. The year 1996 marked the hundredth anniversary celebration of Srila Prabhupada's appearance in this world. A global campaign, headed by His Holiness Lokanatha Maharaja, was a grand success. This year-end 1995 essay emphasizes the importance of Prabhupada's monumental

April, 1995—India: A Padayatra ("walking parade") devotee gathers water from a sacred river in India. Waters from 1,008 sacred wells, ponds, lakes, estuaries, waterfalls, and rivers are brought to Delhi where they are combined, filtered, and distributed throughout the world in engraved silver, gold, or copper chalices. The holy water is used to bathe the feet and murti figure of ISKCON's founder-*acharya,* His Divine Grace A.C. Bhaktivedanta Swami Prabhupada, on the 100th anniversary of his appearance in this world.

contributions to society. Building up to the 1996 observances, *Hare Krishna World* devoted a whole page in each of its 1995 editions to the Centennial celebrations. One of the most amazing events of the observance was the collection of sacred water from 1,008 holy ponds, lakes, streams, rivers, and estuaries in India—a feat not known even to Indian history. Under the guidance of Lokanatha Swami, devotees mixed, filtered, and bottled this water at Centennial headquarters in Delhi and sent it out all over the world. They also made and sent beautifully sculptured and monogrammed kalashes (bronze and silver water pots) to Centennial beneficiaries everywhere.

Hare Krishna World, November/December 1995

As of this writing, the Srila Prabhupada Centennial Celebration has unofficially begun with the great ISKCON tradition of distributing books for the year-end "Prabhupada Marathon." This is a most fitting way to honor Srila Prabhupada—by distributing his teachings and thus helping others.

Srila Prabhupada's book distribution marathon is also for the distributors. One achieves spiritual advancement by helping others change the way they think about themselves and the world they live in. By understanding one's position in the cosmos as God's humble servant, one naturally gains more respect for the universe's other inhabitants, and eventually, by Prabhupada's unparalleled descriptions of the Lord and His pastimes with His associates, one learns to love Krishna.

The natural result of reading Srila Prabhupada's translations of Vedic scriptures and his related works is that one can become free from material illusion and full of hope for a chance to return to the spiritual platform, by hearing from Lord Krishna's pure devotee.

Srila Prabhupada's books also dispel misconceptions, even about ISKCON, the spiritual society he started. In his books, he explains how he expected ISKCON and the Gaudiya Vaishnava system of guru-disciple relationships to continue. He also emphasizes that association with devotees of Krishna is all-important. Although we may encounter great difficulties along the path of devotional service, he reassures us that such service, when fully purified, is the certain method to reinstate us in our eternal relationship with Lord Krishna in His eternal abode of Goloka Vrindavana.

ISKCON devotees are now on the eve of the year-long celebration of his Centennial, which takes place throughout 1996. His Divine Grace A.C. Bhaktivedanta Swami Srila Prabhupada, founder-acharya of ISKCON, was born on September 1, 1896.

Many ISKCON members may feel unprepared for this event. Some haven't yet decided what gift to offer Srila Prabhupada on his hundredth appearance anniversary. To you we say, don't worry—let's do our best and simultaneously depend on Krishna, confident that He will help us glorify His pure devotee.

In the *Bhagavad-gita* Lord Krishna assures us that if we serve with loving faith and devotion, He will help us from within our hearts. He will rescue us from our doubts, our ineptness, and our illusion.

Among the 108 ways to serve the Centennial, as enumerated in a wonderful, small pamphlet issued by global centennial director Lokanath Swami, we learn that we can plant memorial trees, increase our study of Srila Prabhupada's books, get a friend to chant one round of the Hare Krishna mantra on beads, convince parents that their child should attend a Hare Krishna school (*gurukula*), or help build a temple.

Relevance

- Local Centennial Inaugural Functions (December, 1995 through February, 1996)
- Hare Krishna World Convention (Mayapura festival, February 18 to March 17, 1996)
- Padayatra Week (June 2-8, 1996)
- World Holy Name Day (June 9, 1996)
- Maha Vyasa Puja. This event includes bathing his *murti* world wide with sacred waters from 1,008 holy places. (September 6, 1996)
- Srila Prabhupada's Disappearance Day (November 14, 1996)
- New Delhi, Bangalore, Ahmedabad temple and Vrindavana Samadhi grand openings (last part of November, 1996)
- Srila Prabhupada Book Marathon and Gita Jayanti (December, 1996)
- Maha Appreciation Events (end 1996 and early January, 1997)

At a minimum, as ISKCON devotees, we can recommit ourselves to deepen our dedication to our internal spiritual lives by more closely following Srila Prabhupada's teachings.

Even if we've already read them twice all the way through, we can pick up the *Teachings of Lord Chaitanya, The Science of Self-Realization,* or *Bhagavad-gita As It Is,* and read, read, and reread. Each time the experience is fresh, the teachings become clearer, and a deeper sense of understanding, satisfaction, and happiness inevitably result.

ARE DEVOTEES RELEVANT?

Some say that the worst insult is to be told, "You're wrong, your opinions are false, and you don't know what you're talking about." But there is something worse—to be ignored. Sometimes, if we don't say something currently meaningful, people may neglect us. Srila Prabhupada had something to say even about space travel, especially in 1965. Sputniks were deeply on the minds of everyone then. His flagship publication, *Easy Journey to Other Planets,* was testimony to his awareness of the space race that then existed between the US and the USSR. This ICB essay, which is tied to

September 29, 1995—Washington, D.C., USA: Prahlad accepts the Presidential Medal of Freedom on behalf of his deceased grandfather, Walter P. Reuther (charismatic former president of the United Auto Workers union) from US president Bill Clinton and his wife, Hillary. Prahlad's mother, Lekhasravanti-devi dasi (Walter's daughter); her husband, Bhusaya dasa; and other family members also attend. Lekhasravanti joined with Ambarisa dasa, great-grandson of Henry Ford, to purchase the property for the ISKCON cultural center in Detroit. The partnership made headlines because of the history of long and bitter feuding between Ford management officials and Reuther's United Auto Workers union. This adds a spiritual dimension to the Ford and Reuther family traditions.

media relations, discusses the importance of ISKCON members becoming "experts" in different fields and being recognized as such by reporters and news writers. Of course, developing consistent positions on societal questions will take time (this is being written in late 1998). ISKCON will have to articulate its position on topical issues and let devotees know that we have written standard positions. In large part, relevance is achieved when the media seek our answers to important questions of the day. These are likely to include vegetarian and health issues and those of genetic engineering, abortion, animal rights, pornography, drug abuse, hunger, crime, religious strife, and gerontology.

ISKCON Communication Briefings, January/February 1995

What do you think about the new handgun bill? And what about the population conference in Cairo? The earthquake in Japan? Abortion, animal rights, pornography, violence on television, the crisis in education, European unification, the wars in Serbia and Russia, hunger, drugs, crime, terrorism, the desecration of a mosque in India?

These often-asked questions are sometimes met with a shrug or incredulous look, as if none of this really mattered. It wouldn't matter so much if we lived on a desert island instead of on an information superhighway.

The media, one of the most active vehicles on that highway, is at our disposal to carry our message. Newspapers, magazines, and television and radio stations throughout the world are actively and constantly seeking new information packages to deliver to millions of people.

One of the things they constantly seek are "authoritative sources." In fact, many broadcast assignment editors, as well as newspaper and magazine editors, have personal address books, Rolodex card files, or sections of their personal computers that list sources and experts in the various fields they report on.

When a war breaks out, an editor often looks for an academic expert or analyst who can give his or her learned opinion, commentary, or prognosis about the past and emerging events in a region of new conflict. The expert might typically be an author or the head of a university department such as "Middle East Affairs," or the chairman of an "Environmental European Studies" division of a university. Such authors, professors, or department heads appear so often that their faces, voices, styles, and gestures become familiar to a broad swath of the public.

In some parts of the world, priests, bishops, mullahs, or rabbis extensively comment publicly and regularly on events and trends in the news. Such persons become known to the media as "resources" and are thus de facto spokespersons for their faith's point of view. They keep well-informed about current events and carefully develop their public personas. It is they who often help most significantly to keep their religion's agenda up front in the public mind.

ISKCON members, too, can become expert commentators. Their expertise is to develop and expound on the most deeply spiritual perspectives of events, issues, and trends of the day.

This will take special training. Such spokespersons will need not only to be well versed in Vedic knowledge, but also will need to thoroughly understand certain issues, trends, and events, especially those that they can comment upon compellingly.

When such events, issues, and trends involve topics such as abortion, animal rights, vegetarianism, genetic engineering, the environment, crime, intoxication, national conflicts, religious freedom, world hunger, overpopulation, ethics, morality, and personal stress and anxiety, it is possible to develop informed Krishna conscious commentary. Of course, the ISKCON commentator must be sufficiently informed and well-spoken so as to be fully credible. Practice makes perfect.

ISKCON has tended to move in the West from the category of misfit to one of grudging acceptance to one of general acceptance. Even in areas of the West where ISKCON's presence is somewhat cheerfully acknowledged, most people have little knowledge, if any, about what we stand for. A Gallup survey conducted during the mid-eighties in Britain revealed that over ninety-nine percent of the public thought that the Hare Krishna movement had nothing to offer British citizens. This is somewhat disappointing, since ISKCON has been legally incorporated and active in England since 1969. This survey was powerful evidence that ISKCON was simply not relevant to the lives of the British people.

Individual ISKCON members sometimes give unique perspectives on events, trends, or people in the news. Such learned views will be individual, exceptional, and unofficial. A proper system for training experts to write commentary on issues will have to be created and maintained.

As with the Bhaktivedanta Institute, specialized ISKCON groups will become the "spiritual experts" in other areas, such as economics, psychology, rural life, the environment, education, and religious freedom. Books will be written, and institutions and other training facilities will be designed and built.

We will seek and be sought after by the media for learned commentary. This will be a major step toward becoming relevant.

HARE KRISHNA TODAY

Video, it is argued, is today's most comprehensive form of communications. It takes you instantly to faraway places, and dazzles you with beauty, color, and movement. Its voices, sounds, and music captivate your ears; its images change rapidly, engaging your mind and feelings. In a short time, video can convince you to buy a product or service, go somewhere, or think differently. We've tried to put most of these elements together to make "ISKCON's Video News Journal" an exceptional product. It is meant to give first-time viewers an idea of the depth and scope of the Krishna consciousness movement and to show them that we think about things that are critical to our functioning as peaceful, happy, and well-behaved humans. For people somewhat experienced in the Krishna consciousness society, *Hare Krishna Today* (HKT) offers pride of association. I know of no better aid to face-to-face preaching than HKT. It can be used again and again. I developed this ICB article to encourage the widespread use of HKT.

***ISKCON Communications Briefings*, January/February 1995**

One *Hare Krishna World* newspaper or *Back to Godhead* magazine usually includes between 30 and 45 photos, mostly black and white. By contrast, one *Hare Krishna Today* (HKT) video magazine usually comprises 250 different scenes, each a full-color moving picture. These pictures are accompanied by speech, ambient sound, and sometimes additional music. Video is definitely the most comprehensive form of modern communication.

HKT is a half-hour video showcase of ISKCON events, projects, people, temples, and *Bhagavad-gita* philosophy. For those of you who haven't seen HKT, here's a rundown of number seven. The issue begins with Dr. Nelson Mandela's official state visit to the Hare Krishna temple in Durban, South Africa. This sequence is followed by a report on Moscow's Radio Krishnaloka and a story on Germany's Spiritual Skyline (a *sankirtana* bus). Next are a "natural living" segment on the International Society for Cow Protection, a Hare Krishna Food for Life story, and a "temple spotlight" feature on ISKCON San Diego. Aindra Prabhu's twenty-four-hour *kirtanas* at ISKCON's Krishna-Balarama temple in Vrindavana and a *Bhagavad-gita* meditation piece conclude this issue.

Many more "nondevotees" than devotees see HKT. Television stations in the USA and Germany (there is a German language HKT) regularly air HKT. Segments of HKT have been aired in India, and translations are underway for a Russian language version for broadcast in the former Soviet Union.

HKT is in demand. It is attractive because devotees are colorful and interesting. One of HKT's subtle themes is the expression of spiritual perspectives and solutions to material problems. As HKT production continues, this theme will become more apparent. HKT is a powerful outreach program, and ISKCON needs to take more advantage of it.

One of ISKCON Communications goals for Srila Prabhupada's Centennial is to broadcast HKT on 50 cable television channels throughout the world.

IC Global received the blessings of ISKCON's Governing Body Commission in the form of a survey conducted at the 1994 annual GBC meetings in Mayapura, just after GBC members viewed HKT.

Excerpts from comments by GBC members are as follows:

Badrinarayana dasa: "We should get it on cable television, show it to important people, use it at Sunday feast crowds and at home programs."

Bhaktisvarupa Damodara Swami: "The video has great potential in presenting Krishna consciousness in action around the world."

Harikesa Swami: "Everyone likes these. I also like it."

Harivilasa dasa: "It is useful for our congregational members."

Temple presidents throughout the world are enthusiastic to show HKT to great advantage in Nama Hatta preaching. They encourage us to take a copy along when going to someone's home for an evening program, and pop it into their VCR. In half an hour the hosts will get a thorough picture of ISKCON activities all over the world. This will greatly enhance any talk and subsequent discussions with the family.

Also, because television stations around the world are often eager to air HKT or parts of it, it is possible to take a copy to your local station (especially with USA cable stations) and ask to have one or more HKT programs, or parts of them, aired. Usually the station programming personnel will at least view the shows and surprisingly often will arrange to put them on the air. They prefer to show them on a weekly basis.

Copies of HKT for broadcast can be obtained from Avatar Studios at the IC Global Headquarters in Potomac, Maryland, USA.

THEY'RE WAITING FOR US

"Friendship is the real corrupting influence on journalism, and these pressures will never be mentioned. A reporter will never disclose the pervasive influence his friends and dinner companions have on the way he slants a story." This quote comes from David Brooks, a senior editor at *The Weekly Standard.* Whether friends and companions really constitute a corrupting influence or not, the truth is that media people have opinions about everything, just as you and I. There is no such thing as a news story that is not slanted. As many leading *sadhus* would agree, everything worthwhile is based on good relationships (*sambandha*). At the 1998 July 4th holiday celebrations in Washington, D.C., television's News Odyssey reporters covered the ISKCON Rathayatra and Festival of India. The day before, they spent hours in open discussion with Anuttama dasa, ISKCON North America's Communications director. At the festival site, they asked that a large donation box be removed and placed out of camera range. "I don't want viewers to think this is about money," the cameraman said. The following article emphasizes that ISKCON members should generally view the media as partners in spreading *sanatana dharma,* or Krishna consciousness—not people who are out to "get" or "expose" us.

***ISKCON Communications Briefings,* January/February 1995**

Mukunda Goswami, ISKCON Communications Global director, and Anuttama dasa, ISKCON Communications North America director, are both members of the Religious Public Relations Council of America. The most recent issue of the RPRC's Washington, D.C., newsletter, *RPRC Counselor,* discussed the current openness of the news media in America in the following article.

"Writer Notes Window of Opportunity for Religion Coverage"

Neither religion nor the press "is much interested in the First Amendment problems of the other," longtime Washington writer David Anderson told the Washington, D.C., chapter of the

Religious Public Relations Council in June.

Anderson, former religion writer for United Press International and now with Religious News Service, asserted that there is a "window of opportunity" now because "never have the media been so open to the coverage of religion." He added that there is "more ignorance than hostility in the press."

As an example, he pointed to ABC Network's addition of a religion reporter, three full-time religion writers with the *Washington Post,* and noted that "the quality of people covering religion is higher than ever."

At the same time, in relation to the First Amendment, Anderson said there is "no organized culture of disbelief." While both parties tend to "view their expressive rights in fairly absolutist terms," both are changing, asking new questions and using new forms of expressions.

"Capture Religious Awareness, Larson Urges"

In the opinion of a veteran observer and commentator, religious communicators share today "a moment when we have a new religious awareness, but it will vanish unless we do something to capture it." Roy Larson, principal architect of the Center for Religion and the News Media being established jointly by Garrett-Evangelical Theological Seminary and Northwestern University's Medill School of Journalism, both in Evanston, Illinois, spoke at a joint meeting in late September of the RPRC Board of Governors and members of the Chicago chapter. "Flesh and spirit are crying out for more than the secular world can provide," Larson asserted. "I can't imagine a better time to do what you are doing," he told the thirty persons present.

Larson, formerly religion editor of the *Chicago Sun-Times,* is retiring as publisher of the Community Renewal Society's *Chicago Reporter and Catalyst.* He also has been a pastor. The Garrett-Medill Center will serve three general functions, according to Larson. It will be a national information service on religion—a place for creative dialogue between religious leaders and media professionals, and an opportunity for each school's students to enroll in the other's courses.

"I think for many religious leaders the world of the media is kind of intimidating—a hostile world in which they do not feel at home," Larson told a reporter for the *Chicago Reader.* "As a result, I think religion doesn't get the kind of sophisticated, in-depth coverage it should."

A PREACHING INITIATIVE

Very similar to the HKW editorial on page 72, "Putting our Environmental House in Order," this 1995 ICB article makes the case for reading *Divine Nature* and using that book's main themes to awaken people's dormant Krishna consciousness. The book *Divine Nature* includes a bit of history, showing how most people accepted industry for generations, before it began to destroy nature. The famous historian Arnold Toynbee met Srila Prabhupada in 1973, and they agreed on many points. A spiritual, or Krishna- conscious, perspective on the environment is one of the best ways to reach out to thoughtful people.

ISKCON Communications Briefings, May/June 1995

In our last issue of *ISKCON Communications Briefings* we stated that "Individual ISKCON members can give unique perspectives on events, trends, and people in the news of the world." We could have included "issues" in that list of items. One of today's most prevalent issues is the environment. For this reason, the North American BBT has recently published *Divine Nature,* a book written by the editors of this newsletter and devoted to ISKCON's position on the environment.

This publication, subtitled *A Spiritual Perspective on the Environmental Crisis,* can be a powerful instructional instrument for learning how to preach "on the issues." Although the environment is only one of many concerns of the day, the way we approach it with Krishna consciousness helps us learn how to address other issues of the day. Currently, the environment is one of the top five major issues in the world, and experts in sociology say this trend is likely to continue for at least several years.

All problems of the world are due to a lack of Krishna consciousness. "In this material world there is actually no scarcity of anything except Krishna consciousness," Srila Prabhupada writes in a *Caitanya-caritamrta* purport (Adi 9.38).

ISKCON's official statement on the environment is now a seven-hundred-word GBC resolution, passed this year. This position paper clearly establishes our Society's concern with ecological disaster. The resolution also explains that ISKCON is helping to remedy the situation by spreading spiritual knowledge, distributing *prasadam,* and establishing rural communities.

Divine Nature systematically explains how ecological pollution is caused by overconsumption, which is caused by excessive greed, which is fostered by rampant materialism. Materialism easily runs rampant when there is little dominion of God consciousness.

The book's central theme is that each being on the planet can claim only a quota of the earth's resources. But due to greed that comes from godlessness, people are trying to possess and enjoy more than their rightful share of the universe as ordained by higher order cosmic laws.

This point is effectively made in the first verse and purport of Srila Prabhupada's *Isopanisad.* These teachings can help people understand that clear perspectives and solutions to environmental problems are best sought-after in the realm of transcendental knowledge. Even less developed forms of God consciousness—like those followed by Christian communities in Europe before the Age of Reason—tended to act as restraints on materialism.

In the early 1700s, Newtonian physics (followed by the Industrial Revolution) saw a concomitant decline of religion's central role in the lives of individuals and communities. This dwindling of religion and the concurrent rise of industry appear interrelated. Some chroniclers even theorize that they are inversely proportional.

Divine Nature contends that science and even some religious movements have made unholy alliances with a mechanistic, godless view of the world and that all this has greatly accelerated the proliferation of materialistic ways of life.

Historian Arnold Toynbee, writing for the *London Observer* in 1972, described the cause of "the world's malady" as spiritual. "We are suffering," he wrote, "from having sold our souls to the pursuit of maximizing material wealth, a pursuit which is spiritually wrong and practically unattainable. We have to recognize our objective and change it."

When we, as Krishna conscious devotees, identify the core of a problem or issue as spiritual, it rationally follows that the solution must also be spiritual.

Divine Nature can help us explain ISKCON's perspective on the environment in a methodical way. This makes it much easier to enlighten the ever-growing world community of the environmentally concerned.

Preaching about the environment needs to be proactive. It is far better to explain ISKCON's spiritual perspective on the environment and how it is practical before you are asked, "So what practical things are you doing to help anything or anyone?"

We further suggest that you become active in your ISKCON community by separating garbage, reducing the use of plastic, using natural products, stopping the use of Styrofoam plates and cups (a North American GBC resolution restates this), supporting recycling principles in your neighborhood, and doing other things that are consistent with ISKCON's official position on the environment. In this way we will be seen to be "practicing what we preach."

WANTED: OPINION LEADERS

Modern communications methods use "opinion leader" statements as a type of endorsement. An opinion leader need not be

April 9, 1973—Paris, France: Jacques Assouad, mayor of Paris, officially greets ISKCON's founder, Srila Prabhupada, as Yogesvara dasa translates. Although taken aback by Prabhupada's not following the protocol that guests of the mayor should stand in his presence, Monsieur Assouad tells his guest how happy he is to receive a "spiritual ambassadbr" from India and how spiritual a city Paris is.

famous, but he or she should be respected at least as an expert in a specific field. Srila Prabhupada established this principle by insisting that scholarly reviews be printed in his books. He even intimated that he would refuse to compile Vedic literature if there would be no reviews from scholars. Most of the scholars who reviewed Srila Prabhupada's books were not famous. However, they were respected in their fields and among their peers. So their endorsements helped establish that the books were of a high standard, not only for general scholarship, but for sociologists, historians, Indologists, philosophers, and theologians. Opinion leaders in these fields have given Srila Prabhupada's books the stature needed for readers and people in general to take them seriously. The following essay, written for ICB, traces the history of "third-party" responses to Krishna consciousness, from both reactive and proactive positions.

***ISKCON Communications Briefings,* July/August 1995**
Srila Prabhupada and Opinion Leaders

Srila Prabhupada said it many times, in many ways: "Indians are our best allies." This has proven true over and over again—financially, politically, and socially. But Srila Prabhupada also knew that such third-party endorsements were not limited to the Indian community.

He was absolutely convinced that his books needed to be reviewed by scholars. He showed great pleasure when, acting under his direct instructions, his disciples obtained reviews from scholars all over the world. In a letter to Gargamuni, dated September 22, 1969, he wrote, "The methods you have adopted to approach reviewers and convince them to review our books [sic] how much this attempt has been successful? Reviewing is the only way for pushing on any publication."

On January 19, 1975, he remarked in a letter to Satsvarupa Goswami that he wanted the reviews obtained by his traveling library party assembled into a booklet. "If you can send more similar reviews on my books, I would very much appreciate it. I am keeping a folder on such things and we can print a small book to distribute that will contain such reviews so that people will see what a great impression our books have on the intelligentsia of the world."

That year Srila Prabhupada directly ordered the BBT to print with its own funds 270,000 copies of a full-color, twenty-page booklet titled *The Krishna Consciousness Movement Is Authorized.* Seven pages contained book reviews by leading scholars from all over the world. At its expense, the BBT mailed these out to US judges and other important people.

Shortly after Dr. Stillson Judah, professor emeritus of the University of California at Berkeley, published his lengthy book *Hare Krishna and the Counterculture,* Srila Prabhupada read it admiringly from cover to cover.

After a favorable judgment in a famous 1976 "brainwashing" court case, Srila Prabhupada recommended that devotees widely reprint and disseminate part of District Court Judge Leahy's judgment. The passage read, "The Hare Krishna movement is a bona fide religion with roots in India that go back thousands of years."

Before the case came to court, Srila Prabhupada arranged for dozens of leading Indian businessmen to write letters on their letterheads directly to President Richard Nixon. These were used as evidence in a successful campaign that completely exonerated ISKCON from blame.

After his arrival in San Francisco in 1967, devotees showed Srila Prabhupada favorable picture articles in the major newspapers. He immediately ordered hundreds of copies printed, even though the temple barely had enough funds to pay the rent. Srila Prabhupada looked at newspapers as a type of third-party, or opinion-leader, endorsement.

One of Srila Prabhupada's flagship publicity vehicles was the photograph of Indian Prime Minister Shastri with Srila Prabhupada (on the cover of *The Nectar of Book Distribution*), together with Shastri's statement: "His Divine Grace A. C. Bhaktivedanta Swami Prabhupada is doing valuable work, and his books are significant contributions to the salvation of mankind." The late Shastri's statement also included a recommendation that Indian libraries throughout the country purchase Srila Prabhupada's books.

We could recount many other instances which show how enthusiastic Srila Prabhupada was about endorsements from opinion leaders—in academia, religion, government, media, and the legal system, to name only a few.

Definition/Description of Opinion Leaders

Opinion leaders or opinion makers may be defined as believable third parties who have the public's trust in some field of activity. Support from opinion leaders, when properly organized, can be used as Srila Prabhupada wanted scholars' statements used—over and over again. Written support by an authority can be printed and reprinted in the proper context to maximize benefits. Audio or videotaped statements can be played and replayed in many broadcast contexts.

Considering the "mirror-image" effect and Srila Prabhupada's principle of seeing Indian communities as our "greatest allies," we suggest that ISKCON should not underestimate the power of opinion leader endorsements from the Indian communities of the world. An ISKCON backed by 800 million people in India is considered in many important circles a force to be reckoned with.

Within all the publics—including devotees, academics, churches, the government, neighbors, interest groups, Indian communities, youth, devotees' parents, and the greater congregation—opinion leaders can be found.

Since an opinion leader is anyone who helps shape the opinion of a public or group of publics, these publics themselves know best who their opinion leaders are. Columnists are important for the media but are not their only opinion leaders. *The New York Times,* for example, is the collective opinion leader for the media. Government leaders are also opinion leaders for the media.

Opinion leaders for ISKCON include GBC members, temple presidents, and the heads of ISKCON projects. In government, the chief executives, cabinet ministers, committee chairmen, and party leaders are opinion leaders.

Top priority objectives for many temples outside of India today are endorsements from opinion leaders in the Indian community. Endorsements from them help us with Indian communities and "host" communities as well. Local church or religious leaders can also be top priority persons for endorsements. They usually have great influence over their parishioners.

Reactive ISKCON Opinion Leader Activity

When faced with crises generated by detractors, devotees have sought statements and support from academics, judges, prominent Indian citizens, and other "outsiders." In many such cases, they obtained such statements and used this third-party support to successfully help overcome opposition.

For example, in order to support Bhaktivedanta Manor's case to retain the right to public worship in the face of government moves to stop it, devotees sought and gained the support of local borough counselor Frank Ward. Ward even journeyed to India with Manor devotees to help garner patronage from Indian politicians.

Manor campaigners, headed by Akhandadhi dasa, have also obtained backing from Member of Parliament (MP) Keith Vaz. One of Britain's few Indian MPs, Vaz has openly supported the campaign. His written verbal and videotaped statements are nowan integral part of the crusade to preserve the right to public worship. Vaz has even marched, sung, and made speeches at highly publicized rallies protesting government bias. For many Britons, his face has become almost synonymous with ISKCON's fight for religious freedom. Campaigners have also successfully gained endorsements from other MPs from both major political parties.

As these activities indicate, most support from opinion leaders has usually been crisis-driven and unsystematic. ISKCON's opinion leader support has generally relied upon outdated statements by scholars, a handful of celebrities, and prominent people in India. Attempts at third party endorsements usually arise out of urgency, impulse, casual encounter, or accident. Such approval is better obtained from long-term and carefully planned communications, cultivation, and good management principles.

At this writing a crisis is evolving in Russia. We hope that devotees who are learning these techniques and using them in the Russian campaign adopt and convert them to proactive work in the future of the Russian *yatra.*

The Russian parliament may pass a law that would grant the government wide powers to control and restrict all religions. Smaller organizations would be especially vulnerable, and the Russian government would not exercise its new prerogatives against the Russian Orthodox Church, thought by Russian experts to be the principle force behind the law.

The response by ISKCON's North American Communications Office (ICNA) included communications techniques involving opinion leaders. ICNA requested a prominent official in the American Psychiatric Association to fax letters directly to Russian President Boris Yeltsin and Duma (parliament) leader Ribkin. The letter insisted that the law under current consideration violated international principles of human rights. Also, under direction from ISKCON Communications Global, devotees in India persuaded several Indian MPs to write and send similar letters of protest to Russian officials.

Although these efforts in Russia are absolutely necessary and hopefully will be effective, they are initiated by crisis. But if these contacts can be properly cultivated, this reactive activity can be converted into the proactive mode.

Constant gathering and repeated transmission of third-party support messages should take place long before crises arise. Crises can be reduced almost to nil or even avoided entirely. We can learn to prevent rather than react to them. We can safely say this about the proper use of opinion leader statements: the proverbial ounce of prevention is greater than a pound of cure.

Proactive ISKCON Opinion Leader Activity

Although they have been relatively infrequent, ISKCON has made some outstanding exceptions to its conventional reactive mode in third-party endorsements. From these incidents we can learn some of the dos and don'ts about dealing with opinion leaders in the proactive mode.

Some temple leaders have taken the proactive step of inviting local politicians, Indian government emissaries, academics, or other prominent citizens to speak words of support at major festivals like Rathayatra or Janmastami. These appearances have often been picked up by the media and broadcast widely. On some rare occasions, they have resulted in long-term relationships that have helped the movement immensely.

Unfortunately, devotees have not properly recorded or videotaped these appearances and speeches for reuse. Another weakness is that devotees have not systematically directed such opinion leaders to talk on particular subjects or in certain ways. With careful planning, such endorsements can be used to assist in future preaching activities and for responding to problems.

Devotees in many US cities have been proactive in seeking and obtaining official declarations from mayors for major events, especially for Rathayatra festivals. Copies of them have been used repeatedly as support documents for many purposes. These official declarations have been framed and hung in prominent places in temple complexes.

A recent example of proactive opinion leader support occurred on November 6, 1994 at ISKCON's temple in Durban, South Africa. At the invitation of devotees, the country's President, Dr. Nelson Mandela, spoke at the temple's Govardhana-Puja-Diwali Festival during his official state visit. Dr. Mandela's tour of the temple and his videotaped public speech will be used time and again throughout the world because it shows one of the world's most admired and powerful people speaking publicly in support of ISKCON.

For the BBT book *Divine Nature* and the BI publication *Forbidden Archeology* and its condensed version, *The Hidden History of the Human Race,* the authors and their marketing teams obtained reviews from opinion leaders in the fields of science and the environment. Some are printed in the books themselves and in promotional materials. Publicity for *Hidden History* resulted in articles in newspapers and magazines, and many hours of television and radio time.

Devotees in St. Petersburg, Russia, recently acquired a written statement from a prominent government nutritionist, expounding the benefits of the Hare Krishna diet. His statement indicates, among other things, that ISKCON's diet helps reduce heart disease. Russian devotees will print this statement in an upcoming Russian-language cookbook.

Other Opinion Leader Activity and Recommendations

ISKCON members should foresee potential crises long before they occur and obtain statements from opinion leaders as a matter of course for credibility and long-term prevention. Severe problems now surfacing in Russia and England did not occur overnight. In hindsight, even a little anticipation would have helped. Forces of opposition are usually long-known before they become obvious.

A systematic approach to opinion leader support is in line with state-of-the-art communications principles and, as we have indicated, is strongly supported by Prabhupada's life and teachings.

We recommend that qualified devotees, especially those in leadership positions, make time to cultivate local church leaders (especially those involved in interfaith work), neighboring residents and businesses, local politicians, academics, parents, and prominent members of Indian communities (if your temple is not located in India). Any one of these can be an important opinion leader for your center. You need only contact one or two for starters.

After some weeks or months, when you have developed a friendly relationship, you can ask for written or videotaped statements. Cultivation usually goes on for several months before you can obtain an endorsement, and long-term planning is required. Public relations is not a product; it is a process.

Sometimes you are better off writing the statement yourself and presenting it to the endorser to review, change, or rewrite. Some even prefer that you do it this way. Alternatively, you can discuss with the person what you require, for what reason, why it is important, and how such an endorsement will be of service to the public, and then ask him or her to write the statement. All this is in general practice.

By working closely with an opinion leader, you can help to tailor his or her statement to your specific needs. At minimum, you can give potential opinion leaders a set of ideas they can use to formulate a statement. It is also important to explain exactly why you want it and how you intend to use it, now and in the future, so that there are no misunderstandings.

Once an opinion leader has confidence in you, it is not difficult to jointly work out a statement. The time has come to engage opinion leaders in helping to push on Lord Chaitanya's preaching mission.

"US AND THEM": NETWORKERS AREN'T CULTISTS

Living behind tall walls, waiting for Armageddon, caring nothing for those outside the barricades, was the archetypal "cult" projected by the "anticult" movement. Sometimes it is a description of reality. Inner-directed, self-serving groups are often referred to as cults because they are isolationist and vocally disdainful of outsiders. On the first Australian *60 Minutes* broadcast on ISKCON's *gurukula* system, schoolmaster Pariksit dasa, when asked if the children in his school were isolated, replied that they were "insulated, not isolated" and that if protected, like a tree surrounded by a small fence, they would grow up to be healthy and strong. Many preteen Krishna children take part in festivals, distribute books and *prasadam,* go on field trips to historical sites, and in many other ways interact with society at large. In this *ISKCON Communications Briefings* article, I contrast the importance of interacting with nondevotee groups of people with the valid consideration that such activity can be flirting with *maya.*

ISKCON Communications Briefings, September/October 1995

One of the greatest internal stumbling blocks to divesting ISKCON of the damning cult or "sect" label is a persistent devotee mentality that sees devotees and nondevotees in terms of "us and them."

Stereotypically, cults isolate themselves, look down on nonmembers, fear and suspect outsiders, consider their members superior to others, and sometimes (the millenarian groups) hope for an imminent self-destruction of the establishment so they can set up their own new world order.

During a recent discussion on the importance of association, some devotees cautioned about the inherent dangers of bad association. One recalled Lord Kapila's warning in the *Srimad-Bhagavatam* that "By association with worldly people, one becomes devoid of truthfulness, cleanliness, mercy, gravity, spiritual intelligence, shyness, austerity, fame, forgiveness, control of the mind, control of the senses, fortune, and all opportunities."

During the discussion, two other devotees mentioned passages about the risks of nondevotee association:

"It is better to accept the miseries of being encaged within bars and surrounded by burning flames than to associate with those bereft of Krishna consciousness. Such association is a very great hardship" (Madhya-lila, 22.91).

"One should not even see those who are bereft of devotional service in Krishna consciousness and who are therefore devoid of pious activities" (Madhya-lila, 22.92).

So how does one expand Krishna consciousness if even fleeting association with nondevotees is so dangerous?

One devotee in the group then asked, "But couldn't the mailman on the street corner end up becoming your child's guru? Wouldn't somebody have to associate with him?" This statement prompted a deeper look into the Krishna consciousness philosophy and practices as taught by Srila Prabhupada.

During the conversation, another *Bhagavatam* quote surfaced, also quoted from Lord Kapila's teachings but on the other side of the issue: "As the blazing fire of death, I cause fear to whoever makes the least discrimination between himself and other living entities due to a differential outlook" (SB 3.29.26).

Someone else in the room quoted from *Caitanya-caritamrta:* "Instruct everyone to follow the orders of Lord Sri Krishna as they are given in *Bhagavad-gita* and *Srimad-Bhagavatam.* In this way, become a spiritual master and try to liberate everyone in this land"

(Madhya-lila, 7.128). The person citing this verse then read to us the first line of Srila Prabhupada's purport: "This is the sublime mission of the International Society for Krishna Consciousness."

The discussion continued with testimony on both sides of the question. Devotees cited verses, lectures, and conversations in support of the respective viewpoints.

Finally we reached a consensus based on this premise: As loyal sons and daughters of Srila Prabhupada, we are obliged to preach—and that means approaching almost anyone and everyone. But in doing so, one should carefully avoid intimate association with nondevotees, so as to escape contamination.

Approved "association" included devotee parents participating in parent-teachers association meetings (at non-*gurukula* schools), book distributors starting conversations with "whomever they meet," eating in the homes of potential members or devotees in Indian communities, FFL devotees networking with other food providers, temple presidents attending community action meetings in their neighborhoods, and ISKCON leaders establishing relationships with local government officials.

Part of ISKCON's social conscience is to show that our philosophy is practical and that applying it can help solve social and personal problems.

Hare Krishna Food for Life is often used for *prasadam* distribution that benefits the disadvantaged: the orphaned, shut-ins (people who are home-bound due to old age or infirmity), the indigent, the homeless, and the mentally or physically challenged.

The importance of interacting with host communities is beyond ISKCON's need for noncult status. Involvement in the larger community proves that we are enhancing the quality of life. The public should perceive ISKCON as improving society.

Like the distribution of books and *prasadam* as well as participation in *hari-nama* parties and congregational development, our involvement in community activities is also direct preaching. Such involvement includes the all-important one-on-one encounters or personal relationships.

Preaching in community-related affairs also has the advantage of a ripple or domino effect. Convictions that the Krishnas are useful, contributing members of the community spread quickly by word of mouth. Over time, this attitude enables ISKCON devotees to more effectively introduce the movement's philosophy and practices and to thereby more easily "discover" devotees.

Once Krishna consciousness preaching on a community involvement level is well underway, devotees should use their communication skills (like those outlined in the *ISKCON Communications Manual*) to publicize these activities, especially with the media. The manual teaches how to do this in a mature way. When this occurs, the news media and ISKCON mutually benefit; we are not seen as proud or boasting, but as servants of society. By following the methods outlined in the manual, ISKCON becomes known as a service organization instead of as a withdrawn, aloof, uninvolved, and unconcerned religious sect (read "cult").

Service is the key word here. According to Srila Prabhupada, devotional service is the highest welfare work. When Krishna conscious methods are applied in the context of specific service to a community, attitudes and behavior towards ISKCON start to change. Such proactive initiatives break down our "us and them," *kanistha adhikari* mentality, as well as people's "cult" perceptions.

ISKCON leaders can reap great benefits by (1) appropriately engaging in Krishna conscious community service and (2) making this service widely known through a program of media relations. As these two actions rise on leaders' priority lists, perceptions of ISKCON as a cult will fade away.

THE PERFECT SUNDAY FEAST: FOOD FOR THOUGHT

Just let your imagination take over for a minute. Think "what if?" Consider what would make people want to come into a Hare Krishna temple, stay a long time, and come back with many of their friends. What kind of an atmosphere do you envision? What does it "feel" like to be there? How do things look? What are the main elements that make it a memorable event? These were questions once put to devotees by tennis pro Peter Burwash at a North American GBC/TP meeting. Fortunately, I kept my notes, talked them over with others, got some feedback, and incorporated some of these ideas. I refined my thoughts and eventually penned this piece for *ISKCON Communications Briefings.* This is a "fun" article, where you can imagine a brainstorming session with peers or a temple board. The real enjoyment begins, however, when you start to implement some of these ideas.

***ISKCON Communications Briefings,* September/October 1995**

In each ISKCON temple's quest for perfection, one step along the way could be to do one-seventh of the job by having everything "perfect" just one day a week. That could be Sunday, because Sunday is the day most people come and the only day that many people visit. That could be the day that the temple becomes a model showcase for Krishna consciousness. This would require extraordinarily excellent management, but only for one day.

We suggest that the two main goals for the perfect Sunday feast could be these: (1) every guest leaves the temple that day with a full commitment to return soon, bringing along at least one friend who has not yet been; (2) everyone who leaves will seriously begin chanting *japa* or reading Srila Prabhupada's books.

Here are some suggestions for a "Perfect Sunday Feast" based on ideas presented by Peter Burwash on May 25, 1995, at a North American GBC/Temple Presidents seminar in Gainesville, Florida:

Guests are greeted warmly with personal conversation by one or two devotees who've been trained and have practiced what to do.

Each guest prints his or her name, address, phone number, and occupation in a beautiful temple guest book.

Devotees hold excellent *kirtanas* and *bhajanas.* Melodies are simple enough for everyone to follow and sing along with ease.

The *kirtana* leader teaches the congregation how to chant nicely.

He gets them to repeat the words first. Then he claps and sings phrases one at a time and induces them to do likewise. He is friendly but makes it imperative for all to chant and, if possible, dance.

Devotees strategically place signs in building(s) or on grounds so that all guests can know what is going on where and when.

A simple printed Sunday festival schedule is handed out to guests on a small sheet of paper. This information is also posted in strategic places around the temple.

Parking is user-friendly. An attendant directs drivers as to what to do with their vehicles.

All temple residents are to be present in the temple for the whole Sunday program.

All devotees are to be neat, clean, and well-dressed.

Devotees speak with visitors as much as possible so that each guest feels he or she has a friend at the temple.

The mood of all the devotees in the temple community is friendly and festive.

The physical atmosphere of the temple is bright and cheerful. Colorful and tasteful decorations help achieve this mood.

Prasadam is superexcellent. It has been said that *prasadam* is at least half of the total impression created at a Sunday temple visit—or any other Krishna-conscious function.

First-class care is arranged for all young children. What's on most parents' minds these days when separated from their young children in an uncertain environment? Kidnapping. If you're a parent reading this, you'll agree.

The lecture is engaging and interesting. If the speaker deals at least in part with topical issues, that really helps. The lecturer is personal and delivers essential philosophy competently. The time should be limited. Personal stories can illustrate deep philosophical points, thus bringing them to life for the audience. Krsnadasa Kaviraja says, "Essential truth spoken concisely is true eloquence" (Adi Lila 1.106). A talk that "drags on" is a loser. Half an hour is a good limit. The speaker takes into account the needs, interests, and concerns of the audience present. Time left for questions that generate audience participation increases interest and involvement dramatically. Management considers replacing the talk every few weeks with *Hare Krishna Today* or other relevant videos.

If nonparticipative *bhajanas* are to be performed, they should be excellent. It is better to avoid *bhajanas* than to perform mediocre music and song.

Everyone chants one round on beads. This makes for a truly memorable experience. Everyone then has something to take home. But you have to have lots of beads, ideally enough to sell them to those who've been sufficiently inspired by the group *japa* to buy a set of their own. The speaker leads and gets everyone to chant in unison so that all can stop at the same time at the summit bead.

The speakers glorify members of the congregation. Presenters request them by name to step forward and receive awards for such things as paying for the feast that day, arranging home programs, cooking, organizing festival permits, providing financial or other contributions, and for other services. They receive awards of books, garlands, BTGs, HKWs, videotapes, *prasadam,* bead bags, and other gifts as appropriate.

The temple management arranges for activities specifically targeted for young people of all ages such that they too will want to return and not feel alienated by activities aimed only at adults.

Dramas are well scripted and well rehearsed.

Speakers announce all major upcoming events.

The hosts speak in such a way that their words and demeanor help establish strong empathy for the greater congregation—those living outside the temple precincts or immediate environs.

Speakers glorify Nama Hatta and other congregational programs that take place outside the temple complex.

Temple managers schedule lectures and names of the speakers in advance via the temple newsletter, by announcements, by advertising in local newspapers, and other means so that guests can be inspired to look forward to them.

The temple president reads out the temple mission statement—if there is one—to the congregation.

The temple president reads out, and can even elaborate when appropriate, specific ISKCON community goals. He/she may speak of goals as well as the strategies, tactics, and action plans scheduled to achieve these goals.

A "spotter" watches the audience during the talk and notes people who seem particularly interested to hear more. He or she does this by observing the way they look or by noting the questions they ask. After the talk, the spotter can invite these guests to dine on the feast with the speaker and have an informal discussion with him or her.

At the temple entrance the special greeters offer to apply *tilaka* on the foreheads of willing guests.

The temple and grounds are to be spotlessly clean. A *maha* cleanup should be conducted on the previous day or that morning.

TIME, PLACE, AND AUDIENCE

In my view, the essence of preaching according to time, place, and circumstance is contained in this excerpt from Srila Prabhupada's *Srimad-Bhagavatam* purport (1.4.1) and stated in my introduction to this book: "Personal realization does not mean that one should, out of vanity, attempt to show one's own learning by trying to surpass the previous *acharya*. . . . The original purpose of the text must be maintained. No obscure meaning should be screwed out of it, yet it should be presented in an interesting manner for the understanding of the audience. This is called realization." In this *ISKCON Communications Briefings* article, I try to bring out how normal and natural it is to bring Krishna consciousness into almost any situation. Srila Prabhupada was so keen to spread the philosophy and practices of Krishna consciousness all over the world that he sometimes sent his disciples into the most inhospitable places.

***ISKCON Communications Briefings*, November/December 1995**

We do and did it differently in places like Singapore, Thailand,

July, 1966—Orissa, India: Each year in June or July (the exact date is specified by the Vedic lunar calendar), more than one million flock to the Jagannath Puri Rathayatra festival. The annual event, which takes place in the Indian coastal town of Puri, Orissa, is India's largest outdoor celebration. Deities of Jagannatha (Lord of the Universe) and his brother, Balarama, and sister, Subhadra, are hand-pulled, each in a large Ratha, or chariot.

August 15, 1978—Los Angeles, USA: The Los Angeles Rathayatra festival at Venice Beach attracts thousands annually. Although Srila Prabhupada, ISKCON's founder-*acharya,* never personally attended, when he saw photographs of the chariots on this parade, he remarked, "We have never seen such carts!"

Israel, Oman, Saudi Arabia, Bangladesh, Pakistan, Nigeria, Togo, Ghana, Liberia, Gold Coast, and Iran. From *Caitanya-caritamrta* (Madhya-lila 23.105) we read: "Sri Chaitanya Mahaprabhu then told Sanatana Goswami about proper renunciation according to a particular situation, and the Lord forbade dry renunciation and speculative knowledge in all respects."

PURPORT: To broadcast the cult of Krishna consciousness, one has to learn the possibility of renunciation in terms of country, time, and candidate. A candidate for Krishna consciousness in the Western countries should be taught about the renunciation of material existence, but one would teach candidates from a country like India in a different way. The teacher (*acharya*) has to consider time, candidate, and country. He must avoid the principle of *niyamagraha;* that is, he should not try to perform the impossible. What is possible in one country may not be possible in another. The *acharya's* duty is to accept the essence of devotional service. There may be a little change here and there as far as *yukta-vairagya* (proper renunciation) is concerned. Dry renunciation is forbidden by Sri Chaitanya Mahaprabhu, and we have also learned this from our spiritual master, His Divine Grace Bhaktisiddhanta Sarasvati Thakura Goswami Maharaja. The essence of devotional service must be taken into consideration and not the outward paraphernalia. . . . Simply imitating without effect is called *niyama-graha*. . . . We should not follow regulative principles without an effect, nor should we fail to accept the regulative principles. What is required is a special technique according to country, time and candidate. . . . "When one is not attached to anything, but at the same time accepts everything in relation to Krishna, one is rightly situated above possessiveness. On the other hand, one who rejects everything without knowledge of its relationship to Krishna is not as complete in his renunciation" (*Bhakti-rasamrta Sindhu* 1.2.255-6). To preach the *bhakti* cult, one should seriously consider these verses.

In recent times, serious physical violence has occurred against ISKCON devotees in Armenia, Serbia, Ukraine, and Russia. This is far from comforting, not least because it intimates a larger, global trend.

A few years ago, many of us read with muted horror—and perhaps a grain of "I'm glad it's not happening here" relief—that Bahai church members were being mercilessly slaughtered in Iran for their religious beliefs (because they were different from the prevailing Shi-ite Muslim denomination).

Long years of Protestant-Catholic conflict in Ireland claims hundreds of lives. The daily news is dominated by reports of terrible warfare in the former Yugoslavia that is at least partially rooted in contentions that divide Catholics and the Serbian Orthodox Church. Internal religious strife in Russia, Kashmir, Israel, India, and former Soviet republics is becoming more and more common. The ongoing news glut of these and other religiously-based hostilities indicates religious intolerance is on the rise, despite well-meaning efforts to contain it.

Some prejudice stems from doctrinal atheism, but most is rooted in religious bigotry.

Nonetheless, Srila Prabhupada, who gave practical shape to propagating Krishna consciousness universally, expected and wanted ISKCON to develop throughout the entire world. That included finding devotees in places not esteemed for traditions of religious freedom. For example, he fully expected that Krishna consciousness would spread in the former Soviet Union, Pakistan, Bangladesh, Indonesia, Iran, Saudi Arabia, Kuwait, Oman, UAE, Israel, China, Sri Lanka, Fiji, Thailand, and Singapore.

Even in the so-called developed countries of Europe, North America, Australasia, and northern Asia (especially Japan), where religious plurality is mandated by law and widely observed, discrimination is deeply entrenched and, according to many scholars, growing at an uncomfortable rate.

Religious prejudice against devotees takes many shapes: a city government denies permission for a festival, for public chanting, building a restaurant, for public worship, or for constructing *gurukula* facilities; interfaith groups decline ISKCON's bid for membership; anticult groups generate negative media reports; parents resort to violence against, and the kidnapping of, their own children; a landlord refuses to sell property to ISKCON. At the extreme end, armed gangs enter temples, desecrate altars, and assault devotees.

Foreseeing such hurdles, Srila Prabhupada gave many *desa kala patra* (time, place, and circumstance) directions for widening the circle of Krishna consciousness. He showed us how to spread Krishna consciousness within theistic, atheistic, and even openly hostile cultures. He even wanted Krishna consciousness to take hold in regions where Hindus are routinely persecuted. During a visit to Iran, he taught by example how to reach out to the local people.

Surprisingly, his instructions sometimes advised against installing deities, wearing devotional clothing, chanting the holy name in public, or publicly distributing books or *prasadam.*

Special *desa kala patra* considerations are still relevant for more than a fifth of the world's population. The Krishna consciousness process is certainly universal, but sometimes we are puzzled as to how it can take root in certain situations.

With religious prejudice simmering everywhere, special considerations, flexibility, and adaptability are important. Time, place, and circumstance need to be carefully assessed in difficult or unusual preaching environments and, to some extent, everywhere.

Religious prejudice was not unknown in medieval India. Srila Jiva Goswami had to deal with this phenomenon. Understanding the mind of Mahaprabhu, he wrote the *Hari-namamrta-vyakarana,* which expertly transmitted Krishna consciousness through the study of Sanskrit grammar. The Hindus and Vaishnavas of that time (the *patra,* or the audience which Jiva Goswami targeted) were apparently incapable of digesting a completely direct form of Krishna consciousness.

Today, devotees in Mumbai (the new official name of Bombay) produced a half-hour television program called *Aatma.* This show is broadcast seven days a week over a new cable system currently wired to 800,000 city households in Mumbai and 200,000 in Delhi. It is expanding every month and is planning to reach at least 10 major cities by early 1996.

Aatma begins at 7:00 a.m. and is the first program of the In Mumbai and In Delhi portions of the IndusInd Cable Network. Even though shaven-headed devotees preach Krishna consciousness philosophy and chant during most of the program, the phrase "Hare Krishna" is not spoken; but ISKCON—which in India is synonymous with Hare Krishna—and Srila Prabhupada's name appear in the credits at the start and end of each program.

This show was made possible because the devotees involved were willing and able to adjust to specific station requirements so that they would not be seen as pushing their agenda like most religious groups in India do. Also, because *Aatma* occurs in the early morning and is considered family viewing, the programming director believed that a direct approach would have turned audiences off and lost market share.

The *acharyas* point out the need to consider prevailing social customs while preaching Krishna consciousness within the material world. In his purport to the *Caitanya-caritamrta,* Madhya-lila 7.29, Srila Prabhupada writes: "There are many instances of devotional service rendered by previous *acharyas* who did not care about social behavior when intensely absorbed in love for Krishna.

"Unfortunately, as long as we are within this material world, we must observe social customs to avoid criticism by the general populace. This is Sri Chaitanya Mahaprabhu's desire." Action according to time, place, and circumstance (or audience) is part of the "think globally, act locally" maxim, which in many respects touches the very heart of what ISKCON is all about.

"We are the greatest opportunists," Srila Prabhupada is reputed to have said. Spiritual opportunists set goals and develop methods based, to a large extent, on opportunities and resources that are readily accessible. Assessments of the local economic, social, legal, physical, and general human environment often determine to a large extent how ISKCON devotees go about spreading Krishna consciousness.

For example, in Alachua, Florida, an economically depressed area, devotees have employed local residents in a devotee business. This action has compelled local residents to see devotees as contributing significantly to the community. Devotees who moved into dilapidated houses in Detroit and East Dallas improved these neighborhoods substantially and earned written appreciations from local government officials and the media.

Local residents in Venice Beach, California, see the annual Hare Krishna Rathayatra festival as a spiritually uplifting event that brings peace, joy, and wholesome entertainment to an area plagued with drug-related crime, including murders that occur almost every night.

An upscale Hare Krishna restaurant in Oslo, Norway, provides highly nutritious *prasadam* in an environment suitable to its uniquely central location. There, people pay an average of US$10.00 for lunch, and the affluent patrons of Krishna Cuisine consider it a bargain. On the other side of the world, employment of local farmers in Mayapur, India, has greatly endeared neighboring residents to the Mayapura ISKCON community.

In Sukhumi, the (Soviet) Georgia devotees' only activity for more than a year has been to feed war victims, including the old, the young, the immobile, and the infirm. They literally risked their lives by cooking in a house situated almost on the battlefront. Bombs and mortar shells sometimes exploded in their front yard and once in the house next door.

The spreading of Krishna consciousness in Sukhumi took place solely through *prasadam* distribution to people rendered hungry, and often homeless, by the horrors of war. Mayuradvaja dasa, who may be counted among the most heroic Vaishnavas of all time, led the devotees there. When the Sukhumi temple president, Raghava Pandita dasa, was murdered in July, 1995, for reasons unknown, the city mayor and many other leading city officials praised him eloquently at a large public funeral.

On the plains of Siberia, in the jungles of Africa, in frozen polar regions, Amazonia, the Middle East, and on remote Pacific Islands, Krishna consciousness has taken root. If, while adjusting for time, place, and circumstance, devotees uncompromisingly and rigidly uphold the central spiritual tenets and practices of Krishna consciousness, the *sankirtana* movement of Sri Krishna Chaitanya will continue in even the most unlikely places.

CHAPTER 8—1996

Creating an Infrastructure

The year 1996 marked the one hundredth year since Srila Prabhupada's birth in Calcutta. For his centennial celebration devotees staged events throughout the world. And many amazing things just seemed to happen. For example, on February 25, one of the USA's largest television networks, ABC, aired *Mysterious Origins of Man* at 7:00 p.m. Sunday night. The half-hour show featured authors Drutakarma dasa (Michael Cremo) and Sadaputa dasa (Dr. Richard Thompson) talking about their book *Forbidden Archeology.* The

July, 1996—London, U.K.: England's Minister of the Environment, John Gummer, announces that public worship at Bhaktivedanta Manor is fully approved, and a group of young, English-born devotees dramatically proclaim victory. In May, 1996, the Manor's ten-year, high-profile legal battle with the central government finally brings a win for the Krishna devotees.

program also showed illustrations from the book, and narrator Charlton Heston spoke passages from it verbatim. According to polls, the show's viewing audience was nineteen million. In May, the British government gave irrevocable permission for public worship at Bhaktivedanta Manor, thus ending a ten-year struggle. On Wednesday, September 4, the date of Srila Prabhupada's birth, ISKCON staged its Celebration of a Century in Nataji Indoor Stadium in Calcutta, the city of Srila Prabhupada's birth. The very next day, Thursday, India's national TV network, Doordarshan, began its nationwide broadcast of Bhakti Charu Swami's 104-part series, *Abhay Charan*—the dramatized life of Srila Prabhupada. Meanwhile, Bhakti-marg Swami completed his 5,300-mile walk across Canada. Other important events occurred throughout the world that year: an ISKCON farm in Ecuador went "organic," embracing many ecological principles, and a five-day global World AIDS megaconference in Mumbai heard speeches from two ISKCON devotees. The 1996 annual GBC meeting in Mayapura for the first time addressed a wide range of social issues: divorce, abuse, poverty, and various women's issues. ISKCON Houston opened a $1.5 million community center. In October, I participated in a "Hinduism and Ecology" conference in Harvard University's School of Divinity. Here, all thirty-five Ph.D. delegates, including long-time ISKCON friend Diana Eck, helped themselves to a copy of *Divine Nature.*

DOES ISKCON REALLY NEED SOCIAL DEVELOPMENT?

This 1996 *Hare Krishna World* editorial emphasized the need for ISKCON to concentrate on its internal social development. It was a plea to make ISKCON a friendlier, more caring, and happier place to be—where people would feel protected, supported, and able to realize their full potential. I discussed briefly the idea of a social contract in which rights and duties are articulated. As Aristotle wrote, human beings are "political animals," but more to the point, we are all social animals. We require friends, community involvement, people-centered activity, and "support systems." All these needs are solidified in the case for social development. A unified ISKCON means that all social groupings within it feel supported and looked after.

Hare Krishna World, January/February 1996

We have Srila Prabhupada's books, we know we are responsible for our own spiritual life and material karma, and we have been told to be detached from the material world.

Srila Prabhupada established the International Society for Krishna Consciousness. But why do we need a society? And what did Srila Prabhupada mean by "society?" What did he expect from it? How did he want it to grow and develop?

According to dictionaries, a society is a collection of people with shared interests, shared participation in various relationships, shared institutions, shared culture, and shared values. It includes a tremendous range of activities, as it is a compilation of just about everybody doing just about everything.

Social development is important because, in a spiritual society, it can elevate everyone under its umbrella to a higher consciousness. The ongoing development of society, if enlightened, gives individuals an environment conducive for spiritual progress towards the ultimate goal of life—to return to God's kingdom as His pure servant.

At the very least, it should spell out the rules of civilization and enforce them so that its members are somewhat protected from exploitation. What makes it work is a sort of social contract, or agreement, among all levels of members of society, defining and limiting the rights and duties of everyone. Social development is a process by which a social contract is enacted by the members of society, so that all the members (acting in their defined roles) can realize their potentials, aided and strengthened by one another.

We are naturally social beings and need to spiritualize our sociability: *nirbandha-krsna-sambandhe yukta-vairagyam ucyate.* One should use Krishna's property always in Krishna's service. All of us need to know our duty. Lord Krishna in *Bhagavad-gita* tells us to do our duty and not that of another. Social organization insures that all come to know their duty, receive the social facility to do it, and feel secure and peaceful that they belong—they fit in—are valued, respected, appreciated, and loved.

How do you know what your duty is? Some folks seem to be born with a driving sense of what they must do in this lifetime. But such individuals are hardly the norm. The rest of us need parents, teachers, spiritual masters, trusted friends, co-workers, husbands, wives, priests, or counselors to figure out what we are supposed to do and how to do it. And it changes as we change. The psycho-physical characteristics of a 15-year-old student are different from a 65-year-old grandparent. Our natural propensities need to be harmoniously engaged; but how?

We can use the Vedic *varnashrama* system, which organizes society into four categories of occupational activities and integrates this with four fields of spiritual engagement. Vedicly-organized society functioned successfully on this planet for many thousands of years. Its practical format is adaptable to our modern world and is often compared to the human body.

This social body receives direction from its head—the learned (and materially detached) *brahmanas,* or priests and teachers. The arms of the *ksatriyas* protect society, as government administrators and enforcers. Society's stomach is composed of the farmers and entrepreneurs—*vaishyas*—who supply the material goods and services. *Sudras,* who work for others, carry the body on sturdy legs. These four comprise the *varnas,* or occupational categories.

There are also four spiritual orders, or *ashramas. Brahmacaris* are celibate students who devote themselves to spiritual service and study. Most youth go on to marry, thus becoming *grihasthas,* or householders. *Grihasthas* support the other spiritual orders. Retirement in Vaishnava society means increasing devotion to Krishna, once family responsibilities shift to younger shoulders. Retired *vanaprasthas* often go on pilgrimage to strengthen their spiritual resolve. *Sannyasa,* the highest spiritual order (and also the least populated), requires one to renounce all material attachments, including sex and family, to dedicate oneself entirely to preaching.

According to scriptures such as *Bhagavad-gita,* Krishna Himself designed this system for us. It is divine. There are many more practical details that we hope we can editorialize on in future issues. However, the bottom line is that, although these *varnashrama* designations are temporary, all members of society worship Krishna, all are equal as spirit souls, and all can become pure devotees. Everyone endeavoring sincerely to fulfill his or her appropriate social roles is worthy of respect.

We are already beginning to implement some of the *varnashrama* system in modern settings—by performing and training others to perform the above described duties and by developing some of the necessary infrastructures (temples, schools, communities, businesses, etc.). Vedic traditions and culture are taking root in our lives as spiritual observances and arts, Vaishnava fellowship, and volunteerism. But it has been thirty years since Srila Prabhupada started this international society. That's about one generation gone by with only some beginnings in place, so far.

By getting its act together socially, ISKCON can truly lead the world towards peaceful order and God consciousness. Although our missionary tradition dates back 500 years to Lord Chaitanya and we think of Krishna devotees as people who go out into the world "to make devotees," we can also effectively bring others to Krishna consciousness by planting roots.

The activities in the Krishna consciousness movement are moving on two tracks at this time: missionary outreach, or frontline preaching; and perpetuating the Krishna-conscious lifestyle through social development in communities of devotees. One makes devotees, the other keeps devotees.

By developing our social institutions and showing the living proof of Krishna consciousness in the day-to-day fabric of life, we reinforce and support the front line preachers. Healthy, vibrant Krishna conscious communities will give these devotees a practical example to point to, plus the communities can provide financial and moral support for the front liners.

The US National Endowment for the Arts recently did a survey that showed how people are currently less inclined towards philosophical exploration, but more inclined towards cultural exploration. Srila Prabhupada handed us the culture many of them are looking for, and we must develop the society that supports and perpetuates Vedic culture to attract and engage more souls in Krishna's service.

Srila Prabhupada left clear instructions to the leaders of his movement to concentrate on social development after his departure—the 50% of his work that he said he would have to leave for us to do. We need to cross over the distances and differences and identify with one another as a society, so that we can begin to learn from one another, understand each other better, be compassionate and patient, and work together to develop *varnashrama.*

Newsletters and journals circulating throughout ISKCON are earnestly examining this subject, as are devotee discussion groups and conferences. In order to act together, we must first communicate. Our society is spread out all over the world, bridging different indigenous cultures, customs, religions, and languages—and everywhere it is in different stages of Krishna-conscious social development.

We need to refine our definition of carrying on Srila Prabhupada's mission now, during his Centennial birth anniversary. Together, both globally and locally, we must form the social framework that will support the house Srila Prabhupada is building for the whole world to live in.

"WHERE'S THE BEEF" OVER UK "COWSCHWITZ"?

When the lethal Mad Cow Disease or BSE (bovine spongiform encephalopathy) was revealed in England, it was said to adversely affect the $8–$42-billion-a-year British meat industry. Few people, however, seemed to care much about the millions of cows who died or were readied for the incinerator. It was human beings they were mostly worried about (approximately ten people reportedly died from BSE-related diseases). A Hindu group in New Delhi said that British leaders had developed a "culture that runs contrary to the laws of God." As a result of the BSE scare, 174,648 cows were slaughtered and incinerated as of April 1999. As with people (and under the laws of karma), old, infirm, and diseased cows have the right to live out their natural lives. But because most cows are "grown" in man-made feed lots that process them into human food, bovines are seldom extended these rights. The disquieting part of this whole episode was that cows, in a desacrelized Great Britain, were treated as "live" stock (see on page 18 the introduction to "Toward a Consistent Life Policy"), or objects, which could be created by artificial insemination or cloning, or destroyed at will—all for the "betterment" of human society.

***Hare Krishna World,* March/April 1996**

Massive numbers of cows in England suspected to have contracted BSE (bovine spongiform encephalopathy) will soon be slaughtered. The ostensible reason is to protect the populace, at least ten of whom have died by eating BSE-infected cow flesh. But for years, the UK government has compromised and downplayed the dangers of BSE and the beef business.

Recently, politicians proclaimed that BSE arose because beef farmers mixed disease-infested sheep brains into organic cow feed. Officials said that by eliminating this sheep offal, the cow disease would be contained. But scientists have now proved that scrapie, a disease endemic in sheep brains, probably does not cause BSE; the real cause is unknown.

No doubt BSE is dangerous. "The risk to the human population is greater than that posed by AIDS," said leading British microbiologist, Richard W. Lacey, in recently published research. But the hundreds of legal hormones and antibiotics routinely given to food animals are also dangerous. Countless human beings have ingested so much antibiotic-saturated meat that they have developed immunities to standard antibiotics. In other words, antibiotics like penicillin and ampicillin now do not work for large numbers of people. Therefore, government allowances for antibiotics given to feed-lot cows has become a serious health hazard.

It is also a little-known but important fact that slaughterhouses in general are filthy places where hygienic regulations are poorly supervised and feebly enforced. How can one expect a healthy populace when such disease-friendly environments are allowed to proliferate?

Prime Minister John Major called the beef "scare" the "worst crisis in Britain since the 1982 Falklands conflict." But the biggest scare in Mr. Major's mind is not the ethical degeneracy or bad karma of exterminating thousands of sentient creatures suspected of having BSE (his government has claimed, probably erroneously, they will eradicate the disease), but how to pay for disposing of so many extra feed-lot carcasses without further endangering a powerful British enterprise. He is also concerned with declining consumer confidence in an industry that brings in an estimated \$8.5–\$42 billion a year.

Lacey, a professor at Leeds University, and many other British scientists believe BSE causes a fatal human illness known as CJD (Cruetzfeldt Jakob Disease). Besides already having killed at least ten people, scientists say that CJD has an incubation period in humans for from five to thirty years! Thousands, perhaps millions, of skeptical consumers, fearing for their lives, have stopped buying beef altogether. Many thousands of others have stopped purchasing all kinds of meat.

The decimation of six million people in Nazi Germany, 1.5 million in the "killing fields" of Cambodia, and the internecine warfare that killed 200-thousand-plus Rwandans are considered unpardonable acts of cruelty, gross violations of our sacred human rights. But to the UK and many other governments, destroying thousands or millions of "head of cattle" is either reducing "livestock" or processing food—not murdering benevolent living beings.

In a sacrilegious world, nothing is sacred, not even life itself. For the benefit of their subjects, politicians will have to rediscover that divinity exists in all humans and all animals. They will need to recognize the relationship all living beings have with God (or Krishna), the supreme divine. Otherwise, the massacre of millions of innocent creatures for "safety," "taste," and false concepts of food values will continue.

Massive animal breeding belies a spiritual vacuum and callous disregard for life. It took voices from as far away as New Delhi, according to the *London Telegraph,* to remind some British leaders that they have developed a culture that runs contrary to the laws of God. The World Hindu Council in India made a tentative offer to give asylum in England to diseased cows destined for destruction. The BSE phenomenon and the dangers of the beef industry in general have come about because cows should never have entered slaughterhouses in the first place. As with people, old, infirm, and even diseased cows and bulls have the right to live out their natural lives, even if it means doing so in an environment isolated from close contact with humans.

As the Krishna consciousness movement advocates, the cow and bull are among humanity's best friends. They provide fertilizer, fuel, milk products, and even after they die (preferably of natural causes) their skin and other bodily parts are still fully utilizable for many practical products. Oxen, or bullocks, are still an important source of energy. In addition to supplying fuel and fertilizer with their manure, they plow fields, transport goods, and can be harnessed to drive irrigation systems, grain-grinding devices, and wood saws.

Political leaders must understand that human beings need to practice voluntary restraint in order to advance spiritually. Governments also need to be educated about the health threats, environmental degradation, and karmic disasters inherent in the flesh-food industry. Ignorance of this spiritual dimension has also made politicians permissive about obvious public dangers such as drinking, smoking, drug abuse, sexual harassment, hunger, pornography, and many environmental perils. Such permissiveness may be attributed in part to their own indulgence.

Enlightened leaders in business and government would profit materially and spiritually if they would stop the misguided practice of killing animals for food. For example, if Britain as a whole switched to a non-meat diet, all beef farmers could grow grains, vegetables, and fruits. Slaughterhouse personnel could be fully engaged in producing non-flesh foods, including dairies that wouldn't send their non-producing animals to be butchered.

Profits would continue, and probably in a more equally distributed fashion. Moreover, the ethical and spiritual benefits would be enormous. And both industry and government would significantly reduce their burden of karmic debt. The food (absent flesh) would taste much better, more people in the world would be freed from hunger, food bills for the masses would be reduced significantly, decimation of rain forests would decrease, and people would be healthier. In this way, the quality of life would improve.

KRISHNA CONSCIOUS FESTIVALS: EASY ENTRANCE TO A KARMA-FREE ZONE

Written to coincide with Govardhana Puja, Diwali, and Srila Prabhupada's Disappearance Day celebrations, this *Hare Krishna World* editorial focused on three miracles: Krishna's holding Govardhana Hill aloft on one finger for a week, Lord Ramacandra's heroic feats, and Prabhupada's converting beastly humans into godly saints. Following the Vedic (lunar) calendar, the first two events are generally commemorated in November, and since Prabhupada left this mortal world on November 14, 1977, that day is also honored in the same month every year. Because the occasions are festive, and—in the case of Prabhupada's departure—"bittersweet," they are attractive to almost everyone. Once Prabhupada said about his

August 15, 1978—Los Angeles, USA: The first Los Angeles Rathayatra festivals include elephant rides for children.

first "love feast," "No one will refuse an invitation to a place where there is singing, dancing, and refreshments." Colorful Krishna conscious festivals such as these not only commemorate important events but also have a deep meaning and message for contemporary humanity.

***Hare Krishna World,* September/October 1996**

In November, devotees of Lord Krishna throughout the world, particularly those affiliated with the International Society for Krishna Consciousness (ISKCON), will commemorate three miracles.

One occurred in Vrindavana, India, 5,000 years ago. At that time Krishna lifted Govardhana Hill as a young boy and held it on the little finger of His left hand for seven days, balancing the hill like an umbrella and thus protecting all the residents of Vrindavana from a violent storm. The hill, weighing millions of tons, did not disintegrate but remained safely balanced on Krishna's fingertip above the villagers and their cows, defying the laws of physics.

The storm came with unusual fury because Lord Indra, a powerful demigod in charge of the weather, did not understand that this little boy was the Supreme Personality of Godhead. When the residents of Vrindavana were about to worship Indra (as was their custom, to get favorable rains for their crops), Krishna suggested that they worship Govardhana instead, as that is where their beloved cows pastured. Krishna, knowing that Indra was intoxicated with the power He had given him, wanted to test His mighty servant's mettle.

Frustrated by the boy's prowess, Indra finally realized that it was not himself but Krishna who was the cause of all causes, and thus it was Krishna who should be worshiped. Because Krishna is absolute and nondifferent from His pastimes, His devotees remember this event by celebrating Govardhana Puja as one of ISKCON's major yearly festivals. On this day, devotees also perform Go Puja, or cow worship, because Krishna loves cows, which benefit humanity with their milk and labor.

The second miracle involves the pastimes of Lord Ramacandra. The Vedic culture of ancient India provided protection for all living creatures in the Lord's natural order of things. As Krishna protected Vrindavana's residents from Indra's wrath, Lord Rama (of a much earlier age) protected the citizens of Ayodhya. Rama was Lord Krishna appearing in this world as a righteous king to set an example for all leaders. His pastimes are described in the devotional Indian classic, Ramayana.

King Rama protected His subjects from hunger, disease, pestilence, unemployment, and many other types of misfortune. Rama's people loved and worshiped Him because they knew they could trust Him to protect and uplift their society. Unlike many powerful leaders, however, Rama displayed humility as well as power. Therefore, when it became necessary for Him to leave Ayodhya with His stepbrother in charge, Rama was able to relinquish His position for a greater good. While away, He worked with the animals of the forest and His brother Laksman to slay a great demon named Ravana, who had captured Rama's wife, Sita, and terrorized innocent living beings in the region. In order to do this, they threw rocks as stepping stones onto the sea, making a floating pathway to Ravana's island fortress of Sri Lanka.

The Vedic New Year coincides with the triumphant return of Lord Ramacandra to rule His kingdom of Ayodhya after 14 years of exile. Since Rama's return occurred on a moonless night, the city was glittering with lamps, or *dipas,* to light His way. Therefore, this event is known as Dipawali, or Diwali Puja (the Festival of Lights). The citizens had greatly missed their enlightened king, and it was as if Rama's return brought the light back into their lives.

Both Lord Krishna and Lord Rama gave shelter to the citizenry. In *Bhagavad-gita,* Lord Krishna offers protection, saying, *paritra-naya sadhunam:* "I shall give protection to the faithful." The *Srimad-Bhagavatam* recommends that one should "constantly hear about, glorify, remember, and worship the Personality of Godhead (Krishna), who is the protector of the devotees" (1.2.14).

It is miraculous, particularly in the present age, to feel truly secure or happy in the long term about anything. Yet Krishna's protection is only a thought away. Or a Rama away. As Srila Prabhupada explained in a *Sri Caitanya-caritamrta* lecture, "We chant daily, *Hare Krishna, Hare Krishna, Krishna Krishna, Hare Hare; Hare Rama, Hare Rama, Rama Rama, Hare Hare.* Rama means to enjoy life in the Supreme Personality of Godhead. That means dovetail your activities with Krishna consciousness and you will be able to enjoy life eternally, blissfully" (San Francisco, January 23, 1967).

ISKCON devotees know that miracles occur. The very fact that one elderly and ill gentleman from India spread Krishna consciousness throughout the world in a few years, and that this global assault on godlessness continues since his passing nineteen years ago, is itself a supernatural happening. The radical transformation of thousands of lives now committed to spiritual life, many of whom follow vows of strict celibacy as well as eschewing meat-eating, intoxication, and gambling, is Srila Prabhupada's miracle.

He translated the scriptures, broadcast the stories of Lord Krishna and Lord Rama, and gave spiritual shelter to people everywhere, from all walks of life, without discrimination according to sex, class, race, religion, age, income, or education.

On November 14 this year, we observe the anniversary of Srila Prabhupada's passing from this world, when he gave his final lesson: how to leave one's body remembering Krishna. With many disciples by his side and up to his last breath, Srila Prabhupada continued to instruct and encourage his followers. Be Krishna conscious. Cooperate with each other.

Srila Prabhupada endowed uncounted thousands with a legacy of leadership. He has given his followers the scriptures and the tools to lead themselves and society to Krishna's eternal protection. It is their sacred duty to carry on his mission. To do so, ISKCON devotees must also be trustworthy, righteous, enlightened, and patient. Srila Prabhupada instructed his followers to humbly ask people to hear about Krishna consciousness, adding: "You cannot enforce. The atheistic civilization is so strong. So, you are not weak. You are protected by the Supreme. Our mission is not to fight, but to convince" (San Francisco talk, January 23, 1967).

Affiliation with ISKCON is more than escaping the miseries of material existence. The shelter that Lord Krishna offers in this movement is a relationship with Him—the fulfillment of love, support, peace, happiness, satisfaction, and constant personal interaction. It is natural and practical. Vedic lifestyles and social organization account for all our needs and desires. One has only to study Srila Prabhupada's books and lectures to learn how.

Everyone in the material world takes shelter of someone. But a closer look at all the many places one takes refuge—friends and society, fame, intoxication, television, work, and even family and other loved ones—reveals that all such havens will ultimately disintegrate and disappear. It is said that we come into and go out of this world naked and alone.

The *Srimad-Bhagavatam,* recorded in written form about 5,000 years ago, asserts that "materialistic persons complacently believe that their nations, communities, or families can protect them, unaware that all such fallible soldiers will be destroyed in due course of time" (2.1.4).

The *Srimad-Bhagavatam* also reminds us to associate with persons who are purely practicing devotional service in order to find the way out of our constantly crumbling sanctuaries. "One should try to associate with persons who engage in devotional service 24 hours a day" (6.3.28).

Observing Diwali Puja and Govardhana Puja are engaging ways for people to realize and demonstrate surrender to the Lord, by commemorating His glorious activities. In hundreds of ISKCON temples around the world, thousands of people will witness a mountain of eatables, arranged as a replica of Vrindavana's Govardhana Hill. Remembering Lord Rama, they will place candles on the altar and along the walkways of their temples. After chanting the Hare Krishna *maha-mantra* and joining in other ceremonies, they will feast upon a variety of spiritualized foodstuffs.

One of the indirect messages that Govardhana Puja broadcasts is that ultimately there is no such thing as shortages. As stated in the Invocation of *Sri Isopanisad,* God provides for everyone: "The personality of Godhead is perfect and complete. Because He is completely perfect, all emanations from Him, such as this phenomenal world, are perfectly equipped as a complete whole. Whatever is produced of the complete whole is also complete in itself. Because He is the complete whole, even though so many complete units emanate from Him, He remains the complete balance."

Shortages appear because of humanity's greed and lack of knowledge, which breed negative karmic reactions. In Mauritius in 1975, Srila Prabhupada said that the earth could support ten times its population, and modern research has found this to be true. A study by the University of California's Division of Agricultural Science shows that by practicing the best agricultural methods available, the world's farmers could raise enough food to provide a non-meat-centered diet for a world population thirty times greater than can presently be fed. Incidentally, switching to a vegetarian diet would also bring many environmental improvements—less air pollution, water pollution, and destruction of forests, to name a few. And those who choose to eat only food that is first offered to Krishna eat "karma-free."

Lord Krishna—through His pure devotee Srila Prabhupada, His

teaching in Bhagavad-gita that we are eternal, blissful souls (not our material bodies), and His activities—is summoning every human being to take refuge in Him. He cordially invites all persons to chant His holy names and eat sanctified food (*prasadam*) and cast off their karma. Spiritual authorities have recommended these methods as the easiest and best ways for the soul to obtain ultimate protection from ignorance and sinful desires.

The transformation of selfish humans into godly saints is the most astonishing miracle of all.

FROM KNOWLEDGE COMES ENLIGHTENMENT

I wrote this editorial to help devotees develop their enthusiasm for the first World Enlightenment Day—December 14, 1996. The goal was to distribute more of Srila Prabhupada's books than had ever been done before in a single day. Inspirational in tone, rather than detail-oriented, my hope was to deify Srila Prabhupada by showing that the books are universally attractive and that they have widespread application, with a message for everyone. In this way they are like Lord Krishna Himself. Are they the "law books for the future of humanity"? Although these are Srila Prabhupada's words, it's a hard pill for most people to swallow. But these are books that can be admired for the beautiful paintings they contain, their consummate Sanskrit scholarship, their contribution to the world's body of philosophical and theological knowledge, their perspectives on contemporary problems, and their ability to help us maneuver successfully through the material world. This essay speaks of these and many other attributes of Srila Prabhupada's books.

Hare Krishna World, November/December 1996

December 14, World Enlightenment Day for ISKCON, signifies a thrust for radical social change. On this day, thousands of Hare Krishna devotees expect to achieve a world record by distributing the greatest number of Srila Prabhupada's books ever in one day. But what exactly are these books, and what is their value to ISKCON and society at large?

Like everything else in the material world, ordinary books have only transitory value. Even the great classics will one day be reduced to footnotes and ultimately disappear from view. But the devotees who are distributing Srila Prabhupada's books have reason to believe that their efforts will create a much more lasting effect.

Scripture has endured longer than any other type of writing. And among all scriptures, the *Vedas* are the oldest and most voluminous. Of holy books, the most important, relevant, and practical are those rendered by Srila Prabhupada, at least to Hare Krishnas. His works, we say, stand alone.

But who will accept Srila Prabhupada's own assertion that his books would act as the law books for the future of humanity?

Can we say something more objective about his books, beyond declaring that almost everyone who reads them will discover their ultimate worth? How do they influence our world? How will they affect its future?

Here are some facts: Srila Prabhupada's books contribute to the world's philosophical and theological body of knowledge; they enrich the literary heritage of the planet; they provide academics with a reference point to understand the true nature of the Vedic way; they bring personal fulfillment and satisfaction; they help convince us that ultimate knowledge dwells within the hearts and minds of the great sages; they act as an instruction manual by which one can maneuver successfully through the material world; they present perspectives on contemporary problems; they fulfill the desire of spiritual predecessors to spread the message of love of God; they provide an alternative to materialism; they clearly explain the nature of material existence; they answer the most probing philosophical questions, such as "Who am I?" "Who is God?" "What is time, nature, and destiny?" and "Where am I going?"

From 1967 to 1977, despite advanced old age, Srila Prabhupada circled the globe almost continually, lecturing and managing the International Society for Krishna Consciousness (ISKCON), the Hare Krishna movement. Nonetheless, during all this travel, he wrote nonstop.

In his books and in his personal life, he advocated "simple living and high thinking," voluntary simplicity, and a happy, peaceful life with Krishna at the center. He wrote as a full-time practitioner and personally followed the philosophy he preached. In his books Srila Prabhupada teaches a complete science of life. In the 1980s, Srila Prabhupada's books were introduced in many leading universities, finding a home in a large sector of academia.

Most members of ISKCON commit themselves to the philosophy, practice, and spreading of Krishna consciousness because of knowledge gained from Srila Prabhupada's books. Srila Prabhupada called ISKCON the Hare Krishna Movement because he had an agenda for social change. Those who read his books come to understand this and perceive a sense of urgency for propagating Vedic knowledge. Students of Srila Prabhupada's books hope for such change, and many work vigorously for it.

During his time with us, Srila Prabhupada constantly encouraged widespread book distribution as the top priority. He indicated that these writings would gradually effect change. In the preface to his translation of *Srimad-Bhagavatam* he quotes from Canto 1, chapter 5, text 11, where it said that transcendental literature about Lord Krishna brings about "a revolution in the impious life of a misdirected civilization."

Thus, by distributing his books, one is taking part in the process of social change, the revolutionary method of making the material world God-centered and therefore more livable. This, according to Srila Prabhupada, is the highest welfare work.

The publication and distribution of Srila Prabhupada's books form the basis of the Krishna consciousness movement. The knowledge contained therein brings about the impetus for positive change. Although the soul can never be perfectly satisfied anywhere but in the spiritual world, the presence of the spiritual world can be felt here and now by acquiring transcendental knowledge and engaging in bona fide spiritual practices.

World Enlightenment Day, on which ISKCON devotees will distribute more books than ever before in a single day, will emphasize the unique excellence and importance of Srila Prabhupada's teachings and their relevance to a world in transition.

MISSION STATEMENTS: THE WAY FORWARD (PART I)

A many-steepled structure looms high and demandingly above US Highway 495, the fabled Washington "Beltway" that circles the US capital. The building is the Latter Day Saints' (Mormons') showcase temple for the world. On May 4, 1995, the Religious Public Relations Council (RPRC) of Washington, D.C., faxed an invitation to Anuttama prabhu (North American Director of Communications) and me to come to this church on the following Saturday evening at 6:00 PM. As members of the Religious Public Relations Council, we were among the privileged few invited by the RPRC to a twenty-five-person reception for Stephen R. Covey, author, management guru, and practicing Mormon. Mr. Covey was to deliver a speech to several hundred in the main chamber of the church right after the reception. Halfway through the reception, Anuttama talked with Mr. Covey and gave him a copy of *Bhagavad-gita As It Is.* The bald-headed Covey clasped the book under his arm throughout the rest of the reception. I was standing nearby, waiting my turn, when Mr. Covey turned, saw me, and walked over, stretching out his hand to me. We spoke briefly, and when I asked him how a group should formulate its mission statement, he didn't hesitate to tell me the whole process. I remembered it and subsequently followed his advice. With a few of our own communications secrets thrown into the mix, we could say that Stephen Covey helped ISKCON Communications Global develop its first mission statement (which appears at the beginning of this book). Shortly after that happened, I wrote the following ICB article so that ISKCON could use the methodology more universally.

***ISKCON Communications Briefings,* January/February 1996**

Srila Prabhupada laid the groundwork for an ISKCON mission statement. Many progressive organizations use mission statements to help keep their members' attention sharply focused on the group's essential aims, objectives, and action plans.

Prabhupada himself had a mission, but he didn't articulate it into a succinct, single paragraph for everyone in ISKCON to memorize. Time, audience, and circumstance made it seem that this was not so necessary.

Nonetheless, some of ISKCON's most memorable sayings lead us toward a statement of mission. For example: "Books are the Basis; Preaching is the Essence; Purity is the Force; Utility is the Principle."

Srila Prabhupada translates a famous verse in *Caitanya-caritamrta* (Madhya-lila 7.128) as follows: "Instruct everyone to follow the orders of Lord Sri Krishna as they are given in the *Bhagavad-gita* and *Srimad-Bhagavatam.* In this way, become a spiritual master and try to liberate everyone in this land." The first sentence of the purport reads, "This is the sublime mission of the International Society for Krishna Consciousness."

In his memorandum for the original incorporation of ISKCON, Srila Prabhupada enumerates seven key points, all of which are considered ingredients for an ISKCON mission statement. They are:

(1) To systematically propagate spiritual knowledge to society at large and to educate all peoples in the techniques of spiritual life in order to check the imbalance of values in life and to achieve real unity and peace in the world.

(2) To propagate a consciousness of Krishna, as it is revealed in the *Bhagavad-gita* and *Srimad-Bhagavatam.*

(3) To bring the members of the society together with each other and nearer to Krishna, the prime entity, thus to develop the idea within the members, and humanity at large, that each soul is part and parcel of the quality of Godhead (Krishna).

(4) To teach and encourage the sankirtana movement, congre-

gational chanting of the holy name of God, as revealed in the teachings of Lord Sri Chaitanya Mahaprabhu.

(5) To erect, for the members and for society at large, a holy place of transcendental pastimes dedicated to the Personality of Krishna.

(6) To bring the members closer together for the purpose of teaching a simpler and more natural way of life.

(7) With a view towards achieving the aforementioned purposes, to publish and distribute periodicals, magazines, books, and other writings.

The GBC has assigned a committee to produce a mission statement for ISKCON and for the GBC. The first drafts of these two mission statements are expected to be available to all GBC members via the GBC Discussions conference on COM by June 30, 1996. Suggested members of the committee are: Harikesa Swami, Jayapataka Swami, Mukunda Goswami, Sridhara Swami, Naveen Krsna dasa, Damodara dasa, and Vaidyanatha dasa.

All GBC members will then be invited to comment and review these two statements. It will then be this committee's responsibility to produce a final draft of these two mission statements as an offering to Srila Prabhupada on his Maha-Vyasapuja day on September 6, 1996 to receive his blessings. GBC members will then be asked to further refine these two statements such that they will be put into final form no later than the 1997 annual GBC meeting in Mayapur.

A mission statement, by definition, is a condensed, precise statement of purpose. In just a few sentences a group mission statement captures the complete essence and character of an organization—as well as its goals, objectives, strategies, tactics, methodologies, and systems to achieve its aims.

A mission statement can be very short. For example, the mission statement for ISKCON Belfast (Northern Ireland) is "Serving Krishna Together."

Others can be of the more ordinary length, like the one for Srila

Prabhupada's Centennial celebrations in India. "Through a program of major, local, national, and global events and programs, we will present Srila Prabhupada as a servant of Sri Chaitanya Mahaprabhu and as the world's most important spiritual leader today. We will identify him as the Founder-Acharya of ISKCON, highlight his and ISKCON's achievements and philosophy, and portray him as a national hero. We will demonstrate his continuing contributions to the lives of millions of people."

ISKCON's Global Ministry of Communications' statement is slightly longer and reads as follows:

> ISKCON Communications Global (ICG) strives to make a positive difference in the quality of life by benefiting and uplifting the individual and society, following the desire of His Divine Grace A. C. Bhaktivedanta Swami Prabhupada, founder-*acharya* of the International Society for Krishna Consciousness (ISKCON).
>
> ICG protects and enhances the reputation of ISKCON by working to create and sustain favorable environments for advancing the goals of the Krishna consciousness movement. We are committed to achieving topmost standards of excellence through enlightened, effective teamwork, cutting edge communications principles, progressive management systems, and advancements in technology.

MISSION STATEMENTS: THE WAY FORWARD (PART II)
ISKCON Communications Briefings, March/April 1996

Every ISKCON temple and project should have a mission statement. ISKCON leaders can base their decisions on such a statement. They, their temple members, advisors, and congregations can judge their preaching progress and even measure it against their agreed-upon statement of mission.

The best way to produce a group mission statement is to undertake the following procedure:

1. Arrange for a three- to four-hour session when everyone in

your temple or department can participate in your first mission statement session. This will be the first of four mission statement meetings. The venue should be different from the usual meeting or work place, and everyone should agree to free themselves from all other obligations. A large house or spacious apartment is often an ideal setting. There should be no young children present or any other distractions. Participants should free themselves from phone calls and visitors, and should not be reading during the meeting.

In other words, the atmosphere should be absolutely free of distractions so everyone present can fully concentrate on the purpose of the get-together.

It really does take at least four gatherings to produce a truly exceptional, meaningful, and useful mission statement. But only the first needs to be 3–4 hours long. Subsequent meetings should not go more than 1–2 hours.

2. Select a facilitator. We'll call this person the "leader" from now on. Usually the temple president, a department head, or a project head is the best person to perform this important function.

At the first meeting, start by listing activities. For a temple this would include many things, such as preparing offerings, book distribution, *hari-nama sankirtana,* bookkeeping and accounting, scheduling, cooking and cleaning the kitchen, cleaning the premises, scheduling temple classes, and home visits to congregational devotees and members.

Using a flip chart and a marking pen, the leader asks the group to help make a list of all current and future activities. As pages of the flip chart fill up, they are detached and stuck to a wall where everyone can see them, so that the list is easily viewed and remembered throughout the session. At the same time, one person must take detailed notes on a computer, entering everything written on the flip chart sheets, so that all points are preserved. After each session, these points will be distributed to everyone present on hard copy or disk.

3. When the activity list is exhaustive, the leader, with as much group participation as possible, rearranges each activity under a category. One way to do this is to use different colored marking pens, circling the items that come under a particular category with a unique color. For example, all the items that come under Deity worship could be circled with a blue marker. All the items that come under the category of book distribution could be circled with a green marker, and so on. In this way, the group begins to see an emerging picture of functions under various categories. This whole process should take one or two hours.

At the same time, the note taker (we'll call this person "the recorder" from now on) uses a computer to enter all the categories and puts all the appropriate activities under the correct heading as the leader does it on the flip chart. With a computer it is very easy to keep everything neat and clean. In this way, shortly after the session, the participants will get a computer-clean recap of what happened at the meetings. The recorder should distribute the hard copies and/or disks within 24 hours of the session.

4. Next, using the flip chart again, the group should make a list of agreed-upon goals and objectives for the next year. These should be time-bound; in other words, they must have deadlines. For example: (a) By the end of the centennial year, have a well-groomed, excellent *hari-nama* party with flags, *mridangas* with brightly-colored cloth, and first-class singing and dancing going out three times a week; (b) By August of 1996, have a first-rate Sunday feast program in place; (c) By mid-1996, have all the bookkeeping on a computer program; (d) During 1996, establish a Food for Life program that is recognized and accepted by city officials; and (e) Give Krishna consciousness programs in twenty different college classes by November, 1996.

After the leader has written on the flip chart all of these goals, they should be placed under categories, just like the activities were. In fact, most of the goals should fit under the same categories you used for the activities. This process of listing and categorizing goals should take less than two hours. The recorder, using a computer program as with the activities list, can easily fit all the goals under the existing categories. Now you have a complete list of current activities and projected goals for the next year, all under appropriate categories. A clearer picture of the project is beginning to emerge.

5. Even though the current activities and goals are categorized, the leader now helps the group refine things by asking everyone to look for activities and objectives that are redundant, overlap, or should be rephrased or combined. It may even be necessary to change a catagory's name in order to be more precise or comprehensive.

The recorder should ALWAYS operate strictly according to what the group leader and group agrees to. He or she is NOT editing, but RECORDING. The group and the leader in particular occasionally may need to direct or dictate to the recorder to ensure that all the information being agreed to is being recorded strictly on track.

The leader should frequently get nods from the entire group while repeating what has been said and while writing on the flip chart. The leader should always have the group's consensus as to how things are written on the flip chart.

6. The first session is now at an end. The leader announces that the most difficult part is over and that there will be three more, shorter, sessions to develop and finalize the mission statement.

The "homework" assignment: each participant, using hard copy or disk data from the recorder, thoughtfully and carefully writes a proposed mission statement for the whole group (500 words or less) and brings it to the next meeting. The leader schedules the next meeting to take place within a month. If available, the leader may distribute mission statements from other temples or projects.

7. A few days before the second session, the leader collects homework from all participants, copies them, and gives the copies of all the homework to each participant. In other words, everyone gets a copy of everyone's proposed group mission statement. This enables each person to view and digest the mission statements of others before the second meeting.

8. When the meeting day arrives and all are present, the leader initiates a discussion based on the set of mission statements each participant holds and has read, digested, and (hopefully) made notes on.

The single purpose of this meeting is for the group to combine all the mission statements into one composite statement.

During the meeting it is critical that everyone present takes notes, and, of course, the recorder will enter the final wording of the composite statement on disk. The leader should use the flip chart to help reach the combined statement.

If you're really tooled up technologically, you can use a computer with a projector or large monitor instead of a flip chart. But this is only essential for the fourth and final meeting, as we'll explain shortly.

This second meeting should only last an hour or two. Its purpose is to ascertain the salient points participants think need to be retained, combined, deleted, expanded upon, and so forth, to come up with a composite mission statement. You're simply combining all the statements into one, resulting in a concise, single statement using the essential elements from each member's homework.

Work at this until each member of the group is satisfied that the result retains the essence of what the group feels is right. At this time, each member should have the composite statement written down. And of course, for safety and efficiency, the recorder will have it on computer. As with the first meeting, the recorder will distribute hard or disk copy to participants THAT DAY, while it is fresh in mind.

Homework assignment for the third meeting: each participant, using this composite statement, writes another proposed mission statement. In other words, he or she rewrites and refines the composite statement, to make it better. Each member will then possess a revised composite statement, which will be used at the third meeting, to take place in about a month's time.

9. Three days before the third meeting, each member turns in

his or her revised and refined composite mission statement to the leader who immediately copies all of them and distributes them to each member of the group.

10. The procedure of this third meeting is the same as for the second one. In this meeting the leader (with the flip chart or computer screen) and the group and its recorder work together to make a composite of the composites.

Now it becomes clear that the mission statement is getting considerably refined. At the end of the meeting—not to exceed two hours—each person in the group will have written down, in his or her notes, the second composite group mission statement. The recorder has it on the computer and gives copies to group members within twenty-four hours. The leader announces that a fourth meeting will take place in one month.

11. The form of the fourth and final meeting is a repeat of the previous two. This time the second composite statement is refined into a third and final composite. At the end of this composite meeting, what is refined becomes the mission statement for the group.

We strongly recommend that at this meeting the entire group view the final composite on a computer monitor or screen projected from a computer. In this way, the statement can be group-edited in the most efficient way. Group-editing with a computer word processor makes a BIG difference.

Also, at the last meeting's outset, the leader should make it clear that this final meeting is the last opportunity for members to bring up any lingering doubts, thoughts, or fears.

The leader should encourage each person to speak his or her mind, even if the thought deals with very subtle "feelings." It is important at this stage to voice dissatisfaction or even hypothetical ideas that are important to the member but that may seem irrelevant. It is the time for "thinking out loud."

If a member feels there is a particular point, sense, concept, or meaning that needs to be added, he or she should speak out, even though the idea may be unrefined or difficult to express or seems contrary to the main themes. It is important that the group is reminded during this last session that it's "now or never."

The leader should patiently wait—even if it means sitting through a minute or two of dead silence while people think hard and, if necessary, gather up the courage to speak. Even the subtlest perspectives can make a big difference.

If all the meetings and homework are done properly, following the above instructions, members will emerge from this fourth and final session with a feeling of deep accomplishment.

Even the best mission statements are not necessarily etched in stone. It's advisable for the group to revisit them once every six months or so, but only for minor suggestions or to reinforce the existing statement, leaving it exactly as it is. A well-fashioned mission statement should last for at least a year or two.

An excellent mission statement will be one that all participants feel good about. They will want to see it enshrined in a frame and prominently displayed at their work place. They will feel proud to be a part of it and honored that they helped create it.

Mission statements created solely by a director, or group of directors, without participation of other members of an organization, are usually displayed only because the supreme commanders have so ruled. But when statements are created in the way we have described, members never feel the mission was forced upon them by decree. Instead, they see an excellent statement they helped to create and which acts as a beacon to keep them focused on their purpose and as a compass that helps them keep steering in the right direction.

Exceptional mission statements continuously and incessantly inspire creative thinking and activity. They act as a constant reminder of "why I'm doing what I am doing" and have a rejuvenating effect on their creators.

Mission statements can be used in conflict resolution situations. This is because they state common purposes against which to measure "rights" and "wrongs." They help ascertain if a given situation, attitude, behavior, event, activity, or personality is consistent with, contributing to, or distracting from the essential statement of purpose.

A mission statement is also an ideological beginning, upon which even a large group of people can build. Organizations usually take on many projects and have subdivisions. Ideally, each division develops its own mission statement derived from that of the main organization.

Once your statement is in place, details can more easily follow. Among them are job and project descriptions, written policies and procedures, and the tracking of projects, finances, and people.

But the all-important beginning is the mission statement. Once done, everyone directly involved should frame and display it prominently, refer to it constantly, and memorize it. It should become the raison d'etre for your temple, organization, or project.

THE "MIRROR EFFECT" IS CHANGING YOUR LIFE

Srila Prabhupada did many things that were unprecedented. One was beginning a truly global organization—and it all started from what the material world would call "virtually nothing." Srila Prabhupada arrived in Boston, Massachusetts, USA, with US$5.00 worth of Indian rupees and a few sets of books. Yet as early as 1969, a devotee chanting in the streets of London was approached by an American tourist, who asked, "Didn't I see you last week in Honolulu?" The same haircuts, mode of dress, philosophy, and life style were among the few things we held in common in the early days, and there were very few of us. By our visibility, however, we created the sense of a global movement. Srila Prabhupada capitalized again and again upon the "internationality" of his society. The following ICB article highlights some of his most dramatic uses of the "Mirror Effect."

ISKCON Communications Briefings, January/February1996

The grand, unprecedented scale of ISKCON has inspired many

1998—Calcutta, India: Bhakti Charu Swami, with help from assistant director Akeh Ufumaka, directs Jyoti Bagga, who plays Abhay's wife, Radharani, on the set of Abhay Charan, in Calcutta. *Abhay Charan* is a 104-part television series depicting the life of ISKCON's founder, Abhay Charan Bhaktivedanta Swami. Each episode is a half hour long. The serial is based on the authorized biography by Satsvarupa dasa Goswami called *Srila Prabhupada Lilamrita.*

to join Srila Prabhupada's movement.

"They averaged fifteen or twenty thousand an hour," Hrdayananda Goswami said, answering Srila Prabhupada'a question about how many visitors came to Mayapur during the 1976 Gaura Purnima festival.

At a Nairobi lecture in 1975, Srila Prabhupada told his audience, "You are seeing a new thing in the history of the world—Africans, Indians, Americans, and Europeans are dancing." In a letter to Tamala Krsna Goswami he wrote, "Surely we will bring in a new chapter in the history of the world" (January 1, 1970).

Srila Prabhupada made repeated efforts to instill "big ISKCON" consciousness in his devotees. He spoke of ways to "link-up our chain of centers around the world" (letter to Bali Mardan, November 4, 1976). He repeatedly implored devotees, especially ISKCON leaders, to think of the world as a whole, even when preaching locally.

In a letter dated November 18, 1972 to GBC member Jagadisa Goswami, he wrote, "So we shall not think that this is my [GBC] zone, that is his zone, just like the Indian and Pakistan nations are thinking, and then there is war. No. Lord Chaitanya has given us the task to spread His message all over the world, and any process which may be useful for facilitating this business, that we shall gladly adopt, never mind his zone or my zone, that is material designation."

From the very start, Srila Prabhupada called his movement the International Society for Krishna Consciousness. He wanted his movement to be seen on a global scale.

ISKCON's Sridhara Swami regularly asks during his seminars, "What is it that Srila Prabhupada could not do?" The answer was given by Srila Prabhupada himself: "My 'disease' was that I could never think small."

When the cult "brainwashing" propaganda broke out across America in late 1976, along with a burgeoning anticult movement, two prominent devotees were formally charged by a New York court with brainwashing a new recruit. Srila Prabhupada, even while traveling the world as usual, sprang into action and insisted that his disciples do likewise. With this incident, he set the stage for devotees to use ISKCON's internationality to influence judiciaries and governments.

He arranged for dozens of affluent Mumbai (Bombay) businessmen to write letters of outrage (on their business letterheads) to US President Nixon, asking him to intervene. He also requested devotees in Mumbai to organize a massive outdoor protest with written statements and picket signs at the US Consulate in Mumbai.

"It is good that our friends are coming forward to help in Bombay. Let them present a statement that it is a genuine movement. . . . In Bombay there is an embassy branch. Our Bombay friends should go there to express their protest" (letter to Giriraja Swami, November 6, 1976). He wanted the people and courts of the USA to understand that ISKCON had a large following in India, not only of the general populace, but also of elite industrialists.

In July of 1974, when British government officials banned ISKCON's Rathayatra in Trafalgar Square, a London landmark, Srila Prabhupada said, "At least a protest meeting should be done in such a way that the whole world may know that the British government stopped the yearly Rathayatra ceremony of the Hindus." After months of intensive efforts, the government relented and the Rathayatra was celebrated in the Square the very next year.

In these and many other ways, Srila Prabhupada wanted his disciples to capitalize on the fact that ISKCON had a global reach. Even when he was lecturing, giving a *darshan* (audience), talking with a VIP, or counseling a devotee, he was always thinking of ISKCON's progress and problems in far-away places.

He introduced the ongoing book-selling competition on a global scale; he was proud to display what he sometimes called his dancing "white elephants" (Western disciples) to Mumbai festival-goers and Indian temple congregations; he instructed *Back to Godhead* magazine (BTG) editors to publish photos of *sankirtana* parties in different parts of the world; he often spoke of ISKCON's "centers all over the world."

One way to understand the depth of ISKCON's global penetration is through the photographs and brief news articles published in *Hare Krishna World* and *Back to Godhead.* HKW in particular helps to demonstrate that many regional preaching events and victories are not irrelevant, insignificant, or unimportant. In fact, they take on new meaning when seen from the other side of the world or in the context of a global crusade. This phenomenon may be referred to as the "mirror effect."

When the essence of Krishna consciousness is reflected through its preaching in different parts of the world, and when devotees keep in mind, as Srila Prabhupada did, the big picture, the disparate parts fit together into a unified, inspiring whole. This consciousness captures the deepest meaning of the phrase, "act locally, think globally."

In this way, the multidimensional thrust of Krishna consciousness becomes what Srila Prabhupada wanted it to be—a worldwide movement for the respiritualization of humanity.

HEAD-ON (DIRECT) OR HEAD DOWN (INDIRECT)?

This 1996 ICB article analyzes two approaches to preaching: direct and indirect. I conclude that both are important and neither should be emphasized to the exclusion of the other, which too often, unfortunately, happens. The direct approach is what "core" devotees are used to: speaking to visitors, distributing books, giving and hearing classes and seminars, *hari-nama* chanting parties, home visitations. A more indirect approach comes in when our outreach includes restaurants, cultivation of individuals, and participation in community or interest-group meetings. The direct approach tends to involve smaller groups who will hear and assimilate the essential elements of Vaishnava philosophy. Indirect methods tend to involve a larger universe of people who can only accommodate one aspect or a small portion of the Krishna consciousness philosophy, practice, or world view. In this category are those who frequent Hare Krishna restaurants but do not visit temples; those who read books but have never associated with devotees; those who appreciate *hari-nama* parties but generally go no further. A description of the indirect approach dominates this article. I think you will find it interesting.

ISKCON Communications Briefings, May/June 1996

Trikalajna Prabhu developed a friendship with Mr. Goyal, a well-wisher of ISKCON with friends in government. The friendship paid dividends as Mr. Goyal said to Trikalajna one Sunday at the Manor, "I'd like to invite you to the Barnet Anglo-Asian Tory Party dinner next month. Margaret Thatcher will be there. I'd like you to meet her."

Back then, in the mid-80s, the Tory (Conservative)-dominated local government, Hertsmere Borough Council, was determined to stop public worship at the Manor.

At the Barnet dinner, after a brief introduction by Mr. Goyal, Trikalaja handed British Prime Minister Thatcher an envelope and said, "Mrs. Thatcher, you've got to do something about the Hertsmere Council; they're trying to ban worship at our temple." The envelope contained an appeal for help from the British chief executive and background information about the case.

Although he was left only with an "I'll see what I can do" and "I can't promise anything," the incident and the events leading up to it are instructive.

Incidentally, on May 10, 1996, John Gummer, Britain's Minister for the Environment, ruled unequivocally and irrevocably that worship could continue at the Manor. A new entrance road, bypassing the village of Letchmore Heath, became operational in September 1996.

Trikalajna had initially decided to talk with Mr. Goyal as a gesture of friendship to a sincere soul who came to see the Deities and associate with Vaishnavas. Only after several meetings did he learn about Goyal's affiliations with important government leaders. He continued the friendship, considering at the same time that the relationship could lead to important front-line preaching, not least of which would be helping to preserve public attendance at the Manor.

This vision of preaching might be termed the gradual, humble, or "head-down" approach. Slowly but surely, with the ultimate goal always clearly in focus, a relationship developed over a long period of time.

Equally important—and absolutely indispensable—is the more conventional, "head-on" approach. This includes two of the basic *angas* (limbs) of ISKCON: book distribution and *hari-nama sankirtana,* holy-name distribution.

The division between "direct" and "indirect" preaching is not always clearly distinguishable. The direct method sometimes requires waiting, watching, and careful cultivation.

Despite occasional overlapping, studying the two approaches as distinct from one another helps to better understand both. Although the two methods are complementary, each mood has its unique approach and audience.

Delivering essential philosophy by books or speech and sweet *kirtana* has transformed millions of lives and will no doubt continue to do so. Most people have made the transition from material life to Krishna-conscious life through the philosophy presented in Srila Prabhupada's books.

ISKCON temples will continue to be welcome oases in the great material desert. Temples are the bulwark of ISKCON, inspiring millions of people to develop purified Krishna consciousness and preaching capability. Temple lectures have convinced thousands to take up Krishna consciousness seriously. This process must and will surely continue.

The gradual approach, which is readily apparent in *prasadam* distribution and Nama Hatta cultivation, usually requires more time. This more incremental method often involves large numbers of people getting association in the form of *prasadam,* visits by devotees, or newsletters through the mail. The audiences involved here are sometimes those who would not initially buy a book or come to a temple.

Nama Hatta, or congregational preaching and the creation of "cells" and "temples within the home", tends to focus on those who have not visited the nearest temple or who do so only occasionally. But the number of those who have received such visits in their homes is much greater than the number who live in ISKCON *ashramas.*

The "head-on" approach involves our direct contacts with the public, requesting them to purchase books, speaking to Sunday visitors in the temple, or engaging a *hari-nama* chanting party in a busy section of the city.

Using this technique, devotees tend to approach anyone and everyone, according to Lord Chaitanya's order ("Whoever you meet, speak the instructions of Krishna"). From such preaching, many decide to seriously look into Krishna consciousness and even join the movement, up to the point of moving into a temple and/or getting initiated.

Prasadam distribution, on the other hand, is a classic example of a more gradual approach, especially when it occurs in ISKCON restaurants. People who become attached to Krishna through *prasadam* usually become attached gradually—to devotee association, Srila Prabhupada's books, and the devotional atmosphere.

Many restaurant patrons come for months and years before attending a Sunday festival or seriously reading ISKCON literature. Others become devotees only after several years of eating prasadam.

In some restaurant settings, however, devotees meet a patron who decides very quickly to become a serious practitioner. This is an instance of direct preaching within the context of a gradual-approach setting. In general, however, an ISKCON restaurant involves the head-down approach.

Sometimes those who purchase books subsequently receive visits from devotees for many years, and some eventually become initiated. This is a gradual approach that was instigated by a direct, head-on approach.

In 1974, Srila Prabhupada gave a directive through his secretary that ISKCON should not establish more temples in the USA but should open only restaurants with adjoining reading rooms. In this regard, he requested that a letter be "distributed to all GBC members." Paragraph two of that letter reads, "Srila Prabhupada has suggested that rather than opening any more temples in the US, that we open combinations of reading rooms and restaurants."

The letter also included Srila Prabhupada's rationale for this radical directive. "These reading rooms and restaurants will be appreciated by the public as not being sectarian. Our farms can supply the foodstuffs and those who work in the restaurants should be able to eat as much as they like."

Elsewhere in the letter, Srila Prabhupada indicated how this program would counteract negative publicity and enable the public to see ISKCON's cultural position.

Financial support for ISKCON temples varies throughout the world. Some of ISKCON's largest individual donations have come from members who were cultivated over a period of several months or even years, during which time they did not contribute substantially or at all. Also, it is an emerging trend that financial support comes from congregational donors and from devotee businesses.

Since financial support for ISKCON comes increasingly from the "membership" sector of our society, fund raising—which requires careful and ongoing contact—will become increasingly important. In fact, the longest established religious movement in the West, the Catholic Church, receives most of its funding from inheritances.

Networking is another long-range procedure. Attending meetings, making friends, participating in community and interfaith projects, and developing relations with neighbors are all part of long-term, ongoing, reputation-building systems that help create and sustain favorable environments for advancing the goals of the Krishna consciousness movement. These preaching methods help establish a favorable attitude for the acceptance of our philosophy and life style.

Srila Prabhupada himself exhibited both the head-on and head-down approaches to preaching Krishna consciousness—according to time, place, and circumstance. In his Los Angeles garden, he confronted and challenged scholars, almost demanding submission to higher principles; at Bhaktivedanta Manor, he patiently listened to neighbors complain about devotee life styles and philosophy as he tried to establish friendly ties with an inimical audience.

He once spoke to a group of Indian citizens in Delhi, calling them "the greatest offenders" for giving up their Vedic culture. But in Mumbai (formerly Bombay), he lectured patiently to masses at Cross Maidan, apparently oblivious to the hundreds of men, women, and children who were coming and going and talking incessantly during his speech.

In the context of book distribution, small books like *The Higher Taste, Chant and Be Happy, Coming Back,* and *Divine Nature* are designed to lead readers to Srila Prabhupada's books and to the practice of devotional service.

Pamphlets, newsletters, posters, advertisements, *Back to Godhead*, and *Hare Krishna World* act as bridges to Prabhupada's books and the serious, committed practice of Krishna consciousness.

Following the instructions of Lord Krishna (*ya idam paramam guyam*), Lord Chaitanya, and Srila Prabhupada, ISKCON will continue to approach conditioned souls both directly and indirectly. But the purpose will remain the same: to get them started on their path back to Godhead—in whatever way works best.

NEAT, CLEAN, AND GREEN

Srila Prabhupada's teachings warn us more than once that we should beware of the vox populi (voice of the people). It is fraught with defects because of humanity's inhuman condition in this age. But, seen in terms of time, place, and circumstance, this warning has different meanings. Wrong cognition and negative attitudes by the public can ruin a reputation and impede progress of the *sankirtana* movement. "Somehow or other we should not become unpopular in the public eye," Srila Prabhupada wrote in a January 9, 1975 letter to Rupanuga. In the "developed countries," people tend to make judgments and form lasting opinions based on external observations. In India, a *sadhu* is traditionally unkempt in his outer appearance. He might have a day's or more growth of beard, wrinkled clothes, and dirty feet from walking barefoot. In developed countries, a devotee is expected to be well groomed; otherwise people will reject his or her words without ever really listening to them. In all cases, Srila Prabhupada was greatly concerned about his movement's reputation. In the same letter to Rupanuga he wrote, "If we do something which is deteriorating to the popular sentiments of the public in favor of our movement, that is not good."

ISKCON Communications Briefings, May/June 1996

How you dress, speak, walk, talk, what your living place looks like, what kind of car you drive, how well you listen—all these things matter a lot more than you think.

Unfortunately, many superficial aspects of our lives are often the only basis for judging character in this age. These fleeting first impressions often become the basis for opinions that shape the way people think about us. "First impressions are the last and lasting," it is sometimes said.

As stated in the *shastras,* in Kali Yuga a *brahmana* will be recognized simply by his wearing a string across his torso. In spreading Krishna consciousness effectively in this age, one should carefully note the phenomenon of superficiality. Another shastric reference refers to a black spot on a white tablecloth and compares it to a *sannyasi* displaying improper external behavior.

Especially in the developed countries of the world, but also everywhere, the importance of dressing nicely (one of Lord Krishna's opulences as described by Rupa Goswami) and making all of ISKCON temples appear pleasing cannot be overestimated.

Thousands of people will judge us on these things and carry their impressions with them throughout their lives. For Srila Prabhupada's centennial, a noble aim is to make long-term commitments to keeping his temples immaculately clean inside and out, nicely painted, and the grounds presentable in a first-class manner.

Another related issue is the creation of an environmentally friendly atmosphere in the temple. This is especially important in the so-called developed countries, which consume most of the planet's energy and shamelessly waste vast amounts. Simple acts, like separating garbage (paper, glass, and metal) and avoiding Styrofoam cups are noticed and noted by many thoughtful members of the public who visit temples.

There is an unfortunate tendency to think that because we are meant to be absorbed in transcendence, such things don't really matter. In this day and age, keeping up good appearances for the general public is critical. We may not care for public opinion, as Srila Prabhupada has sometimes said, but that is a reference primarily to philosophy, not lifestyle. "Cleanliness is next to Godliness," he frequently reminded us.

Sometimes ISKCON members have dealt roughly and insensitively with members of the public. Navina Nirada and other devotees now conduct courses throughout the world, teaching devotees how to interact with the public—especially in book distribution situations—so that our reputation doesn't suffer.

In a letter to Rupanuga (January 9, 1970) Srila Prabhupada writes, "If we do something which is deteriorating to the popular sentiments of the public in favor of our movement, that is not good. Somehow or other we should not become unpopular in the public eye." And in *Caitanya-caritamrta* he writes, "There are many instances of devotional service rendered by previous acharyas who did not care about social behavior when intensely absorbed in love for Krishna. Unfortunately, as long as we are within this material world, we must observe social customs to avoid criticism by the general populace. This is Sri Chaitanya Mahaprabhu's desire."

OPINION LEADER ENDORSEMENTS

This 1996 ICB perspective is a further evolution of the 1995 story I wrote in ICB entitled, "Wanted: Opinion Leaders" (ICB, July/August, 1995). In this article, I give some practical guidelines on how to acquire an opinion leader statement, how to use it, how to videotape it, and how to get endorsers to be more involved. I also suggest methods for developing such statements for future use.

"Srila Prabhupada on Reviews," taken from the front page of this ICB, introduces the topic, as we read how he suggests that a small book be printed containing book reviews, "so that people will see what a great impression our books have on the intelligentsia of the world."

"Srila Prabhupada on Reviews":

Srila Prabhupada understood the importance of opinion leader endorsements, and when it came to publishing and distributing his books, he insisted on large numbers of reviews by scholars from all over the world. "I was very pleased to receive the review on the first volume of the Third Canto of *Srimad-Bhagavatam* written by Professor Mehta from the University of Windsor. If you can send more similar reviews on my books, I would very much appreciate it. I am keeping a folder on such things and we can print a small book to distribute that will contain such reviews so that people will see what a great impression our books have on the intelligentsia of the world" (letter to Satsvarupa Maharaja, January 29, 1975).

He also wrote in a letter to Brahmananda on December 19, 1968: "My only suggestion for this selling is to get the book widely reviewed in different papers, and that is the only standard method of promoting these publications By such reviews, as soon as there is some demand, all the book sellers will purchase from the publisher at least three copies each. That is the way of propagating sales organization."

***ISKCON Communications Briefings*, July/August 1996**

Srila Prabhupada did it. Printed them right in his books—reviews by scholars. He insisted on them. He even formed a library party, one of whose primary missions was to obtain reviews of his translations and purports. On his specific request, the Bhaktivedenta Book Trust published *Krishna Consciousness Is Authorized,* a booklet that contained many book reviews and other endorsements. In these and many other ways, Srila Prabhupada showed the need for opinion leader endorsements.

Although we included a short article on opinion leader endorsements one year ago in ICB, we consider the practice serious enough to present what we consider an important, more informed presentation of this principle.

Bhagavad-gita As It Is also establishes the principle: "Whatever action a great man performs, common men will follow. And whatever standards he sets by exemplary acts, all the world pursues" (3.21).

It is not that ISKCON hasn't been using such endorsements. But we've done so in a haphazard, slipshod, and unsystematic way. In one sense there is nothing wrong with that. Excerpts of decisions from judicial verdicts, scholars' praises, religionists' appreciations, politicians' plaudits, celebrity backing, and judges' decisions have been used widely and have appeared in many ISKCON publications.

Today, however, a more disciplined approach to opinion leader endorsements is necessary.

Appreciations from "third parties" can be used time and again and are actually a stimulating way to spread Krishna consciousness. You can begin to acquire opinion leader endorsements by examining your temple's strong points. Is your temple advanced in book or *prasadam* distribution, academic preaching, community relations, *hari-nama,* congregational development, government relations, or in other activities? If so, you may look for people related to these preaching fields to offer "official" compliments.

It's important to note that an "opinion leader" is not necessarily a celebrity, or even a mayor, city council member, or even a leading business figure. An opinion leader is someone who is respected in a particular field.

For example, a well-known nutritionist could champion ISKCON's diet in a letter; the director of a city's welfare division might be willing to support ISKCON's Food for Life program; a trusted city employee might offer to stand behind ISKCON for successfully promoting clean living—a life style free from drugs, illicit sex, and gambling.

Taking a progressive approach, Australian devotees, in May of 1996, requested and obtained a focused statement from leading Australian nutritionist Rosemary Stanton, who mentioned ISKCON by name in a written endorsement. She will be further contacted by Taittreya dasi in Australia, who obtained the endorsement.

Stanton's statement included the following words: "I support vegetarian choices, because I think some forms of raising animals for food are environmentally disastrous—lot feeding, for example. A well-selected vegetarian diet is also healthier than the diet of most Australians."

Opinion leader statements should be obtained by viewing the endorser as a devotee, not as a tool for spreading Krishna consciousness or even as a sympathizer. When cared for in a personal manner, they will see such service as an important development in their own spirituality. When we care for their Krishna consciousness, their words of support gradually become their devotional service.

Under the expert guidance of a devotee, opinion leaders can become serious about the Krishna consciousness philosophy, practice, and/or world view and begin to develop a service attitude. When this happens, he or she will not only allow their opinions to be used, but they will even ask for them to be used and suggest how, where, and when they could be better used. The secret is to develop a Krishna conscious relationship with them.

We may remember how personal Srila Prabhupada was with Dr. Stillson Judah. He read Dr. Judah's book *Hare Krishna and the Counterculture* cover to cover and developed a personal relationship with the professor. On several occasions afterward, Dr. Judah helped Prabhupada in various ways to spread Krishna consciousness.

Validations by leaders can be widely utilized. They can be used as an integral and helpful part of ISKCON temple newsletters, for congregational preaching, for work with government authorities, for academic conventions, for Food for Life, for selling books, for news releases, and for many other outreach programs.

Opinion leader approval can be obtained not only as written statements, but also as videotaped statements. You need to get professional help to produce a statement on videotape.

If a videotape opportunity arises, we recommend you contact the ISKCON Global Communications Ministry, ISKCON Communications North America (also located at ISKCON Potomac), or ITV in Los Angeles. Video endorsements can be used in a variety of ways.

If you are developing your congregation, you will find that most of them have a VCR and will be happy to watch any video you bring to their home.

A videotaped opinion leader support statement should be less than eight minutes in length.

Videotaped statements often involve prominent personalities. For example, a famous scholar may agree to make a videotaped statement for use at a seminar or interfaith conference. If the scholar is well-known enough, the videotaped statement can be shown on a big screen as the keynote address.

Other uses for videotaped statements include incorporating them into ISKCON video productions; showing them to devotees and your congregation at the Sunday feasts; taking the tape with you to television shows on which you will be interviewed; setting up continuous viewing at festivals; and showing the tape to other devotees to encourage them to produce similar videos.

Vaishnavas should see each opinion leader endorsement as an ongoing process, not as a product.

AN EMERGING UNIVERSE OF DEVOTEES

The June 1996 issue of Jayapataka Maharaja's *Congregational Preaching Journal* got me excited. I had no idea how Krishna consciousness could grow so expansively through congregations, even under unfriendly governments! The numbers showing exponential growth are impressive. But what's even more important is that this manner of increasing Krishna consciousness could be the primary way the world's teeming masses can become Krishna conscious. Jayapataka Maharaja sometimes asks his seminar attendees the following question: "How many temples did Chaitanya Mahaprabhu start?" Correct answer: "None." Although temples will always remain the bulwark and inspirational wellspring of the Krishna consciousness movement, we may see massive "conversion" take place mainly through the organic system of congregational growth.

***ISKCON Communications Briefings,* September/October 1996**

Today more initiated ISKCON devotees live outside of temples than in. This fact is changing the way ISKCON looks and works.

ISKCON's Nama Hatta program, spearheaded by Jayapataka Swami, has reached impressive levels in Eastern India. Congregational Preaching (CP) is now recognized as an increasingly important method for spreading Krishna consciousness to every town and village and every home in the world. In fact, the future of ISKCON—its growth—will depend to a large extent upon congregational development.

In some countries, Christian preaching is officially banned, and thus Christianity has remained a timid minority. But even in such places, some Christian preachers have undertaken congregational development through the "cell church" method. The "cell technique" of congregational preaching is a form of Nama Hatta preaching that Jayapataka Maharaja teaches in seminars all over the world.

Part of the process is known as cell replication. "Cells," in Jayapataka Maharaja's words, "are the small parts our body is made of. They reproduce and multiply by dividing into two. In the same way, Nama Hatta cell groups are the basic units of an organized congregation. The cell group grows by making new devotees, and when it reaches fifteen members, it divides into two. Both groups go on growing and multiplying. Cells are also called 'bhakti-branch groups.' This name is in relation to the metaphor of the Chaitanya tree, as presented in *Caitanya-caritamrita,* Adi Lila."

A cell group usually consists of five to fifteen devotees. They nurture one another and meet weekly. Each group has a leader and an assistant leader. When the group reaches fifteen members it divides into two groups, with the leader starting a new cell group, choosing a new trainee-assistant. Meanwhile, his or her assistant in the original cell takes charge of it and arranges for a new assistant there. This is the basic principle.

Of course, there is a lot more to it, but "the secret," says

Jayapataka Swami, is taking personal care of every devotee in our congregation.

With proper training, cells can and should double at least every year. When the principles that make this possible are put into action, a Nama Hatta group of only two cells with a total of twenty devotees (ten in each cell) will, in ten years, become 2,048 cells with 20,480 devotees. A community with ten cells, consisting of 100 devotees altogether, can become 10,240 cells in ten years—with a total of 102,400 devotees! If the cells can replicate twice a year instead of once, the numbers of devotees could reach into the millions.

Several unique advantages of Nama Hatta preaching for ISKCON were brilliantly described by Kaunteya dasa of ISKCON Zagreb (Crotia) in the June 1996 issue of Jayapataka Maharaja's *Congregational Preaching Journal.* He explains how ISKCON temples can take great advantage of this system. Here's an excerpt:

Efficient in Training

Temples don't have enough manpower to personally train each devotee of the congregation. Therefore, the congregation often remains undeveloped. The Nama Hatta cell group focuses on training: a "devotee sponsor" is assigned to every new member for personal supervision and guidance. The new member is given homework—reading passages from scriptures on philosophy and conduct. His understanding is regularly tested in the weekly discussions. A special emphasis is put on learning how to preach by going out with more expert devotees.

Focuses on the Individual

Someone visiting a big temple may just get lost in the crowd, without getting the personal care needed. Temple devotees often don't have the time to speak with guests or to engage them. In the Nama Hatta cell groups, the focus is on the individual; thus everyone is taken care of. The progress of every member is closely monitored, and in case of difficulty the leaders take immediate steps to offer assistance.

Effective in Engaging People

Who could coordinate, directly from the temple, the individual service of hundreds and thousands of congregational devotees? How many people can a few temple devotees effectively engage and coordinate? To organize the congregation in cell groups is the best way to effectively engage everyone in devotional service.

Economical

To open and run a temple requires lots of money. If we calculate how much we spend for each person we engage in practicing Krishna consciousness, we'll find that one devotee is worth a lot of money, in terms of what is spent just to bring the message to him or her. To start and operate a cell group costs practically nothing; the cell devotees already take care of themselves. They don't cost the temple anything except a little supervision. Cell groups are self-sufficient and low-budget. They give very big preaching results for very small investments.

Upward Mobility

In the temples, the positions of responsibility are already taken, and it is often difficult for qualified congregational devotees to develop and exhibit their full potential. The Nama Hatta Cell Program gives ample opportunity to expand one's service; cells multiply very fast, and more and more leaders are needed at every level of the structure. A qualified preacher who is successfully managing many cells may become a temple president in the future.

Fosters Good Relations

Have you ever heard of an ISKCON temple under financial strain? The congregation often feels burdened by the often-insistent collection schemes, but when the temple organizes cell groups, the devotees of the congregation appreciate that the temple is taking care of them. The congregational devotees don't feel any more as if they were only financial contributors. This generates a feeling of gratitude and an atmosphere of cooperation.

Removes "Us and Them" Feelings

Discrimination between temple devotees and devotees of the congregation evaporates quickly, because the members of the cells are obviously advancing and preaching. Terms such as "part-time devotee" or "friend of Krishna" soon disappear from the vocabulary.

Creates Sense of Belonging

The essence of community is a sense of belonging. There are primary and secondary affiliations. Secondary refers to groupings that are formal, utilitarian, and impersonal, such as school classes, business firms, labor unions, etc. Primary groups are small, intimate, and informal, such as one's family. Primary affiliations are usually more important to a person than his secondary associations. The cell is a primary affiliation. The powerful camaraderie created among the members of a cell group cannot take place when people only assemble in large groups.

Changes Values

The small group setting promotes personal value changes. Regular personal contact with sincere devotees inspires people to change personal standards and accept Krishna consciousness.

People may hear in a lecture in the temple that they should do this and that, but many may think, "Well, that's okay, but it doesn't really apply to me." Dealing with people personally, on a one-to-one basis, has a much bigger impact.

Two new cell members, for instance, may talk together: "I am smoking twenty cigarettes a day," one says, "how can I be a devotee?" "I used to smoke forty," the other says. "I am still smoking five, but I am chanting four rounds and trying to give it up. It is a gradual process; we should keep trying."

Not Limited by the Size of the Building

Only a limited number of people can fit in a temple. When the maximum capacity is reached, where do you put the people? A temple in a city of one million may have space for, say, one thousand people. What about the rest? Cell groups meet in private homes, and when they reach fifteen members, they multiply. Thus, the congregation can expand without being conditioned by the size of the building.

Avoids Culture Shock

In non-Hindu areas, sometimes new visitors feel uneasy and out of place in the totally new atmosphere of a temple. In attending home programs, they feel more comfortable and less intimidated. It is also easier to invite someone to an informal home meeting. Many people hesitate to go to a Hare Krishna temple but can easily agree to go to someone's home.

Highly Accessible

In big cities, to go to the temple often takes a long trip if there is a temple in that area. Nama Hatta cell groups can be started in every area and thus become easy to reach. It is closer for the congregational members to go to the cell meetings and easier for the preachers of the cell to meet with the people they are cultivating. This creates a wide area coverage; Krishna conscious association becomes available "next door."

Self-Perpetuating

Growth and multiplication are built-in features of the Nama Hatta Cell Program. Expansion is such an integral part of the whole method that those cell groups that do not grow are sometimes dissolved by spiritual authorities.

Deep Penetration

Nama Hatta cell groups penetrate deeply into the structures of the city. They operate on the cutting edge of the world, in touch with all ethnic, social, and economic communities. Cell members live and operate in all spheres of society. The preachers from the cells can reach people in a more informal way than in traditional preaching and often have easy access to important people who are difficult for temple devotees to reach.

Versatile

Nama Hatta cell groups can be geared to cater to people with different natures and interests—children, teenagers, professionals, etc.—who otherwise find it difficult to get involved in the existing temple programs.

CHAPTER 9—1997

Players on the Field

The Second World Conference for the Synthesis of Science and Religion, headed by Svarupa Damodara Goswami, took place in Calcutta in January of 1997. Also, ISKCON devotees opened a full-service hospital near an ISKCON temple just outside of Mumbai. Treatment methods include allopathy, Ayurveda, homeopathy,

April 7, 1997—Durban, South Africa: South African President Dr. Nelson Mandela and Kwa Zulu-Natal Premier Dr. Ben Ngubune stand on stage with ISKCON devotees at the Hare Krishna Food For Life Children's Rainbow Festival at Durban's Kings Park stadium. Over 60,000 schoolchildren born of African, Indian, Dutch, and British families perform and attend. Hare Krishna devotees provide *prasadam,* or spiritualized food, for everyone. Dr. Mandela, who addresses the crowd, calls the occasion "the happiest moment of my life." Event organizer Kapiladeva dasa, not pictured here, reiterates on stage that the Hare Krishna goal is to make Durban a "hunger-free zone."

herbal, naturopathy, and acupuncture. One of the year's biggest events happened in May when South African president Nelson Mandela danced on stage at ISKCON's Children of the Rainbow Festival, organized by Kapiladeva dasa and Indradyumna Swami, in Durban's Kings Park Stadium. The president, addressing the 40,000-plus crowd and the media, praised ISKCON. In September, the Indian government issued a five-rupee postage stamp with an image of Srila Prabhupada, made from a painting by US-born Puskara dasa. Russia passed a new law that could severely restrict religious practices of new or newly-arrived religions. In November, devotees entertained hundreds with a choreographed *kirtana* at the Washington, D.C., National Cathedral's annual interfaith concert. Arsonists burned a barn at the ISKCON New Talavan (Louisiana) rural community; neighbors helped raise funds and donated hay.

EUTHANASIA AND BEYOND

Disgusted with the never-ending string of news stories about "mercy killing" and courts not prosecuting doctors and survivors, I decided to write this editorial for *Hare Krishna World.* It has become almost a human right to take one's life, and doctors' assistance has become part of that "right." This essay, also published in *Back to Godhead* magazine, argues against this trend. The basic justification for euthanasia and doctor-assisted suicide is mitigation of pain and suffering. The following perspective posits that such killing only brings increased pain and suffering, as the law of karma takes its toll on those who transgress it.

Hare Krishna World, January/February 1997

Supporters of assisted suicide would have us believe that artificially determining one's death is a right rather than a criminal act. As euthanasia has been elevated to the status of an ethical issue, traditional concepts of suicide and homicide have become blurred by phrases like "doctor-assisted suicide" and "mercy killing."

In January, contending forces pushed the issue all the way to the US Supreme Court, where lawyers argued the legality of euthanasia. A decision is expected in June or July.

Australia's Northern Territory, one of the largest and most independently-minded states "Down Under," legalized voluntary euthanasia last July.

Advocates of doctor-assisted suicide say its purpose is to end unremitting and excruciating pain often associated with diseases like terminal cancer.

But does doctor-assisted suicide really stop pain? According to Vedic wisdom, the answer is no. Suicide does not stop pain at all, but rather prolongs and even increases it. From the *Vedas* we learn that the eternal soul, or *atma,* lives on after death. "For the soul," the *Bhagavad-gita* informs us, "there is neither birth nor death." The soul reincarnates, or transmigrates from one body to another, at the time of death.

The *Vedas* also inform us about the law of karma, a higher-order system that prohibits the killing of living beings, including oneself. Civil law throughout the world has generally prohibited murder and suicide.

According to the law of karma, the soul is put into the human body to reform and ultimately attain liberation, or a spiritual body free from birth and death. The soul's term in the human form is a type of captivity. The length of a soul's stay in a particular body, and the happiness and suffering it gets while residing there, are determined by its previous activities. To kill oneself or someone else and thus interrupt the soul's prescribed period of embodiment is against natural laws, or God's law, and generates further reactions or penalties.

By karmic law, one who commits suicide becomes a ghost. A ghostly or astral "body" is composed of mind, intelligence, and false ego. The soul living in such a subtle body keeps its personality, physical desires such as thirst, hunger, and sex drive, and desires for human relationships. Because of the soul's disembodied state, however, it cannot satisfy these desires. The astral body can travel rapidly, far and wide. Ghosts routinely wander for years, their natural desires raging and unfulfilled. In an effort to fulfill their desires, ghosts sometimes haunt or "possess" another person's body.

So while suicide may apparently give relief from physical or mental suffering that may have lasted for days, months, or years, a lifetime of unabated misery is destined to follow.

Involuntary euthanasia, or doctor-assisted killing without the patient's consent, also transgresses universal law. Physicians who commit such acts are unnaturally ending the soul's prescribed term in a particular body. According to karma, the lives of such doctors will be cut short in their next birth, often by acts of violence. In the Netherlands, even though euthanasia and doctor-assisted suicide are formally illegal, the courts have been allowing many exceptions to the law, and every year there are one thousand documented cases where doctors cause or hasten death without the patient's request. Almost routinely, such violations go unpunished. Unlike secular law, however, karma is infallible and inescapable.

Karmic considerations aside, what may be even more surprising is that most of those pushing to legalize euthanasia are not doing so to relieve unremitting and excruciating pain. Studies in the US and the Netherlands show that pain is not the only motivating factor among patients requesting euthanasia. The most comprehensive study of the Dutch experience with euthanasia is the 1991 Remilink Report, which showed that "pain was a factor motivating requests for euthanasia in less than half of all cases. More importantly, pain was the sole motivating factor in just 5% of euthanasia cases." A study of physicians who are caring for nursing-home patients in the Netherlands found that pain was the main rationale in only 11% of euthanasia requests.

In the US, a Washington State study of physicians who performed euthanasia or assisted suicide found that pain figured in only 35% of the requests. According to Harvard Medical School Professor Dr. Ezekial J. Emanuel, euthanasia is "a way of avoiding the complex and arduous efforts required of doctors and other health-care providers to ensure that dying patients receive humane, dignified care."

To legalize euthanasia would be tragic. The main reasons for which people want euthanasia—depression, isolation, psychological maladjustment, and lack of care—reveal a pervasive spiritual vacuum. In an increasingly secular society, God has been consigned to a minor role. Godlessness has bred callousness and a lack of genuine care for the dying by friends, relatives, and doctors. As the world becomes more materialistic and divorced from spiritual principles, the laws of God and the inextricably related elements of gratitude, tolerance, self-control, peacefulness, family unity, and human kindness retreat further and further into the background.

The science of Krishna consciousness, which includes knowledge of the soul and karma, needs to be pervasively and systematically taught throughout the world. Only such education can rejuvenate a desacrilized society and return us to our normal, natural position of love, with an understanding of who we really are and where we are going.

Whatever the US Supreme Court, the Australian Parliament, or other government bodies decide, involuntary euthanasia and doctor-assisted suicide are likely to proliferate. Without understanding the nature of the self and its movements through time and space, more people will blindly try to reduce suffering by acting in ways that will only serve to prolong and increase it.

RELIGIOUS INTOLERANCE IS EVERYONE'S PROBLEM

"What is your attitude toward other religions?" a questioner at a public festival asked one of ISKCON's lecturing leaders. "We have an equal attitude toward all faiths. We think they're all inferior," came the joking reply. The speaker went on to explain the nonsectarian nature of Krishna consciousness. But there is a ring of truth in the first statement by the ISKCON Swami. This editorial takes a hard look at ISKCON members' attitudes toward other faiths. It's easy for majority religions to label ISKCON a "cult," claiming that its members think they are superior, recruit ruthlessly, think they are above the law of the land, and refuse to enter into dialogue with host religions. The unfortunate truth is that some ISKCON members and groups were displaying these very symptoms. When this article was written, the European Parliament, probably influenced by majority denominations, was making resolutions against "destructive cults." In more than one country, they included the Hare Krishna movement in the "destructive" category. This editorial is an appeal to devotees to maintain an open attitude toward other faiths and to discuss similarities without diluting or compromising the philosophy of Krishna consciousness.

***Hare Krishna World,* May/June 1997**

Despite the extinction of Soviet communism and efforts to establish the "global village," religious intolerance is on the rise, according to the United Nations' latest report on the topic.

The European Parliament, which issues a common European passport, promises a single currency for member states, and predicts massive trade reforms, has just passed a resolution about "new religions."

These violations, the resolution says, are "all the more serious" as they "sometimes involve minors." The document calls on member states to "take whatever action is needed to combat violations of fundamental rights perpetrated by certain sects. The legal basis and grounds therefore exist for them (sects) to be prohibited." Strong stuff that governments are considering prohibiting religion, something one would expect only of atheistic totalitarian regimes.

But fundamentalism and fanaticism are not only in the province of religions that rule. Violence, human rights abuses, "us and them consciousness," and claims of superiority can be as prevalent within minority or "hosted" religions as they are in "host" religious communities. Interestingly, the Euro-Parliament outlines many problems that ISKCON itself is grappling with. And, let's face it, some sects can be downright dangerous.

The United Nations report speaks of hostility suffered by sects because of "major religions'" tendency "to oppose anything unorthodox." At the same time, however, it mentions how "new religions" or "sects" are causing problems and recommends that they moderate their stance in relation to the "longer-established religions."

From one perspective, the majority religions hold the power in this game. Nonetheless, the smaller, lesser known, new-on-the-scene religious organizations can also be their own worst enemies.

Sects who claim superiority, recruit ruthlessly, think themselves above the law of the land, and refuse to talk with host religions are easy targets for right-wing protectors of established faiths.

Although Srila Prabhupada repeatedly instructed his disciples to be ideal citizens, mistakes have been made, and ISKCON has had its humbling experiences. Partly as a result of a civil lawsuit in which a US jury fined ISKCON for sheltering a female runaway teenager, the movement established a policy requiring minors to provide written parental consent before allowing them to live in temples. Interfering between a child and his or her parents, no matter how justified it may seem at the time, is unacceptable. (ISKCON later settled out of court for considerably less than the jury award.)

Owing to this and other hard lessons, ISKCON has begun to develop sound social policy that is faithful to Srila Prabhupada's teachings. Policies regarding property, marriage, children, education, careers, other religions, the environment, and a variety of other concerns are being formulated one after the other as our Society comes of age.

Religious bias looks for extremism. It's a way that people react to the new and misunderstood. Therefore, victimization by intolerant majorities can be significantly reduced by astute social policy, interfaith dialogue, historical presentation, and well-thought-out responses to controversy.

Why should our movement formulate social policies when systems like *varnashrama* (the Vedic social system defining spiritual orders and occupational duties) are already known and recommended? This ideal system seems far removed from our present social reality. We have to make strides to align our society with the system ordained by Lord Krishna Himself in *Bhagavad-gita.* We must also peacefully coexist with our host societies while not compromising our principles—not an easy task.

How would Srila Prabhupada react to our efforts?

In a *Sri Caitanya-caritamrta* purport (Madhya-lila 7:29), he writes, "There are many instances of devotional service rendered by previous *acharyas* (spiritual preceptors) who did not care about social behavior when intensely absorbed in love for Krishna. Unfortunately, as long as we are within this material world, we must observe social customs to avoid criticism by the general populace. This is Sri Chaitanya Mahaprabhu's desire."

Regarding the end justifying the means, Srila Prabhupada wrote in a letter to Rupanuga, dated January 9, 1975: "Regarding the controversy about book distribution techniques, you are right. Our occupation must be honest. Everyone should adore our members as honest. If we do something which is deteriorating to the popular sentiments of the public in favor of our movement, that is not good. Somehow or other we should not become unpopular in the public eye. These dishonest methods must be stopped. It is hampering our reputation all over the world. Money collected for feeding people in India should be collected under the name ISKCON Food Relief."

These, among many of Srila Prabhupada's teachings, are taken as *shastras* (authorized injunctions) to help ISKCON not only survive but to teach others while minimizing resistance.

The people of the world are in dire need of spiritual knowledge about how to solve their problems. Coming through the chain of spiritual masters from God Himself, ISKCON has something to offer to society at large, not only philosophically and theologically but also socially and behaviorally. The Krishna consciousness movement can provide solutions regarding economics, the environment, family, drug abuse, sexual promiscuity, and education. We must master these solutions within our own Society, and we must do the needful to help others—even our so-called detractors—to be receptive to this information. The world should not be deprived of this knowledge due to miscommunication or because devotees are not practicing Godly ways themselves. The followers of Srila Prabhupada must become expert at communicating this knowledge, as well as exemplifying it, for the benefit of all people.

It is essential to contribute to the world's theological body of knowledge through meaningful and informed interfaith dialogue; to talk with avowed detractors, to formulate policies about recruiting, possessions, careers, education, marriage, and children, and to become known as an educational institution.

According to *Srimad-Bhagavatam,* religiosity, personified by Dharma, the bull, is standing on one last leg. This leg stands for truth and is wobbling precariously.

ISKCON is realizing that one of the things that distinguishes us as a religion instead of a sect or cult is to be more forthcoming about internal affairs, to network appropriately, and to become part of the communities we live in, insulating, rather than isolating, devotees. This puts us in a strong position to present Lord Krishna's instructions.

ISKCON VIS-À-VIS SECULARISM: LONG JOURNEYS BEGIN WITH THE FIRST STEP

Secularism (godlessness) has come to rule US society in a way that the nation's founding fathers would never have approved. A primary purpose of the First Amendment was to protect religion from too much government intervention. In his book *The Culture of Disbelief,* Steven Carter lists many US court decisions that overtly or covertly deny freedom of worship. The Reverend Martin Luther King was the last spiritual leader to be a national hero and the only religious figure for whom the US has declared a national holiday. Because King fought for the rights of Afro-Americans, he was deified in the US, but his religiousness was minimized. Srila Prabhupada could see through pronouncements about the separation of Church and State in the US It was clear to him that in the name of separation or single-faith domination, America had become godless. And with godlessness inexorably comes hedonism—a proliferation of crime, violence, drug abuse, immorality, and degeneracy. This editorial appreciates Srila Prabhupada's unflagging determination to reverse this unfortunate trend.

***Hare Krishna World*, July/August 1997**

In the early 1960s, the phrase "under God" began to disappear from some US schoolchildren's daily mandated group recitation of the Pledge of Allegiance to their nation's flag. Strangely, parents and children alike, for the most part, quietly accepted this act of treason against the Almighty.

From the very start, the United States has prided itself in championing "freedom of religion." That supposedly translates into the right to choose one's own faith, in lieu of forced acceptance of a state religion. "Separation of church and state" in the USA has achieved almost sacred status. But should this exclude proclaiming God as the Father of a nation? We think not.

While promoting denominational diversity, secularism and religious bigotry have flourished in America. Religious principles have been set aside, forgotten, and pushed into the province of the feeble-minded and superstitious.

In his book *The Naked Public Square,* Reverend Richard John Neuhaus argues that in the free speech arena, religion has become a societal taboo, even though the US Constitution ostensibly vouchsafes freedom of religious speech.

Powerful economic forces in the early part of the century have aided the removal of God from American intellectual society. For example, the Rockefeller Foundation abundantly funded research into the Big Bang theory. This concept of universal origins effectively elbows God into the outer darkness. According to the *Forbidden Archeology* authors, Drutakarma dasa and Sadaputa dasa, the stated goal of the Rockefeller Foundation "reflected the implicit goal of big science—control, by scientists, of human behavior." Since then, many influential figures have voiced their fears that a religious public will be a fanatical, irrational, unpredictable, uncontrollable, and dangerous element in society.

In 1965, Srila Prabhupada walked into one of the most secular citadels on earth, the United States of America. He emphasized and reemphasized that in order to change American society, the International Society for Krishna Consciousness (ISKCON) would have to successfully challenge and alter fundamental ideologies. He persistently targeted secular-minded philosophers, theologians, scientists, historians, psychologists, religious leaders, and sociologists.

Recent decrees enacted by the European Union and Russia even further minimize God. These laws attempt to put "undesirable" or "strange" religious organizations under government control. They covertly give the majority or ruling churches dominion over denominations.

Srila Prabhupada's and ISKCON's challenge has always been to bring God back into public life. "I have come to teach you what you all have forgotten," he announced to a crowd of news reporters on his first visit to London in 1969, "and that is God!" Perhaps for the first time, an Indian "beggar" was throwing down the gauntlet before the all-powerful West.

And he often cited one of the great tragedies of our time—the partially successful attempt of Indian politicians to make their own country godless. British-educated Jawaharial Nehru, one of independent India's early leading statesmen, initiated a trend favoring modern materialistic technology over India's timeless culture and commitment to Vedic philosophy. The belief that science, technology, and material progress will ultimately solve all of India's problems has increased over the years. Srila Prabhupada found this trend of Indians renouncing their own culture and embracing a culture that pursues only material enjoyment to be misguided.

However, the Hare Krishna movement continues to make progress within an increasingly secular world. For its challenges, for exposing the folly of wanton materialism, and for reminding people about the miseries they bring upon themselves, ISKCON may not enjoy mass popularity. Nonetheless, its members remember Srila Prabhupada's uncompromising drive to respiritualize human society and his great happiness at seeing even incremental progress.

For each soul who changes his or her concept of enjoyment from material to spiritual, a great internal celebration takes place. A still higher victory is changing the quality of life of a whole population through spiritual understanding. It is possible, by the mercy of Lord Chaitanya and the purity and commitment of His followers, to make Srila Prabhupada's vision for such a change become a reality.

May, 1992—Calcutta, India: Mother Teresa shows surprise and gratitude for the gift of a cake and promises local membership director Achyuta dasa and his wife, Madha-devi dasi, that she will save the garland for Mother Mary in Calcutta. The garland is from the temple deity figure of ISKCON's founder-*acharya,* His Divine Grace A.C. Bhaktivedanta Swami.

LADY DIANA AND MOTHER TERESA: LOST OR LIBERATED?

Eleven months after the death of Princess Diana at age 36, the Church of England's Bishop of York warned, "We should be careful that she is not worshiped." But the tidal wave of populist sentiment could hardly be affected, especially by a clergyman whose denomination will have lost twenty-five percent of its members by the year 2000. A very different kind of soul, Mother Teresa (who died a week after Diana after living for 87 years), was generally regarded as a modern-day saint. People even from the ranks of the rich and famous and from all parts of the world flew to Calcutta to do volunteer work at her hospital and to attend her funeral. Princess Diana and Mother Teresa were arguably the two most loved women in the world. This HKW editorial speaks about the association these two highly public figures had with devotees. One can deplore an outbreak of over-emotionalism over their deaths—what one sociologist called "mourning sickness"—but in praying for a better future for these two departed spirits, we can mitigate the sorrow felt by millions.

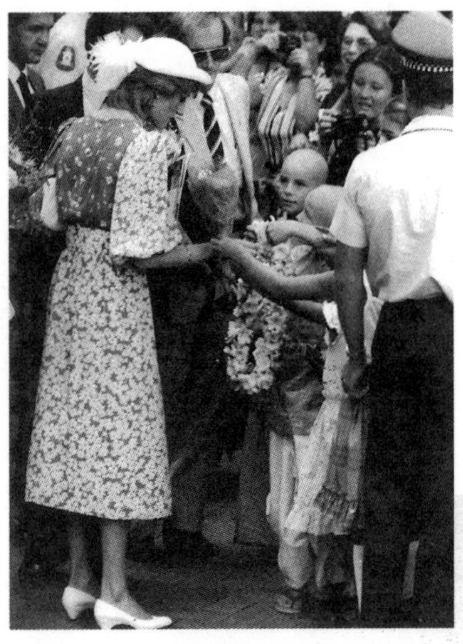

April 4, 1983—Australia: On her visit to Australia, Princess Diana defies police barriers to accept a garland from Dhanvantari, as young Sri Prahlada dasa looks on.

***Hare Krishna World,* September/October 1997**

According to the philosophy of transmigration, the souls of Diana, Princess of Wales, and Mother Teresa have probably arrived at their new destinations by now. But where are they, and what kind of births are they about to take? And why should we care? Do we care as much about the other thousands of people who die every day?

Diana campaigned against Bosnian land mines, AIDS, and homelessness. She planned to send her children to work for a time in Mother Teresa's Calcutta mission. Although her personal behavior caused some to see her more as a sensualist than a noblewoman, this didn't detract from her overwhelming popularity.

Most people probably thought of Mother Teresa as a modern-day saint, but some in India understandably found it deplorable that she converted many Hindus to beef-eaters.

Interestingly, Diana, to whom most "commoners" could not

get close enough to talk, had some brief association with a devotee in Brisbane, Australia, circa 1981.

Sri Prahlad, then an eight-year-old, shaven-headed gurukula student, recalls waiting along a procession route for hours with other *gurukula* schoolchildren. They had with them gifts for Princess Diana and Prince Charles. Their presentation included Radharani's huge garland from the New Govardhana school Deity, some books for newly-born Prince William, and a bouquet.

Sri Prahlad: "I don't know how Pariksit (the headmaster) ever thought we would meet them. There were thousands of police on foot and overhead in helicopters. Suddenly, the Princess was there. Pariksit pushed Tulasi forward with the bouquet, and a policeman immediately and violently pushed her back. The Princess saw it. Although she was all the way on the other side of the street, she made a beeline towards us. Tulasi gave her the bouquet, and then the Princess bent over with her head down to receive Radharani's garland.

"But Danvantari, who was holding the garland, wouldn't give it to the princess. All morning Pariksit had told him to give the garland to Prince Charles, who was still on the other side of the street. The Princess repeated several times, "Put it over my hat." Finally Danvantari put it on her. Then I gave the Princess the books and we all said Hare Krishna. She smiled, thanked us, and went on her way. The next day a photo of me and the Princess appeared and the caption said, 'Princess Stops to Talk with Krishna Children.'"

Mr. Gulu Lalvani was reported by the *London Express* in September as saying that Diana "shared his Hindu belief in reincarnation."

Mother Teresa's association with ISKCON devotees includes encounters with Bhakti Charu Swami, Nrsimhananda dasa (of ITV), Adridharana dasa (ISKCON Calcutta temple president), Jalakara dasa, and Hari-dhama dasa.

On a flight from Calcutta to Mumbai, Nrsimhananda found Mother Teresa sitting directly behind him and Bhakti Charu Swami.

It was springtime, 1996, and, as Nrsimhananda spoke with the nun, she remembered meeting with him only two weeks before. He gave her an *ISKCON World Review* (now *Hare Krishna World*).

Nrsimhananda: "She took the time to read about devotees, and there was no mistaking that I was a Hare Krishna devotee from the get-go. After a few minutes her aide tapped me on the shoulder."

Mother Teresa had questions, and she spoke about the "good work" that ISKCON was doing around the world. They talked for some time; then Bhakti Charu Maharaja reminded Nrsimhananda that Mother Teresa's agenda was quite different, and that there were philosophical differences between her and ISKCON.

Nrisimhananda: "He was right. Yet, I could not deny the experience of connecting spiritually with this dedicated soul. We did have in common our desire to serve God, whether we were in the mode of goodness, passion, or ignorance. I love my own carnivorous mother dearly. What can be done? We live in a contradictory world. Mother Teresa was another vivid example of the incomprehensible machinations of karma."

Hari-dhama, who met Mother Teresa in January 1996, in Calcutta, remembers: "I told her about Srila Prabhupada (ISKCON's founder). She had heard of him and expressed her admiration for the courage he showed when crossing the ocean to teach those lost and confused children of America about the ancient wisdom of India."

According to *Srimad-Bhagavatam,* Sri Havir says to King Nimi that a devotee, or *madhya-lilama adhikari,* is generally supposed to regard people as innocent and in need of association (11.2.45). Both Mother Teresa and Lady Diana can fit this category. Also, because both had an urge to see improvement in the material quality of life, there was an apparent mix of the mode of goodness in their materialism. Further, their association with Krishna's devotees, albeit rather brief, augers well for their future.

In a lecture in Honolulu on February 5, 1975, Srila Prabhupada said about distributing his books, "If he reads one line, his life will be successful. This is such literature. Somehow or other, small book or big book, if it is given to somebody, he'll read someday."

We read in *Sri Caitanya-caritamrta* how even brief association with Vaishnava devotees of Krishna brings "all success" and attainment beyond the "heavenly planets," "liberation," or "worldly benedictions like material prosperity" (Madhya-lila 22.54-55). Srila Prabhupada once even went so far as to agree that the potency of one bite of *prasadam* (food offered to God) could assure a human birth (*Bhagavad-gita* 19.6 lecture, February, 27 1975). That exchange, which took place at the end of his lecture, also includes this statement: "You can see practically, all of you, what you were and what you are now."

Although one can take birth as a dog in one's next life (Srila Prabhupada quoted an astrologer's conclusion that a prominent Indian politician was reborn as a "dog in Sweden"), even a dog can attain liberation, as was the case with one who got Lord Chaitanya's benediction through devotees like Sivananda Sena (*Caitanya-caritamrta,* Antya-lila, Chapter l).

"A Vaishnava is described as *paradukha-dukhi* because, although he is never distressed in any condition of life, he is distressed to see others in a distressed condition." (*Srimad-Bhagavatam* 4.6.47 purport).

It is the duty, then, of Hare Krishna followers to not only hope but also pray for better destinations for the souls of Princess Diana Spencer, Mother Teresa, and others.

CAN MORALITY BE ABSOLUTE?

In this age of duality and disquietude, morality has become relative. Values, judgments, and authorities are not in vogue. Even convicted criminals seem to have rights to judge society and its laws. What is right for one person is wrong for another. It is chic to defy authority, discredit accountability, and oppose teachers. *Bhagavad-gita,* however, presents an absolute morality grounded in spiritual understanding. This spiritual and foundational principle is that one should "give up all other duties and surrender unto the lotus feet of Krishna" (18.66). Thus the *Gita* establishes that God in His personal form is the ultimate law. The oft-quoted *Srimad-Bhagavatam* maxim, *dharma tu saksad bhagavat-pranitam* (6.3.19), asserts that ultimate morality ("real religious principles") is enacted by the Supreme Personality of Godhead. This absolute nature of morality is impossible to fully grasp without understanding its spiritual basis. Morality of the material world, this HKW editorial advocates, can and must be linked to the complete morality of the Personality of Godhead. Only then can morality be absolute.

***Hare Krishna World,* November/December 1997**

The revered Vedic text *Sri Isopanisad* indirectly calls almost everyone a thief, because we declare complete ownership over all we possess instead of giving God that prerogative. We don't recognize Him as the ultimate owner of everything. But does this mean that we have no propriety whatever, even over our own bank accounts, families, and means of support? Establishing what is moral, even when God is in the picture, is not a simple matter.

Living in a secular world, we find that morality is constantly marginalized. When questions of ethics and values arise, it is the fashion to either avoid them or to create new ones and live by them. The US, for example, is sharply divided over the abortion issue. Even the infamous ritual murderer, Charles Manson, now serving a life sentence in prison, believes that he was justified in his acts because he considers society itself to be immoral.

Some are satisfied with relativistic morality, while others feel they are grappling with the "problem of morality." Becoming more apparent is the inability to pass on relative morality to future generations. Many are concerned that their own children, at tender ages, are taking shelter of drugs, violence, sex, and self-abuse.

Interest groups in the US are crying out for the teaching of "values," for "standards" in schools, and for "decency" in television. Many Catholic schools in the US have met with success in advertising "schools with values," even attracting many non-Catholic students.

Certain people find it convenient to relativize morality within a philosophy of "spiritual" impersonalism. But such concepts tend to give credence to the "everything is one" theory in which one may love or kill without benefit or consequence because there is no ultimate person to whom we must account.

Without a systematic conception of Krishna or God consciousness, morality is paradoxical and elusive. We question what is right in a secular society whose basic purpose is to improve entertainment, intoxication, gross national product, personal wealth, education, beauty, and other hallmarks of material progress.

Morality can be a perplexing issue. We discover that what is right for one often encroaches on someone else and thereby turns into immorality in the mind of another. There is constant tension between individuals, communities, and nations. Violence is all too commonly based on doing what is seemingly the "right thing."

Invoking the higher order laws of the universe such as those found in the *Manu Samhita* and other Vedic books, Lord Krishna sets absolute standards for morality. Throughout Vedic writings, one finds a wealth of insights into right and wrong. In fact, most civil law is based on these edicts, which prescribe punishments for such things as pillage, murder, adultery, embezzlement, and violence.

The primary book of Krishna consciousness, *Bhagavad-gita* (Song of God), exercises some of the most difficult of all questions of right and wrong. On the battlefield, Arjuna finds himself opposite his own relatives and teachers. Ultimately, on learning that the war and its outcome are predestined and that he will not fulfill his Godly obligation by inaction, and that good will triumph over tyranny, Arjuna fights. In the end, everyone benefits. In the dialogue of *Bhagavad-gita,* Lord Krishna establishes that the ultimate morality is to follow His direction, but only after careful questioning and mature understanding.

Generally, Lord Krishna follows and teaches the principles of *ahimsa,* or nonviolence, but He sanctions violence when one's life or family are threatened, when one is attacked with deadly weapons, or when one's possessions or properties are stolen. There must be exceptions to *ahimsa* in the material world. For civil safety, it is necessary to maintain police or other armed forces.

According to the Vedic authorities, Krishna is the Supreme Lord, the cause and maintainer of all creation. Although the context of *Bhagavad-gita* may be considered highly exceptional and extreme, it establishes Lord Krishna's position as the ultimate judge of right and wrong. This book stands as the greatest treatise on morality known to the world.

But where does that leave us—souls endeavoring to make ends meet in the material world, often struggling with questions of right and wrong? Srila Prabhupada (the founder-*acharya* of the International Society for Krishna Consciousness and author of *Bhagavad-gita As It Is*) has recommended that his followers be adored as honest. When asked on a TV interview in Gainesville, Florida (June 27, 1971), "How would I recognize a true follower of the Krishna consciousness movement by his behavior?" Srila Prabhupada answered: "He will be a perfect gentleman. That's all. You cannot find any fault in him."

In his rendering of *Sri Caitanya-caritamrta,* Madhya-lila (7.29), Srila Prabhupada makes this comment in his purport: "There are many instances of devotional service rendered by previous *acharyas* who did not care about social behavior when intensely absorbed in love for Krishna. Unfortunately, as long as we are within this material world, we must observe social customs to avoid criticism by the general populace. This is Sri Chaitanya Mahaprabhu's desire."

Here Srila Prabhupada makes a clear distinction between past and present by referring to the "previous *acharyas.*" In other words, one does not introduce Krishna consciousness in the same way at different times. *Bhagavad-gita* was spoken 5,000 years ago, and most of our previous *acharyas* lived and taught in times, places, and circumstances radically removed from our own.

We can see throughout the life of Srila Prabhupada, our present *acharya,* that abiding by social conventions, including financial practices, organization, use of technology, neatness in personal appearance, use of medicine, excellence in book printing, and following civil law codes, was central to his success and that of his movement.

Yet, through all of this, his spirituality, purity, and illuminating writings remained unaffected and uninterrupted. He led the way on all fronts, showing that Krishna consciousness answers all our uncertainties, including those about right and wrong.

And no one—as *Isopanisad* intimates—has to be a thief, even while living in this material world. One of the *Vedas'* most important teachings to us is to have complete faith in the present *acharya.* Srila Prabhupada is that present *acharya.* He propagated Krishna consciousness with many modern possessions and even concepts of possession, but was never attached to them. We aren't wrong for using them as long as we, like Srila Prabhupada, are detached from them and willing to engage them in devotional service to the Lord—the ultimate provider, proprietor, and judge.

DELIGHTING THE CONGREGATION

Glimpsing the future, I projected in this two-part ICB article that congregations would become the main support for ISKCON centers. Temples would have to gear up to sustaining and developing their primary source of income. Many ISKCON centers would see that the nonresident Indian (NRI) community makes up the majority of their congregations and often provides most of the center's income. Although NRI communities are small or nonexistent in most non-English-speaking countries, rules for delighting the congregation are universal. These standards include regular home visits, expert database management, engaging temple newsletters, great *prasadam,* super Sunday festivals (including meaningful and exciting engagement for children and teens), Vedic hospitality and general friendliness (everyone in the temple gets into it), excellent temple management and leadership, regular performance of Vedic ceremonies for Indian communities, and a clear and obvious commitment to serve.

***Hare Krishna World,* May/June 1997**

PART I: As more temples become dependent on their congregations, financially and otherwise, an emerging stability surfaces. To get a little support individually from a lot of people is equal to, if not greater than, getting a lot of financial support from just a few people. The "little support" includes contributions of money, time, and services, donations of goods such as *bhoga,* as well as people power and brain power (as in advisory committees). A truly healthy, congregationally-based institution will generate its basic subsistence from hundreds, or even thousands, of small monthly donations.

In this way, some temples have excelled. ISKCON of Bangalore, Chowpatty (in Mumbai), and Houston, Texas, are three noteworthy examples of temples that are doing well with their congregationally-based support. Within these three temples there is a strong drive, everywhere evident, to constantly serve and unify the congregation. Congregational members, including initiates together with noninitiates, serve on various boards and committees and are active at many levels. In these temples, one also finds formal and informal "support systems" for *brahmacaris, brahmacarinis, grihasthas,* students, businessmen, elderly members, women, children, and others.

ISKCON Bangalore is advanced in data-based management. Each day, its thousands-strong database generates birthday congratulations that are then mailed out by Bangalore devotees. Members of the Indian public, both inside and outside of India, enjoy contributing to their local temples on their birthdays.

Every time a donation is sent in by mail or a check is put into the hundi (temple donation box), the Bangalore temple sends out a handsome thank-you letter, signed by a principal temple devotee.

Temples advanced in congregational development are attentive to visitors. Any and all guests, even first-timers, are seen as potential members of the congregation. Therefore, permanent systems are in place for making them feel at home and wanted, giving them some *prasadam,* and obtaining their names and telephone numbers.

Temples that excel in congregational development have adequate facilities for members' temple needs. Such temples provide appropriate, clean, and welcoming space for ceremonial functions: grain, wedding, and hair-cutting ceremonies, and many other occasions. When temples manage these nicely, members become grateful, more attached to the devotees and the temple, more inclined to aspire for spiritual advancement (some for initiation), and more liberal in making financial contributions.

The vision of the *madhya-lilama adhikari—isvare tad-adhinesu balisesu dvisatsu ca, prema-maitri-krpopeksa yah karoti sa madhya-lila-mah* (*Srimad-Bhagavatam* 11.2.46)—is that he or she shows mercy to the innocent.

Enlightened temple dwellers see anyone who crosses the temple's threshold as a devotee, one who should be treated with the utmost of care and attention. Also, congregational members or first-time visitors who bring their children to the temple need good facilities for them, especially during Sunday festivals. Sunday schools and other recreational/educational activities are required for young children.

Another, and perhaps the most vital, aspect of congregational development involves regular visitations to congregational members' homes. Sometimes only two devotees are necessary. Preaching done in this way is the bread and butter of congregational development. During home programs, temple devotees engage their congregation in *kirtana, japa,* reading, service, and often Deity worship.

As important as home visits are the regular production and mailing out of a monthly temple newsletter to all congregational members. Each month this vitally important publication should feature a particular congregational family, include pictures, provide something for the children, list upcoming temple holy days, festivals, and other events, and be graphically eye-catching. It can also contain topical and intellectually stimulating articles.

Ideally, such a newsletter should be accompanied by ISKCON's global newspaper, *Hare Krishna World,* and its magazine, *Back to Godhead.* The newsletter should give readers an inside look at the temple; it should be fun to read, relevant, and newsy. The Chowpatty temple in Mumbai sends one out every week!

Most religious organizations depend on their congregation for support. ISKCON is inexorably moving in that direction. Therefore, it is important for us to sharpen our expertise in the area of congregational development. Bangalore, Houston, and Chowpatty are good models to follow. There is also much to learn from a few other ISKCON temples which excel in consistent congregational growth. There is also a global body of fundraising knowledge to which the organization known as ISKCON Foundation provides access.

Through implementation of a regular home visitation program, the distribution of an appropriate monthly newsletter, provision of adequate temple facilities for congregational functions, adoption of proper devotee attitudes and behavior, expert data-based management, consistency and efficiency in temple administration, and demonstration of a strong commitment to serve, temples and their growing numbers of devotees will benefit immensely. They will be able to procure their basic maintenance and solve the problems of finance, people power, and brain power. Moreover, gifts "in kind," as well as many other facilities and endowments, will be showered upon the temple.

PART II: In the last issue of *ISKCON Communications Briefings,* we learned about the importance of basing an ISKCON temple's maintenance on many small donations; the need for an expertly managed data base; reciprocation with members; home visits; the necessity of adequate temple facilities for members; and the importance of appropriate service attitudes. Here, in Part

II of "Delighting the Congregation," our presentation will be concluded and summarized.

Temple devotees should acquire birth dates of husbands and wives, children, their parents, and when appropriate, the passing dates of parents and grandparents. They should then enter this information—along with other pertinent facts gleaned from continuing visits—into a database.

Devotees might also acquire and enter as data information various types of service members would like to render. Additionally, congregational members' hobbies, vocations, and charitable interests may be input.

Throughout the world, many organizations other than ISKCON are vying for membership, loyalty, and contributions from the Indian public. In this sense, ISKCON is in competition. But more importantly, ISKCON has a way of giving back by delighting members with its unique excellence in the philosophy, vision, and practices of Srila Prabhupada.

What prevails over and above competition is our commitment to ISKCON's unique advantages: Vaishnava hospitality; the view that all innocent people should receive mercy and compassion, as well as care and attention; the world's best-tasting food in *prasadam*; regular home visits; a most ambitious and effective mission to change the quality of life on earth (Srila Prabhupada's mission); a comprehensive philosophy of God-consciousness; the most easily practiced and appropriate yoga and meditation systems for the age; and the happiest and most satisfying activity a human being can engage in—devotional service to Lord Krishna.

Therefore, ISKCON members should be confident that they can provide the greatest value to members. Topping the list is friendliness, the individual and ongoing care that only genuine, heartfelt Vaishnava hospitality can provide.

Our faith in that tradition, so painstakingly described by Srila Prabhupada and Krishna dasa Kaviraja in *Caitanya-caritamrta,* along with our ability to practice it enthusiastically, makes all the difference; hence, the "competition" can become irrelevant.

Any temple, and especially those located where there is a community of NRIs (non-resident Indians), can and should practice state-of-the-art congregational development.

Temples that want to excel in congregational development should have first-class systems in place for:

1. Ongoing daily home visits and information-gathering therein.

2. Consistent and expert database management, including regular mail-outs such as birthday acknowledgments, reminders, thank-you letters and, most importantly, a high-quality, monthly newsletter.

3. Regularly performed ceremonial functions such as weddings, hair-cuttings, and grain rituals.

4. Expertly greeting all new and regular congregational members when they visit the temple, as they often do, without prior notice.

5. Providing all visitors with, at the very least, friendliness, hospitality, and tasty *prasadam.*

6. Excellent Sunday festivals.

MANAGING CONFLICT

In this 1997 ICB article I floated the concept of "force-field" communications. This theory is based on the principle of "driving forces vs. restraining forces." The latter—be they ISKCON breakaways, non-Vaishnava organizations, or individuals—are defined as those who oppose ISKCON with destructive, as opposed to constructive, intentions. Almost all organizations, especially high-profile ones, face committed opposition which never goes away or disappears, just as all fire is covered with smoke and all endeavors are tainted with fault. Restraining forces are a bit like the hecklers and pickets one sees at rallies, or the ubiquitous mosquitoes that infest even the most sacred parts of the planet. Constant proactive precautions are taken to minimize the effects of restraining forces.

The art of leadership includes managing the forces that seek to hurt and destroy. In the essay, I analyze certain oppositional operating principles and tactics. I also explain how ISKCON has dealt with opponents in the past and how it sometimes deals with them in the present. Also included are some tips for devotee spokespersons in dealing with hostile media interviews. Enlightened and powerful internal organization—including reform as necessary—is often required to deal effectively with adversarial elements.

Hare Krishna World, May/June 1997

In the 1940s, an American sociologist posited what some communications specialists call the "force-field" theory. This perspective accents the fact that both "driving" and "restraining" forces are constantly at work in the course of advancing any idea, product, service, or philosophy. In other words, there is always opposition to

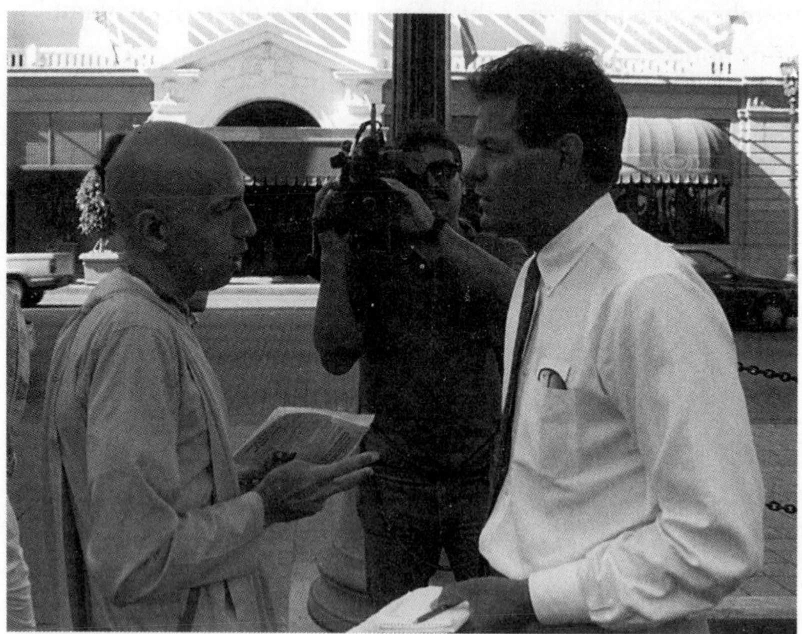

August, 1989—San Diego, USA: Mukunda Goswami, Director of ISKCON Communications, talks to a San Diego news reporter about the George v. ISKCON appeal. The case settled out of court in June of 1993.

every endeavor—like fire covered with smoke and endeavors by fault.

According to force-field philosophy, opposing forces like gravity and centrifugal force, action and reaction, positive and negative, Krishna and *maya* will eternally exist, and one can choose between them.

In the case of ISKCON, many opposing forces are at work, some powerful and some weak, some external and some internal. They tear at the fabric of the movement. Some are overtly hostile and others only subtly so.

To keep this discussion focused, we shall designate "opposing forces" as those whose primary aim is to harm Srila Prabhupada's movement or its reputation, even if they claim that their ultimate aim is reform. We are talking about truly destructive forces. We shall not discuss constructive criticism because, when considered properly, it is a beneficial, driving force for ISKCON.

ISKCON's restraining forces cannot be ignored, nor will they go away. Some might disappear, but others would soon fill the vacuum and might be even more malicious than their predecessors.

In July 1977, Srila Prabhupada predicted that, as our movement grew, its adversaries would increase: "They're feeling the weight of this Hare Krishna movement." Prabhupada, with his inimitable wisdom and far-sighted vision, was predicting that as ISKCON grew and penetrated, its detractors would also grow.

Opposition reached frightening proportions when in the early '80s, a US jury ordered ISKCON to pay $32 million to a young girl named Robin George, who claimed ISKCON devotees had brainwashed her. Fortunately, in the higher courts ISKCON won that issue and settled others for a far lesser amount, but the settlement costs and legal fees were substantial. ISKCON has to deal with those who challenge it.

Sometimes, internal conflicts are made public and used against ISKCON. Some of the Hare Krishna movement's principal antagonists thrive on making propaganda out of hearsay, as well as out of real incidents of internal misbehavior. Their operating principle is to "give the dog a bad name and hang it." Such distortion has no redeeming value; its aims are primarily destructive. Other hostile forces work more behind the scenes, attempting to influence governments to control, restrict, reduce, and in other ways impede the growth of ISKCON's missionary activities.

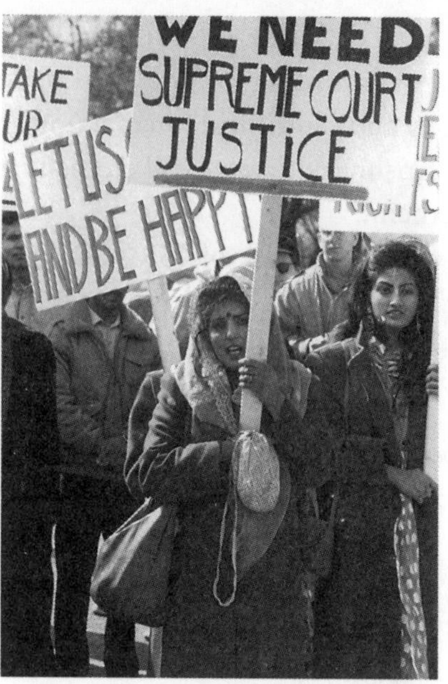

February 28, 1990—Washington, D.C., USA: When George v. ISKCON reaches the US Supreme Court, followers hit the streets of Washington. Karuna Sankhla (center) with elder daughter Vrinda (right) hold signs in front of the National Archives, home of the original US Constitution and the Bill of Rights.

Members of established religions sometimes covertly try to persuade governments, academics, and their own members that ISKCON is intrinsically evil. Sometimes this propaganda stems from our own lack of cooperation with them, and from not being forthcoming enough. We live in a world in which denominationalism long ago replaced genuine religious principles. Outside of India, members of major religions who cling persistently to sectarian ways see newly arrived religious orders like ISKCON as serious threats to their well-being.

To counteract its opponents, ISKCON has many courses from which to choose. It may ignore such attacks, which is, in less serious cases, often most effective (this is like ignoring a disobedient child who is seeking attention); it may belittle; it may counterattack with words; it may play legal hardball; it may implement discussion with detractors; or it may prepare its own members to develop a particular set of goals, strategies, and action plans to effectively deal with the forces of opposition. Any one or combination of these strategies can be effective.

Generally, in dealing with adversaries, ISKCON should seek the aid of communications specialists. Protecting our reputation is fundamental to advancing Krishna consciousness. With proper aid and assistance in place for managing conflict, ISKCON will continue to move forward, despite continued opposition from within and without.

For example, Srila Prabhupada said we would be victorious against accusations of "brainwashing," but that we would have to employ organization and intelligence. Sometimes opposition causes us to alter the way we operate, but this should never be done at the expense of compromising fundamental principles. For example, as a result of the Robin George case, ISKCON's Governing Body Commission implemented a policy whereby ISKCON must obtain written consent from parents of any minors proposing to live in an ISKCON temple.

Anti-sect proponents in Germany compelled ISKCON's leading German devotees to establish a formal position regarding members "surrendering" their possessions. In both cases, the written guidelines were not at odds with our philosophical principles, because they were carefully thought out and weighed against ISKCON's philosophy.

At times, ISKCON has filed lawsuits against attackers to protect itself, to punish the wrongdoers, to ward off future attacks, and to secure the advantages and protection provided by government law. In more cases than not, such lawsuits have been successful.

Currently, ISKCON's biggest external battles are raging in Europe. The Euro-Parliament recently passed a resolution regarding "new religions." The new document expresses "great concern" about the "unlawful and criminal activities perpetrated by certain sects, and the violations by some of them and of their members' psychological integrity."

These "violations," the resolution says, are "all the more serious" as they "sometimes involve minors." The document calls on member states to "take whatever action is needed to combat violations of fundamental rights perpetrated by certain sects. The legal basis and grounds therefore exist to provide for them (sects) to be prohibited."

One-on-one conversations with government officials, as well as with academic representatives and religious leaders, is one slow but sure method of convincing European nations that ISKCON is beneficial and conducive to the civil behavior of their population—an ostensible goal for all national governments. ISKCON's reasoned, patient, and written policy-level responses are convincing. ISKCON Communications Europe is leading the way in developing such relationships and written policies.

Saunaka Rsi, European Communications director, helps to provide other European communications directors with practical, reasonable approaches to effectively counter some of the most common accusations that misleadingly portray ISKCON as a "sekt" (the European equivalent of "cult"). First, he advises giving general responses along these lines:

—Much of the information is clearly the result of a speculative approach, betraying a distinct agenda/bias.

—Much of the information that reflects reality is considerably outdated.

—I would call for a more scientific and objective study, as these accusations are very far from reality. Here is a specific accusation with his recommended response.

Accusation: "Children have to learn the following four things, according to the teachings of the founder of ISKCON: always think of Krishna; become a servant of Krishna; work for Krishna; follow the instructions of Krishna."

Saunaka's Advice/Response: "Actually, everyone has to learn these things, according to the teachings of the founder of ISKCON. Please substitute the word God for the word Krishna—which is simply a normal suggestion for a spiritual leader." This is a good response.

The following short positioning statements have been utilized and taught to spokespersons by ICG and IC specialists throughout the world.

Surprisingly, because of their controversial nature, some of these questions are still frequently asked. We recommend that ISKCON representatives give short answers, along the lines of those given below, and then skillfully and quickly move on to the main points they have planned to make. Always plan exactly what messages you want to get across. For television, you may only get time to emphasize three points; so make them, and make them briefly and clearly!

Question: "Does not singing and dancing in public put people off, thereby defeating your purpose of winning people over to your point of view?"

Suggested Answer: "The public chanting of the Hare Krishna mantra has been going on for thousands of years in India. It is an integral part of our philosophy, and it glorifies God. It's a natural expression of our love for God."

Question: "Isn't public soliciting or begging for money off-putting to the public?"

Suggested Answer: "All religions depend on donations. In the past, some of our devotees were overly zealous in approaching the public. We are sorry for that. Now we are much more careful about training our volunteers. If anyone ever experiences a problem with one of our members, we encourage that person to immediately contact our local leadership so that we can rectify it."

Question: "Aren't you a cult?"

Suggested Answer: "We are a culture with roots in India dating back to 5,000 years ago. Ours is a cultural movement meant for the respiritualization of society. As a culture, we have a religion, a community, arts, and all of the aspects that define a culture."

Question: "News reports show that Krishna leaders have been tied to murder, drugs, abuse, and other criminal activities. Is this true?"

Suggested Answer: "Our tenets forbid drugs, alcohol, and violence. As these problems are worldwide in scope, and our members come from a cross-section of society, we are, unfortunately, not immune to these all-pervasive social concerns. In general, however, our members are well-behaved citizens who live very clean lives."

Question: "Your prominent temple in West Virginia was particularly known for violence, and even murder. What about this?"

Suggested Answer: "The temple leader was a renegade whose behavior violated our beliefs, practices, and ethics. He was expelled from our religion in 1987. We worked cooperatively with the police in their investigation."

Question: "Reports show that, after joining the movement, a teen-age girl named Robin George sued your society for millions of dollars. What happened there?"

Suggested Answer: "This person came to us of her own free will, asking for sanctuary. She had an unhappy home life and was angry with us for sending her back. Allegations of brainwashing and false imprisonment were thrown out by the higher courts. Ultimately, we settled other issues out of court. However, as a result of her litigious action, we now only accept members who are over eighteen years of age, unless they have parental permission."

Question: "News records describe an ISKCON drug scandal in Laguna Beach, California. What was all this about?"

Suggested Answer: "This occurred in 1977, over twenty years ago. It was an unfortunate situation, but it's now water under the bridge for us. Our Society was in its infancy then. Now, our members and leaders are scrutinized much more carefully."

Question: "In general, what has been done to correct these types of situations which harm your reputation?"

Suggested Answer: "Please keep in mind that, in the West, we are only thirty years old. We have made some mistakes, but we have also learned a lot. In each of these unfortunate incidents, our leaders have taken strong, corrective measures to ensure that these events will not be repeated. We now have a Justice Department in place, and our Global and National Governing Body Commissions hold regular reviews and apply disciplinary action when basic principles of conduct, ethics, or the law are violated."

THE MEANING OF EMPOWERMENT

"After some time the Lord would embrace these people and bid them to return home, having invested them with spiritual potency" (*Caitanya-caritamrta, Madhya-lila* 7.99). This is the basic principle of empowerment, which I discuss in this ICB article. Also (in a shaded box on the front cover of ICB Vol. 10, No. 3) we published part of a letter in which Srila Prabhupada explains in his own words the principle of empowerment as it has flowed from Bhaktivinoda Thakura all the way down through Srila Prabhupada's grand disciples and beyond. Empowerment equates with purity. It includes managerial consistency, enlightened leadership, and proper understanding of the concept of guru.

In a letter to Hansadutta, dated March 12, 1970, Srila Prabhupada writes, "Our London Deities are certainly very, very nice; and everyone is captivated by seeing the smiling face of the Lord. It is very enchanting. Now everything is there and you are also experienced, therefore go on opening branches—as many as possible—and preach *sankirtana* movement to your best capacity. Srila Bhaktivinode Thakura entrusted the responsibility to my Guru Maharaja, and he also, in his turn, empowered us to do the work. Similarly, I am requesting you, all my European and American students, to spread this movement city to city and village to village and make all people of the world happy. Actually, they are missing the central point—Krishna. Therefore they are unhappy. Let us inform them about this missing point, and certainly they will be happy."

ISKCON Communications Briefings, May/June 1997

Purity, it is said, is the force in advancing the Krishna consciousness movement. By becoming pure, one becomes spiritually powerful. Increasing Krishna consciousness in the world always pleased Srila Prabhupada.

Sri Chaitanya Mahaprabhu, who established no temple at all during His time on earth, empowered his followers to spread Krishna consciousness throughout southern India. When the *brahmana* named Kurma asked if he could leave his family and home, Sri Chaitanya Mahaprabhu replied, "Don't speak like that again. Better to remain at home and chant the holy name of Krishna always" (*Cc Madhya-lila* 7.127).

Srila Prabhupada writes in the purport to this verse, "This is the instruction of Sri Chaitanya Mahaprabhu. If this principle is followed by everyone, there is no need to accept *sannyasa.*"

He writes in the purport to the next verse, "This is the sublime mission of the International Society for Krishna Consciousness." This verse (*Cc Madhya-lila* 7.128) reads: *yare dekha, tare kaha 'krsna'-upadesa amara ajnaya guru hana tara' ei desa,* or "Instruct everyone to follow the orders of Lord Sri Krishna as they are given in the *Bhagavad-gita* and *Srimad-Bhagavatam.* In this way, become a spiritual master and try to liberate everyone in this land."

Srila Prabhupada continues, "The Krishna consciousness movement is trying to elevate human society to the perfection of life by pursuing the method described by Sri Chaitanya Mahaprabhu in His advice to the Brahmana Kurma."

Followers of Sri Chaitanya and Kurma would empower some, who would then empower others, thus setting in motion a chain reaction that would eventually bring millions of people into devotional service of the holy name. The following series of verses in the seventh chapter of the *Madhya-lila* of *Caitanya-caritamrita* further demonstrates this principle.

Verse 99: "Chanting this verse, Lord Sri Chaitanya Mahaprabhu, known as Gaurahari, went on His way. As soon as He saw someone, He would request him to chant *'Hari! Hari!'* Whoever heard Lord Chaitanya Mahaprabhu chant *'Hari, Hari,'* also chanted the holy name of Lord Hari and Krishna. In this way they all followed the Lord, very eager to see Him. After some time the Lord would embrace these people and bid them to return home, having invested them with spiritual potency."

Verse 100: "Being thus empowered, they would return to their own villages, always chanting the holy name of Krishna and sometimes laughing, crying, and dancing. These empowered people used to request everyone and anyone—whomever they saw—to chant the holy name of Krishna. In this way, all the villagers would also become devotees of the Supreme Personality of Godhead."

Purport to verse 101: "In order to become an empowered preacher, one must be favored by Lord Sri Chaitanya Mahaprabhu or His devotee, the spiritual master. One must also request everyone to chant the *maha-mantra.* In this way, such a person can convert others to Vaishnavism, showing them how to become pure devotees of the Supreme Personality of Godhead."

Lord Chaitanya's view and personal expression of spiritual empowerment was to act in a materially unmotivated way, desiring only to liberate conditioned beings by inspiring them to take up the practice of chanting the Hare Krishna *maha-mantra.* From the *Caitanya-caritamrta* it appears that such inspiration can take place en masse through preaching done by householders, who are, in current times, too often thought to be in disadvantageous or subordinate positions for the spreading of Krishna consciousness.

ISKCON is equipped and ready for more passengers to step aboard and participate in the great empowerment adventure.

BUILDING CHARACTER

I wrote this article for ICB because of the gap that often appears between philosophy and practice. Being saintly also means to be perceived as saintly. In addition to thinking saintly, we have to act saintly inwardly and outwardly. Thousands of personal exchanges take place every day between devotees of Krishna and members of the public. People quickly form opinions about what kind of people we are. The sum total of these exchanges makes up our reputation. Srila Prabhupada often recalled that "even a small black stain on a white tablecloth spoils the whole thing, just as a minor transgression by a renunciant can destroy his or her reputation." It is especially important that, in our many personal exchanges, we act appropriately and inspire people to look further into Krishna consciousness. In this ICB analysis, I praise ISKCON Book Distribution Minister Navina Nirada for producing and teaching world wide his course on book distribution, where aims, values, character, and behavior are the essential lessons.

ISKCON Communications Briefings, July/August 1997

The *Random House Dictionary* defines ethos as the "fundamental character or spirit of culture; the underlying sentiment that informs the beliefs, customs, or practices of a group or society; the distinguishing character or disposition of a community, group, person, etc."

Does ISKCON have an ethos? Do we need one? Are the ISKCON members' present nature, character, and behavior appropriate and consistent? Do they need to be? If so, how important is our conduct?

If what we say in the news media, at interfaith or academic conferences, and at other public meetings is not consistent with our day-to-day behavior in public, our reputation will suffer.

Sometimes, due to the improper behavior or character of one person, a negative article appears in the press, despite the fact that the majority of ISKCON devotees are of good character. The reason for this is given in the Vedic literature and often cited by Srila Prabhupada, who repeatedly told us that just as a small, black stain on a white tablecloth spoils it, a minor behavioral discrepancy by a *sannyasi,* or anyone dressed in religious garb, can destroy his or her reputation."

Each individual should have unassailable character and behavior. Srila Prabhupada wanted this. I have quoted him several times before as saying "My disciples act in such a way that no one can find any fault in them" (television interview in Gainesville, Florida, June 27, 1971).

We are constantly and critically judged by how we speak to shopkeepers, how we dress, how we treat telephone inquirers and visitors to our temples, how we drive our cars, how we carry ourselves in public, how we treat our children, and how we make announcements to devotees and the congregations in our temples.

Is it possible that our character development has not kept pace with our preaching accomplishments? Srila Prabhupada is quoted as saying, "We will be judged by our character, behavior, and preaching." The order he chose here is interesting.

ISKCON book distributors meet hundreds, if not thousands, of people daily and engage in philosophical exchanges with them. Therefore, what devotees say, how they act, the neatness of their appearance and dress, the attitude they project, their character and integrity reflect upon our organization and influence others. The composite of these traits is, in one sense, ISKCON's reputation.

If ISKCON's book distributors come across as friendly, saintly, empathetic, patient, humble, and intellectually astute, receivers of books are not only more likely to read them, but also will tend to do so with an eye to acquiring the qualities they observed in the book distributor.

Navina Nirada's book distribution course teaches, above all else, the qualities of a devotee. It instructs students how to act and present themselves in a way that brings out their saintliness, making it obvious to all that they are of high character. The course includes instruction on dressing, answering questions, fielding insulting remarks, as well as being consistent, concerned, and compassionate. The course is the first of its kind in establishing a model pattern of behavior for ISKCON devotees.

Many temples require that their book distributors complete this course before they are allowed to pass out Srila Prabhupada's books. This year, in fact, the ISKCON Governing Body Commission (GBC) voted into effect a new law that reads as follows: "That the five-day seminar course established by the Global Book Distribution Minister (Navina Nirada) is accepted as the official training course for all ISKCON book distributors. This course is to be taken by all: (a) new regular book distributors within the first twelve months of their book distributing career; (b) regular book distributors by Gaura Purnima, 1998; (c) part-time book distributors are strongly encouraged to take this course. The Global Book Distribution Minister (Navina Nirada) is responsible to supervise the standard and content of the Book Distribution Graduate Course, promote it, and ensure the requirements of this resolution are met."

As for reputation management, the task is not limited to ISKCON Communications specialists, but rather, it is a responsibility for all ISKCON members to assume.

This book distribution training, combined with other educational courses currently in development, along with an enlivened understanding, comprise the beginning of an ethos for ISKCON.

WHAT THE *CAITANYA-CARITAMRTA* SAYS ABOUT WRITING

Writing, especially for publication, requires spiritual realization, aptitude, skill, technical know-how, understanding, knowledge, the ability to analyze, and lots of practice. In this short ICB article, I have republished a section from the *Caitanya-caritamrita,* in which Srila Prabhupada analyzes a verse and explains the basic elements of written composition, according to the *Vedanta-sutra.* I included this as one of the many instructions that aspiring ISKCON writers should be aware of. Because this one is found in our own scriptures, I thought it appropriate that it become part of *ISKCON Communications Briefings,* as well as ISKCON's body of knowledge about composition.

ISKCON Communications Briefings, **November/December1997**

Adi-lila, 7.106: The Lord said: "Vedanta philosophy consists of words spoken by the Supreme Personality of Godhead Narayana in the form of Vyasadeva."

PURPORT: *Vedanta-sutra,* which consists of codes revealing the method of understanding Vedic knowledge, is the concise form of all Vedic knowledge. It begins with the words *athato brahma-jijnasa* ("Now is the time to inquire about the Absolute Truth"). The human form of life is especially meant for this purpose, and therefore the *Vedanta-sutra* very concisely explains the human mission. This is confirmed by the words of the *Vayu* and *Skanda Puranas* which define a *sutra* as follows:

alpaksaram asandigdham
saravat visvatomukham
astobhamanavadyam ca
sutram sutra-vido viduh

"A *sutra* is a code that expresses the essence of all knowledge in a minimum of words. It must be universally applicable and faultless in its linguistic presentation."

Anyone familiar with such *sutras* must be aware of the *Vedanta-sutra* which is well known among scholars by the following names: (1) *Brahma-sutra,* (2) *Sariraka,* (3) *Vyasa-sutra,* (4) *Badarayana-sutra,* (5) *Uttara-mimamsa,* and (6) *Vedanta-darsana.*

There are four chapters (*adhyayas*) in the *Vedanta-sutra,* and there are four divisions (*padas*) in each chapter. Therefore, the *Vedanta-sutra* may be referred to as *sadasa-pada,* or sixteen divisions of codes. The theme of each division is technically called *pratijna,* or a solemn declaration of the purpose of the treatise.

The solemn declaration given in the beginning of the *Vedanta-sutra* is *athato brahma-jijnasa,* which indicates that this book was written with the purpose to inquire about the Absolute Truth.

Similarly, reasons must be expressed (*hetu*), examples must be given in terms of various facts (*udaharana*), the theme must gradually be brought nearer for understanding (*upanaya*), and finally it must be supported by authoritative quotations from the Vedic *shastras* (*nigamana*).

Summary:
1. *Pratijna.* Solemn declaration of purpose.
2. *Hetu.* Reasons must be expressed.
3. *Udaharana.* Examples must be given. Various facts should be cited.
4. *Upanaya.* Theme gradually brought nearer for understanding.
5. *Nigamana.* Supported by authoritative statements from various *shastras.*

From the material body of knowledge:
1. State the answer/problem/theme/message.
2. Amplify.
3. Give a few examples.
4. Wrap-up.

CHAPTER 10—1998

A Global Perspective

In February Saunaka Rsi organized a two-day conference, "Religion, Community, and Conflict," in Armagh, Northern Ireland. Several organizations, including the World Conference on Religion and Peace and the Irish School of Ecumenics, co-sponsored the event. Speakers included the head of the Anglican Church in Ireland (a Protestant denomination); Archbishop Dr. Robert Eams,

April 5, 1998—New Delhi, India: Atul Behari Vajpayee, Prime Minister of India, addresses a select group of religionists, business elites, government officials, invited media, and other guests as he inaugurates ISKCON's Glory of India Vedic Cultural Center at its grand opening in New Delhi. Others who address the assembly are former US Congressman Steven Solarz and the youngest member of Britain's Parliament, Clare Ward. In addition to her own words of praise, Ward delivers a message of salutation from British Prime Minister Tony Blair.

head of the Catholic Church in Ireland; and Archbishop Dr. Dean Brady. Several other prominent scholars and theologians took part. In Mayapura, the ISKCON GBC added a new member, Malati dasi, the first woman to have a seat on the ruling commission. ISKCON women held a conference in Los Angeles that drew over 100 people, many from far-away countries. India's newly-elected Prime Minister, Atal Behari Vajpayee, inaugurated ISKCON New Delhi's four-acre Glory of India complex on April 5, 1998, Lord Ramachandra's Appearance day. The *Hare Krishna World* (HKW) newspaper printed Vajpayee's speech verbatim and pictured him on the front page. British schools released a religious education book, dedicated to ISKCON members Rasamandala and Indriyesha. The textbook includes many pictures supplied by ISKCON. A Mayapura interfaith conference of Hindus, Muslims, Christians, and Jews examined common ties.

OPRAH'S BEEF WITH MEAT IS MORE THAN OFFAL

This HKW editorial gives a Krishna-conscious perspective on a legal dispute that erupted between US beef-industry magnates and one of the world's most popular entertainers. Although Oprah Winfrey won the first round in a Texas Federal Court, an appeal there and re-filings in a State Court appeared likely to keep the controversy brewing. Indirectly, Ms. Winfrey represented millions of non-flesh-eaters throughout the world, and, in the early court decisions, won her right to vilify hamburgers as part of freedom of expression in the US But big beef was saying no. The public unfolding of this controversy could highlight the dangers of beef consumption and further hurt the troubled industry.

Hare Krishna World, January/February 1998

"Therefore, if people are to be educated to the path of Godhead, they must be taught first and foremost to stop the process of animal-killing."—Srila Prabhupada's purport to *Srimad-Bhagavatam* (1.3.24).

"The only Mad Cow in America is Oprah," said a bumper sticker seen in Amarillo, Texas, USA. "Amarillo loves Oprah," read another.

Daytime television star Oprah Winfrey, the highest-paid entertainer on the planet, and arguably the world's most loved woman, has been hauled before a Texas federal court for bad-mouthing beef. Because of Ms. Winfrey's popularity, the legal case is extremely high-profile. Its venue is amidst the world's greatest concentration of cattle feeders, in a state where the laws have made Ms. Winfrey liable for allegedly demeaning meat.

On April 16, 1996, twenty million viewers heard her declare, "It has just stopped me cold from eating another burger! I'm stopped!" The show discussed how BSE, or "mad cow disease," killed twenty humans in England. The victims had eaten contaminated beef. BSE is said to have occurred because offal, in the form of ground-up sheep brains, was fed to the cows.

The program featured two guests: former cattleman turned vegetarian advocate Howard Lyman and US Department of Agriculture BSE expert William Hueston. Relatives of the deceased were shown close up in the audience, weeping. Plaintiffs Paul Engler of Cactus Feeders Inc. sued Lyman as a codefendant along with Winfrey.

Thirteen states in the US have passed laws that can make a person liable for vilifying food groups. The ultimate question in this case would seem to be about whether "agricultural disparagement laws" are constitutional or if they contravene the free speech clauses of the US Constitution's First Amendment. But there are deeper issues.

Before long it may be proven that meat consumption is more dangerous to human health than cigarette smoking, and this case is grist for the mill. The health question is not limited to beef's correlation with "mad cow disease." It links meat to cancer, heart attack, stroke, and many other life-threatening conditions. To prove this, medical research is well under way, and government officials regularly hear about the health hazards of meat. Now the multibillion-dollar entertainment industry is involved. In a roundabout way,

Oprah represents millions of anti-meat advocates.

What does all this have to do with the Krishna consciousness movement? People who read this newspaper and ISKCON's *Back to Godhead* magazine tend to forswear flesh consumption, since this prohibition is a first principle to developing Krishna consciousness. One thing is certain: a substantial reduction in the consumption of flesh, especially of beef, indicates a public that is more ready and able to assimilate spiritual knowledge.

In his purport to *Srimad-Bhagavatam* 1.3.24, Srila Prabhupada writes, "Therefore, if people are to be educated to the path of Godhead, they must be taught first and foremost to stop the process of animal-killing."

Of course, being merciful and kind to animals is only one step in a long journey. Vegetarianism alone does not provide a complete answer. Howard Lyman, who in May of last year addressed ISKCON's North American Governing Body, feels that unless there is a spiritual underpinning to the vegetarian movement, it will flounder. The Krishna consciousness movement's answer is to widely distribute spiritual sanctified food, or *prasadam* (literally, the Lord's mercy), and the 16-word Hare Krishna chant of purification.

If beef eventually becomes as passe as fur is in England and Holland, and as cigarettes are becoming in the USA, the Krishna consciousness movement will have an open invitation. Devotees would introduce "karma-free" spiritual food on an unprecedented scale with cookbooks, restaurants, cooking classes, home programs, and feasts forming the front rank.

As the "big entertainment vs. big beef" courtroom drama unfolds, we watch with muted interest. One hopes a nation will begin to awaken to the dangers and evils of flesh-eating. But even if such added exposure brings people only one step closer to breaking the meat habit, members of the Krishna consciousness movement will find a new opportunity for transcendental knowledge to take root more firmly in the public mind. When this happens, there will be great benefit to both the individual and society.

LOST CIVILIZATIONS: SOCIETIES WITHOUT SPIRITUAL VALUES

At the center of corruption in leading political circles is a lack of spiritual insight. The following editorial provides commentary on today's dearth of values and principles. Particularly in the developed or civilized world, most people feel lost or full of fear and false hopes. One of their greatest problems is that they have few people to look up to, especially in government. Today's political leaders have private as well as public lives. This editorial suggests that members of the public should demand that their political authorities become spiritual. I argue that leaders should be of good character and think of the welfare of their subjects as more important than their own. Heads of state share in the collective karma of their subjects. "To give protection to the general mass of people who are citizens of the state," says the *Srimad-Bhagavatam* (4.20.14), "is the prescribed occupational duty for a king. By acting in that way, the king in his next life shares one-sixth of the result of the pious activities of the citizens. But a king or executive head of state who simply collects taxes from the citizens but does not give them proper protection as human beings has the

May, 1983—London, England: At the Great Children's Party in London's Hyde Park, England's prime minister Margaret Thatcher embraces "Krishna," played by Yamuna-devi dasi. Mrs. Thatcher asks, "Why are you blue?" Yamuna's reply: "Because Krishna is blue."

results of his own pious activities taken away by the citizens, and in exchange for his not giving protection, he becomes liable to punishment for the impious activities of his subjects."

Hare Krishna World, March/April 1998

Television has provided humanity with novel ways of supporting fundamental human needs. In the privacy of their homes, people identify with soap opera stars, heroes who always win against the odds, sports stars, rock idols, and the ineffable, unrufflable hosts who always have the right word or phrase for any situation. Oddly enough, the ubiquitous tube seems to help to satisfy people's inescapable craving for recognition and the need for role models, support systems, and psychological shelter.

Television aside, most people's deepest needs are met by family members in early life and role models and close friends in later life. Many are made to feel secure and supported by leaders in business (often their bosses), government, religion, psychology, academia, and the arts. The need for understanding, support, and recognition is a fact of life.

Although many might deny it, following the leader is an integral part of human existence, almost a reflexive action. The *Bhagavad-gita* informs us that "Whatever action a great man performs, common men follow. And whatever standards he sets by exemplary acts, all the world pursues." Whether admitting it or not, everyone needs to look up to someone. And in today's world this may be a woman or a man. We need to feel that we matter, that we can make a difference, and that we are cared for.

Also, our values, character, and behavior tend to be patterned after the company we keep or hold most dear. One serial killer's defense was that he witnessed so much violence on television that his murders could not be his own fault. Conversely, those who have excelled in disciplines like medicine, the arts, or sports often point to role models whose lives and instructions inspired them and who were in large measure responsible for their success.

What is missing in our mentors and leaders, however, is unimpeachable character and values (see excerpts from the *Washington Post* on Bhakti-tirtha Swami). We tend to look to the leaders of countries to instill in us a sense of confidence.

We were pleased to note that in his speech at the opening of ISKCON's new temple in Delhi, newly-elected Indian Prime Minister Atal Behari Vajpayee said that "the motive of today should be *yogah karmasu kaushalam*"—the great art of doing work connected with God—as recommended in the *Bhagavad-gita.* He went on to recommend that this principle be applied on a national scale to create a "new work culture" for his country. This presentation was reminiscent of many of India's rulers in the distant past, pious kings who embraced God consciousness as the center of civilization.

Unfortunately, most of today's political leaders do not have such a moral and spiritual vision. In the *Srimad-Bhagavatam,* an important Vedic scripture, Prahlad Maharaja says, "Persons who are strongly entrapped by the consciousness of enjoying material life, and who have therefore accepted as their leader or guru a similar blind man attached to external sense objects, cannot understand that the goal of life is to return home, back to Godhead, and engage in the service of Lord Vishnu. As blind men guided by another blind man miss the right path and fall into a ditch, materially attached men led by another materially attached man are bound by the ropes of fruitive labor." (SB 7.5.31)

By contrast, the *rajarshis,* or saintly rulers of ancient Vedic civilization, to whom Mr. Vajpayee was indirectly referring, were known as God-conscious kings who upheld universal principles of religion. In their realms there was no unemployment, and every citizen felt protected and satisfied. The elders, women, and children were always protected, such that everyone realized their true potential. Complete protection meant that a soldier or policeman would sometimes have to sacrifice his life for others to live.

In his purport to *Srimad-Bhagavatam* 1.18.41, Srila Prabhupada writes: "In the Vedic way of life, the king is trained to become a *rajarshi,* or a great saint, although he is ruling as king. It is the king only by whose good government the citizens can live peacefully and without any fear. The *rajarshis* would manage their kindgoms so nicely and piously that their subjects would respect them as if they were the Lord."

As Bhakti-tirtha Swami would tell us, today's citizens need to call loudly for new ethical standards and ideal character in government leaders. We need to find ways to induce our political leaders to become more spiritual. This is important because such figures set criteria for all the rest of a nation's leaders. It is also essential that a nation's people themselves become more spiritual, as they must take more responsibility for the leaders they elect.

A society without godly principles, a secular society, is necessarily bewildered about values. The rebirth of a nation where God is at the center of individual lives and public affairs will bring about true freedom and a practical reprieve from constant fear and false hopes.

CAN NUCLEAR BLASTS CREATE "FRIENDS" AND "ENEMIES"?

Taking many of us completely by surprise, weeks after her Prime Minister inaugurated ISKCON's Glory of India project, India launched an underground nuclear bomb test. Days afterward, Pakistan responded in kind with underground tests of its own, in May 1998. India's rationale was to protect itself against China and Pakistan, and Pakistan justified its tests by saying it had to match India. The tests, coupled with the long-standing quarrel and three wars fought between India and Pakistan since 1950, made headlines all over the world. The US promptly slapped economic sanctions upon both countries, casting an unsettling pall over longtime hopes for improved India-US relations. India's action was viewed with disdain by the United States.

Hare Krishna World, May/June 1998

When India and Pakistan detonated nuclear bombs in underground tests, the West reacted sharply. The United States quickly planned to cut off loans, investment, and aid to both countries. It began to see them both as "enemies," or at least potential enemies. Pakistan was previously considered an "old ally" of the US.

In a May 15 CNN interview, US President Bill Clinton said that America and India should be "close friends and partners for the twenty-first century." And almost in the same breath, he declared India to be on the "wrong side of history." India said that its reason for testing first was to protect itself from Pakistan.

About ten weeks later, after a lot of finger-pointing, hand-wringing, and posturing, the front-line furor over the India and Pakistan atomic tests subsided. The US Congress was in the process of giving the Clinton administration permission to lift sanctions against these two countries, and at the same time, leaders of India and Pakistan agreed to continue high-level talks started in Sri Lanka on July 30. But on the first day of August, an India-Pakistan skirmish killed at least 87 people in Kashmir, and both countries, at least for the time being, seem to have given up on the South Asian Association for Regional Cooperation Peace Talks.

The world's people are crying out for peace, yet nations and even religions constantly perceive one another as "friends" or "enemies." These circumstances reveal an abysmal state of spiritual bankruptcy.

People have been relegating God to a position of decreasing prominence in human affairs. At the same time, peril increases proportionately. An important inverse correlation exists between the two phenomena: spiritual decay and growing danger. These two are now in advanced stages. God is hard to find, and the "nuclear clock," alarmists would tell us, is at 11:59:59 PM.

Theologically speaking, there is one human family of which God is the head, the original progenitor or Father of all living beings. The mission of ISKCON is to bring our awareness of God to the forefront of world consciousness. In every scripture, God claims to be the ultimate owner of everything. He also establishes that the final human purpose is to surrender oneself to Him.

Some citizens in the neighbor nations India and Pakistan think the two countries are eternal enemies. Such persons defy essential principles of religion and spiritual life. A central Koranic phrase reads, "There is no compulsion in religion."

From the spiritual point of view, our "best friends" can be our "worst enemies" and our "worst enemies" can be our "best friends." For example, when we are praised by our "friends" we tend to feel proud, important, powerful, and attractive. Spiritually, this is unhealthy and augurs for an uncomfortable day of reckoning, a reality check on where we're "really at." When our "enemies" insult those of us who are aspiring to be transcendental, we tend to feel humbled and seek rectification and improvement. This is good for us. Such criticism leads us further into the spiritual consideration that "friends" and "enemies" can be interchangeable or senseless designations.

Here's a real-life example. Before 1947, hundreds of millions of Hindus and tens of millions of Muslims lived in India relatively peacefully—as friends. Admittedly there were some skirmishes and incidents of carnage, but both held that there was one God, named Allah and Krishna, and the purpose of life was to develop love for Him. But when the British-orchestrated partition (India for Hindus and Pakistan for Muslims) occurred, "Hindu-Muslim" war broke out and hundreds of thousands were killed. Friends, even members of the same family, became enemies. Although the reasons were ostensibly religious, the real motives were economic, political, and social. Thanks to their former British rulers, residents of the subcontinent began to identify themselves as a particular faith—the enemy of the other faith.

Those who consider themselves to be connected eternally with God and who recognize themselves as soul, or spirit, see all beings on even terms. The *Bhagavad-gita* indicates that a learned person sees equally all types of humans and animals. Srila Prabhupada writes in *Srimad-Bhagavatam* (4.9.33, purport): "Either materially or spiritually we are basically one, but we make friends and enemies as dictated by the illusory energy."

Hundreds of millions are failing to realize a first principle in spiritual life: "I am not an American," "I am not an Indian," "I am not a Pakistani." "I am not this body."

Glossary

Acharya — One who teaches by example; an extraordinary spiritual teacher.

Aham brahmasmi — Literally this means "I am spirit" and refers to the philosophy that one is not the body but a spirit soul.

Ahimsa — Non-violence; within Vaishnavism this particularly refers to the violence of interrupting a soul's journey toward God, as in the killing of animals for fun, food, and fur.

Apasampradaya — Drawing conclusions that are not accepted by a bona fide disciplic succesion.

Arati — A ceremony in which different articles, such as a *ghee* lamp, flower, and water are offered to Deities. *Mangala aratika,* at 4:30 AM, is the first ceremony of the day in ISKCON devotional life.

Ashrama — Often used to refer to accommodation for spiritual seekers and devotees; each of four divisions of the human life cycle meant to elevate one to spiritual consciousness.

Bhagavat Purana — Considered the most exalted of the eighteen *Puranas* (also known as the *Srimad Bhagavatam*), it contains the most confidential information about Lord Krishna and His devotees and delineates the process of devotion by which one can know Him.

Bhagavad-gita — Literally, *The Song of God.* The revered spiritual discourse between Krishna and Arjuna in the *Mahabharata* epic. One of the basic scriptures of the International Society for Krishna Consciousness (ISKCON).

Bhagavatam — (see *Srimad Bhagavatam* and *Bhagavat Purana*)

Bhajana — Literally, worship; melodic personal or group singing of devotional songs, sitting and accompanied by instruments.

Bhakta — A male member of ISKCON who is aspiring to become initiated into the Vaishnava *sampradaya* of ISKCON. *Bhaktin* designates female members.

Bhakti — Devotional service to God (Krishna).

Bhakti-yoga — A spiritual discipline by which one can recover his/her lost relationship with God through devotional service.

Bhoga — Literally means "enjoyment" and refers to foodstuffs and other items set aside for offering to God, e.g. food not yet prepared or cooked.

Brahmana — One of the four social orders of society; a spiritually trained man or woman who performs the function of a teacher or priest.

Chaitanya, Lord — A full manifestation of Lord Krishna who appeared in sixteenth century Bengal to propagate the chanting of the Hare Krishna mantra.

Caitanya-caritamrita — A narration of the life and activities of Lord Chaitanya Mahaprabhu; Bengali literary work by Krsnadas Kaviraja Goswami.

Dasa/Dasi (male/female) — Servant of God.

Devotional service — *Bhakti*, or activity which helps one to develop love for God.

Disappearance (as in "Srila Prabhupada's Disappearance") — When the soul leaves the body, a person is no longer in our mortal view. Traditionally, it is an alternative word for "death," generally used when referring to a saint, or a pure devotee of God.

Divine Couple — The Supreme Personality of Godhead and His eternal consort, Srimati Radharani, who is the personification of His internal potency.

FOLK — An acronym for Friends of Lord Krishna: an outreach program to engage and encourage those interested in Krishna consciousness.

GBC — An acronym for Governing Body Commission; a committee established by Srila Prabhupada to oversee and manage his organization, ISKCON. It is the ultimate managing authority and regularly undergoes reform and revision to better perform as Srila Prabhupada desired.

Gurukula/gurukulee — A school for children growing up in the Vaishnava tradition. Originating in India, these schools—once just for boys—teach Vedic knowledge and are run by the spiritual master—hence the name, meaning "school of the guru." Outside India, accommodation has always been made for both sexes in ISKCON *gurukulas,* and all schools incorporate a full curriculum. Those who have attended such schools are called ex-*gurukulees.*

Hari — A name for Krishna which means "one who removes obstacles in spiritual life."

Hari-nama — Literally means "the name of Hari." A congregational activity in which members chant the holy name and dance in public, particularly on the streets, for their own spiritual benefit and that of others.

Istaghosti — A discussion on the philosophical and practical teachings of the spiritual master, Srila Prabhupada, by devotees, in a group session.

Janmastami — An important festival day that commemorates Lord Krishna's appearance on earth 5,000 years ago.

Japa — Soft chanting of mantras told on beads.

Kali Yuga (age of) — The earth is currently 5,000 years into the Age of Kali, which is characterized by quarrel and hypocrisy. It lasts in total 432,000 years and is characterized by a progressive decline in God-consciousness. Within Kali Yuga there is a period known as the Golden Age, a time of great spiritual renewal.

Karma — Literally, activity. Often this term refers to reactions accrued from one's activities, both good and bad. (See "Euthanasia and Beyond" [page 204] for a fuller explanation of this complex subject. *Karmic debt* and *karma free* refer to how we build up reactions to our activities, or become free from such reactions.)

Kirtana — The congregational chanting of the holy names of God.

Krishna — The Supreme Personality of Godhead; the name Krishna means "all attractive" and is the name used for God within the ISKCON Vaishnava tradition.

Krishna's lila — A transcendental activity performed by Lord Krishna Himself and/or with His associates, close friends, and family members.

Mantra — Literally, "that which frees the mind" and refers to transcendental sound vibrations that awaken spiritual consciousness.

Maha-mantra — Literally, the "great mantra for deliverance", or Hare Krishna Hare Krishna Krishna Krishna Hare Hare, Hare Rama Hare Rama, Rama Rama Hare Hare.

Maya — "That which is not." The misidentification by the soul as the body, and activities performed in that consciousness.

Mridanga — A two-headed clay drum traditionally played in *kirtan.* Also refers to a modern fiberglass drum constructed in the same form as the clay drum.

Padayatra — Literally, "foot parade;" travelling festival with *kirtana,* teachings, and *prasadam* distribution, traditionally including an ox and cart.

Parikrama — The circumambulation of a sacred space.

Prabhupada — A.C. Bhaktivedanta Swami, the founder-*acharya* of ISKCON and leading exponent of Krishna consciousness in the world.

Prajalpa — Unnecessary talking about mundane subject matters; gossip.

Prasadam — The remnants of food, prepared for and offered to God, that possess spiritual benefit for anyone who eats it.

Rajarshi — A spiritually exalted monarch, especially in Vedic scriptures.

Rathayatra — Literally, "chariot parade." An annual chariot festival that originated in Jagannath Puri, India.

Sadhu — A saintly person.

Sampradaya — A bona fide disciplic line of gurus and their disciples.

Sanatana dharma — Eternal religious principles based on devotional service to God.

Sankirtana — The distribution of spiritual knowledge; in

ISKCON, traditionally refers to book distribution and/or congregational chanting and dancing in public.

Sannyasi — A member of the *sannyasa* order; renunciate or monk.

Shastra — Revealed scriptures.

Srimad-Bhagavatam — See *Bhagavat Purana.*

Tilaka — A clay marking that sanctifies the body as a temple of Vishnu or Krishna.

Vaishnava — A devotee of Vishnu, or Krishna.

Vaishnavism — The branch of *sanatana dharma* enumerated by the Vaishnava *sampradayas,* based on *bhakti-yoga,* where devotion to Krishna as the original Personality of Godhead is central, with Vishnu being another name for Krishna in his role as maintainer of the universe.

Varnashrama — The Vedic social system that organizes society into four occupational and four spiritual divisions for the progressive spiritual development of all. Since Lord Chaitanya's time, and certainly within ISKCON, this is based on qualification, activity, aptitudes, talents, and inclinations, not on notions of birth and caste.

Vrindavana — The transcendental abode of Krishna; a city in the district of Mathura in Uttara Pradesh, India, where Krishna manifested His earthly pastimes 5,000 years ago.

Yatra — Literally, "parade." A place where devotees assemble. Usually refers to a large group of organized devotees, such as the Australian *yatra.*

Yoga — A spiritual discipline for approaching God; literally means "to connect."

Yogi — One who practices yoga.

Index

ICG Mission Statement

ISKCON Communications Global (ICG) strives to make a positive difference in the quality of life by uplifting and benefiting the individual and society, following the desire of His Divine Grace A.C. Bhaktivedanta Swami Prabhupada, the Founder-*Acharya* of the International Society for Krishna Consciousness (ISKCON).

ICG protects and enhances the reputation of ISKCON by working to create and sustain favorable environments for advancing the goals of the Krishna consciousness movement. We are committed to achieving topmost standards of excellence through enlightened, effective teamwork, cutting-edge communications principles, progressive management systems, and advancements in technology.

Bhagavad-gītā As It Is

By His Divine Grace
A. C. Bhaktivedanta Swami Prabhupāda

OVER 40 MILLION COPIES IN PRINT!

The *Bhagavad-gītā*, a 700-verse section of the epic *Mahābhārata*, is the concise summary of India's spiritual teachings. Remarkably, the setting for this classic is a battlefield. Just before the battle, the great warrior Arjuna begins to inquire from Lord Krishna about the meaning of life. The *Gītā* systematically guides one along the path of self-realization. It is the main sourcebook for information on karma, reincarnation, yoga, devotion, the soul, Lord Krishna, and spiritual enlightenment. *Bhagavad-gītā As It Is* is the best-selling edition in the world!

"Bhagavad-gītā As It Is *is a deeply felt, powerfully conceived, and beautifully explained work. I have never seen any other work on the* Gītā *with such an important voice and style. It is a work of undoubted integrity. It will occupy a significant place in the intellectual and ethical life of modern man for a long time to come.*"

— Dr. Shaligram Shukla, Assistant Professor of Linguistics, Georgetown University

---

Available in deluxe or standard editions,
both with full translations and elaborate purports.
DELUXE: Hardbound • 6½" x 9½" • 1,068 pages
29 full-color plates • $24.95 • ISBN 0-89213-268-X;
STANDARD: Hardbound • 5" x 8" • 924 pages
14 full-color plates • $12.95 • ISBN 0-89213-268-X

Mahabharata

abridged

Condensed

The Greatest Spiritual Epic of All Time

Retold by Krishna Dharma

The original *Mahabharata* is the longest epic known to man. It is composed of 100,000 Sanskrit verses, making it eight times longer than *The Iliad* and *The Odyssey* combined. Anyone interested in this celebrated epic will especially enjoy this authentic new version. Although abridged into a highly readable novel, none of the essential details have been sacrificed. Krishna Dharma brings the characters, stories, and teachings of this great classic to life with clarity and vibrancy. He has opened wide the doors of the literary and spiritual treasure-house known as the *Mahabharata*.

"Dharma successfully captures the mood and majesty of a rich and ancient epic, and in the process, does full and complete justice to the critical elements of the complex story. . . . A well-wrought saga that will be appreciated by Western readers and admirably serve to introduce a new generation to the rich spiritual, cultural, and historic legacy of India."

— The Midwest Book Review

Available in unabridged or condensed versions.
UNABRIDGED: Hardbound • 6" x 9" • 960 pages
16 full-color plates • 20 line drawings • $39.95
ISBN 1-887089-17-9; CONDENSED: Hardbound
6" x 9" • 296 pages • $19.95 • ISBN 1-887089-25-X

Book Order Form

☎ Telephone orders: Call 1-888-TORCHLT (1-888-867-2458).
Have your VISA, American Express, or MasterCard ready.
✲ Fax orders: 559-337-2354
✉ Postal orders: Torchlight Publishing, P. O. Box 52, Badger, CA 93603

▲ **World Wide Web: www.torchlight.com**

Please send the following:	**Quantity**	**Amount**
❍ ***Bhagavad-gita As It Is***		
Deluxe (1,068 pages) — $24.95	x________	= $________
Standard (924 pages) — $12.95	x________	= $________
❍ ***Mahabharata***		$________
Unabridged (960 pages) — $39.95	x________	= $________
Condensed (296 pages) — $19.95	x________	= $________
❍ ***Inside the Hare Krishna Movement*** — $19.95	x________	= $________
Shipping/handling (see below)		$________
Sales tax 7.25% (California only)		$________
TOTAL		$________

(I understand that I may return any books for a full refund—no questions asked.)

❍ Please send me your catalog and info on other books by Torchlight Publishing.

Company____

Name____

Address____

City ______________________________ State________ Zip__________

Payment:

❍ Check / money order enclosed ❍ VISA ❍ MasterCard ❍ American Express

Card number____

Name on card_______________________________ Exp. date__________

Signature____

Shipping and handling:

USA: $4.00 for first book and $3.00 for each additional book. Air mail per book (USA only)—$7.00. **CANADA:** $6.00 for first book and $3.50 for each additional book. (NOTE: Surface shippimg may take 3–4 weeks in North America.) **FOREIGN COUNTRIES:** $8.00 for first book and $5.00 for each additional book. Please allow 6–8 weeks for delivery.